Willard L. Sperry

American University Studies

Series VII
Theology and Religion

Vol. 90

PETER LANG
New York · San Francisco · Bern
Frankfurt am Main · Paris · London

William L. Fox

Willard L. Sperry

The Quandaries of a Liberal Protestant Mind 1914-1939

PETER LANG
New York · San Francisco · Bern
Frankfurt am Main · Paris · London

Library of Congress Cataloging-in-Publication Data

Fox, William L.
    Willard L. Sperry : the quandaries of a liberal
Protestant mind, 1914-1939 / William L. Fox.
       p. cm. — (American university studies. Series VII,
Theology and religion ; 90)
      Includes bibliographical references.
      1. Sperry, Willard Learoyd, 1882-1954.
2. Congregational churches — United States — Clergy —
Biography.   3. Theologians — United States — Biography.
I. Title. II. Series: American university studies.
Series VII, Theology and religion ; v. 90.
BX7260.S715F68   1991   230'.58'092 — dc20   90-21612
ISBN 0-8204-1429-8   CIP
ISSN 0740-0446

CIP-Titelaufnahme der Deutschen Bibliothek

Fox, William L.:
Williard L. Sperry : the quandaries of a liberal protestant
mind, 1914-1939/William L. Fox. — New York; Bern;
Frankfurt am Main; Paris : Lang, 1991
   (American university studies : Ser. 7, Theology and
religion ; Vol. 90)
   ISBN 0-8204-1429-8
NE: American university studies / 07

© Peter Lang Publishing, Inc., New York 1991

Printed in the United States of America.

To Lynn

Acknowledgments

The author gratefully acknowledges permission to reprint previously published material from the following:

Macmillan Publishing Company, *Reality in Worship: A Study of Public Worship and Private Religion* by Willard L. Sperry, 1925 (copyright renewed 1953).

Harper and Row Publishers, *Yes, But-, The Bankruptcy of Apologetics* by Willard L. Sperry, 1931.

Harper and Row Publishers, *Summer Yesterdays in Maine: Memories of Boyhood Vaction Days* by Willard L. Sperry, 1941.

Harper and Row Publishers, *Thirteen Americans: Their Spiritual Autobiographies*, Louis Finkelstein, ed., 1953, 231-251.

In addition, quotation from the Willard L. Sperry Papers has been granted by permission of the Harvard University Archives, the Andover-Harvard Library and Lady Henrietta Wilson.

CONTENTS

PREFACE xi

1 Early Intimations of Religious Thought 1

2 Oxford: The Central Stream 31

Introduction to a Serious Theological Life 35

The Synoptic Problem 39

British Theological Modernism 44

Non-German Channels of Influence 53

An Unexpected Source: George Tyrrell 57

3 Developing A Theology of Second Thought 67

Yale and Ministry 67

First Stage Pulpit Theology: Pacifism 79

After the War: Afterthoughts on God and Human Nature . . . 88

The Paradox of Religion 96

4 Inside the Church 109

Complementary Loyalties: Harvard and the Church 112

A Dean's Musing on the Ministry 120

Defining the Significant Form: Worship 126

We Prophesy in Part: Preaching 143

5 Outside the Church 151

Fresh Sources of Calvinism 151

Secular Models of Theology 157

Contra Accommodation 164

The Illiberal Liberal 169

Theological Outlines of Immortality 185

EPILOGUE 191

NOTES 201

INDEX 233

PREFACE

INAUGURATING THE AYER Lectures at the Colgate- Rochester Divinity School in 1929, Willard L. Sperry, already Dean of the Harvard Divinity School for seven years, allowed that "we are living in one of those periods of history... when prophecy seems to be in temporary abeyance." Mingled with his thought at the time was the memory that "ten or fifteen years ago we had dared hope that we might be on the edge of some general revival of religion. That hope was probably based on ignorance of what wars do to the souls of men."

Recognizing that he was part of a generation that longed for a prophetic word because "there was no open vision," Sperry devoted his life to "thinking out loud" in writing, teaching and preaching about the problem of reading the "signs of the times." Sperry not only looked for a prophet upon the American religious scene, he looked for and tried to express that wise man in himself, because "our religion will more and more part company with the soberer thinking of the country unless it also gets wisdom."[1]

Since Jeremiah no prophet has been eager for the role, and either natural modesty or sage reluctance prohibited Willard Sperry from disclosing any self-image, prophetic or not. Unlike most prophets, however, he did not lack for recognition in his own country or during his "myriad days." Besides holding his high post at Harvard for more than thirty years, longer than anyone before or since, while combining the deanship at the Divinity School with the ministry at Memorial Church in the Harvard Yard, Sperry received prestigious lectureships and honors that are primarily reserved for the most accomplished persons. Yale (D.D., 1922), Amherst (D.D., 1923), Brown (D.D., 1928), Williams (D.D., 1935), Harvard (S.T.D., 1941) and Boston University (D.Litt., 1939) bestowed upon him honorary degrees. Princeton and Bowdoin had voted him degrees, but illnesses prevented him receiving them. He was elected a Fellow of the American Academy of Arts and Sciences in 1927 and for many years belonged to the famed Century Association of New York City. He published more than a dozen books, often in unrelated fields, including the subjects of theology, worship, preaching, religious education, Christology, a history of religion in America, a literary biography of William Wordsworth, and a memoir of Maine in the 1890s.

Sperry's list of publications in magazines and religious journals is no less impressive and equally varied in theme. Showing the competence of a philosopher, many of his essays in periodicals dealt with a wide array of topics such as pacifism, the relationship of science and religion, literary criticism, Anglo-American relations, ecumenism, democratic theory, euthanasia and bio-medical ethics. Some of these pieces have been rightly judged to be ahead of their times in anticipating the direction of moral and religious problems which settled into American public consciousness by 1960.

Eugene Exman, who was Sperry's editor at Harper's, offers a tenable and lofty tribute to Sperry as a writer:

> Dean Willard L. Sperry, of the Harvard Divinity School, never had Fosdick's readership, but in urbanity and scholarship and style he was unequaled. For many years he was my trusted adviser, reading manuscripts... Sperry directed many important books and authors to Harper's...[2]

Sperry's friend and neighbor on Francis Avenue in Cambridge, Massachusetts, Howard Mumford Jones, of the Harvard Department of English, wrote him upon first reading the announcement of the Dean's retirement, saying, in part, "when I think of all I have read that you have written, and remember the clean, easy prose, the good sense, the humor, the urbanity, none of it concealing a confident Christian faith, I can only marvel at your industry and your tact."[3] D. Elton Trueblood, the Quaker leader, admired Sperry over many years "as a speaker and writer," who left a great mark on him.[4] John Wesley Lord, the Methodist Bishop of Boston, wrote at the occasion of Sperry's retirement, "I have always felt that Dean Sperry was a leader who stood in the Grand Tradition of those who, by the character and culture, they possess, add luster and worth to the holiest things in life."[5]

Praise for Willard L. Sperry from his contemporaries was uniform: he was a master of the English essay and an eloquent preacher. An Anglican bishop lauded Sperry's collection, *Sermons Preached at Harvard* (1953), in an effulgent review for *The American Oxonian*, saying, "in fact these sermons are not only relevant to the age in which we live, but even more they have the timeless spirit of the ages."[6] As recently as 1987 Sperry's "tradition and character" have been eulogized in the conventional way of noting past praise-worthiness. Alan Seaburg commends Sperry as a neglected religious writer and to endorse him this way is also "to discover his simplicity, his unity as a person and as a Christian minister, and as a preacher..."[7] All of this may be true even if derived from a convivial, but diffuse mythology grown around a man who was decent and of whom there is much good report. Unfortunately, the sum is also a type of excessive adulation which hinders a measured assessment of his intellectual contributions.

Sperry needs to be considered more for his intellectual power and yield, his qualities of prophecy than for the genteel manner of expression which characterized his style and admitted him to an elite circle of well-rounded litterateurs.

Meanwhile, scholars have begun to rediscover Sperry as a harbinger of liberal Protestant reactions to the twentieth century. Paul A. Carter in his book *Another Part of the Twenties* (1977) relies on Sperry in matters of religion to dispel the popular notion of the decade as solely the story of "the beautiful and the damned." Carter, for instance, applauds the republication of Sperry's works because it will give "students of the history of religion in America" one of the better authors of the twenties.[8] William R. Hutchison edited an anthology entitled *American Protestant Thought in the Liberal Era* (1968), which has gone into at least one reissue. Willard Sperry appears therein with many better known Protestant leaders under the section heading, "Complications." Sperry also figures prominently in Hutchison's major treatise, *The Modernist Impulse in American Protestantism* (1976). Sperry's thought, not just his "tradition and character" are beginning to be taken seriously by historians studying the period.

It seems for the most part that by the end of his career and the time of his death in 1954, Sperry was forgotten as an important liberal Protestant voice of the twenties and thirties. How he has been recognized since is significant, because he has been remembered mostly as the Dean who presided over an historic Divinity school through its time of internal exile under the ambivalent administration of James B. Conant, President of Harvard through most of Sperry's tenure. Howard Mumford Jones, for instance, intimates Sperry's feeling at the end of his final term, implying that Sperry left more than a few things at Harvard better off forgotten:

> I suppose, like, it seems to me most who toil at the enigmatic institution known as Harvard University, you are afflicted with a sense of not having succeeded in your post as you had wanted to. I think Harvard has a curious facility in inducing thoughts of failure in its staff.[9]

Any recovery of Sperry's "serious" life, apart from his administration of a department of university life, begins, as scholars detect, in a de-mystification of the congenial man of letters, and turns to his prophetic qualities. Further, prophets are not always in sync with their times which proves them all the more fascinating. What Sperry was saying in critical, if also prophetic, terms, more than how well he said it, forms the first line of suspicion, which at some deeper level of investigation would convey that something or someone has been overlooked. The first part of the task in this investigation is to follow the hunches of scholars such as Hutchison and Carter who hint strongly, without proving it themselves, that there is in Willard Sperry an articulate representative of liberal Protestantism during its crisis years. In other words, the preliminary, but not primary reason for this study of Sperry is that since his death popular references to him have almost always been along the lines of one good man writing about another. His urbanity is never at issue here. What merits exploration, however, is what he says and when he says it, particularly against his own background and that of his times. This treatment of Sperry, therefore, is an exercise in intellectual biography within the specific context of the time just before 1914, during the Great War and up to 1939. These are not artificial boundaries, but are years that bracket an experience for an entire generation and are a constant reference mark for the scholar probing the religious thought of the first half of the twentieth century.

The first problem of the study, consequently, is to cut through the honeyed words about Sperry that have appeared as a kind of roadside historical marker. The second and major task is to put his thoughts up against the historical continuities of the liberal Protestant tradition as defined by scholars studying the period. In doing this Sperry becomes a test case for considering the varieties of liberalism delineated in general by Kenneth Cauthen, William R. Hutchison and others. Inevitably Sperry, for comparison's sake, is examined in context with contemporary thinkers such as Walter Lippmann, Reinhold Niebuhr and Harry Emerson Fosdick. Finally, he is also considered as being symptomatic of something complex and "profoundly serious" in American culture and theology, a dilemma once posed in liberal Protestantism between neo-orthodoxy and humanism. Sperry seems to have been a liberal who surveyed and staked out the middle-ground, the most difficult territory to defend when coming between polemical antagonists. And in the reconstruction of events, the middle-ground has often disappeared, having been effaced by more visible and vocal disputants in the version which comes out in the historical wash. Neo-orthodoxy, for instance, dominates the theological history of the thirties, but with the exception of Princeton, Drew and Union Theological Seminary in New York City, the older liberalism was still in place through the forties at many schools, including Yale, Harvard and Chicago. In the battle for attention neo-orthodoxy had won, but there were middle-ground liberals, such as Sperry, who held sway longer than has been generally acknowledged.

The principal significance for American religious history is that Sperry is representative of a normative pattern that existed within liberal theology. His struggle to interpret the general concerns of religion in a modern setting with an ancient idiom of faith symbolized the sticking "points in modern American Christianity, where our creeds and our culture come into contact." He indicated often that he "tried to follow the battle to the places where there is a real issue, where too meagre accounts of religion may lay us open to danger."[10] It is his response to changing theologies and new cultural demands as a liberal Protestant which shapes the argument that Sperry's strenuous pursuit of the "real issue" is illustrative of what some of the best thinking of the time was contemplating.

He represented the draw bridge spanning the two centuries coming together at 1900 (or arguably, 1914). His theological heritage ran deep into the romantic past, coursing its way through the New England theology, brushing against Finneyite Congregationalism, dipping into Carlyle's romantic spiritual autobiography, *Sartor Resartus*, digesting the Anglican liberalism at Oxford and being absorbed by the lost cause of Roman Catholic Modernism. He is a period figure as he once admitted to his daughter and only child, Henrietta:

> My dear, I often feel that you were born into a very thankless and hard period of the world's history—that those of us who got some roots struck in before 1914 were by contrast very lucky. It's your life that has been complicated, not ours. Please believe that we owe you a lot and you don't owe us, as a generation, very much. That is always in the back of my mind. We want to do all we can to help you in any way. I said this at Vassar, at Commencement, a year ago [1939], and the old folks there simply said "Amen."[11]

The fatherly disclaimer notwithstanding, Sperry's intellectual life was far more "complicated" than his noble concession to a child of the twentieth century allowed. On the contrary, one could argue that because he had "roots struck before 1914," and therefore, began life with expectations that on hindsight seemed naive, far more treacherous ground had to be covered than those seekers starting after 1914 who also tried to reach the end point of "Amen." Sperry, after all, was on the scene for a half century, trying to hold and restore the liberal middle ground that at various times was invaded by humanism, neo-orthodoxy, variations of Thoreauvian individualism and off-shoots of mysticism. Sperry had a commanding view from his position at Harvard, which by no means insulated or exempted him from the ongoing theological dialectic.

Sperry's dilemma, of course, was not unique, but his situation was demonstrably most unusual. His intellectual life had the constant double facing of British and American theological values which were not always compatible. Not only did that difference exist, but also his American point of view was regularly informed by British social and cultural conventions which were sometimes at odds with American casualness. Forty years after going up to Oxford he remembered

> ...one of my pals in the first Rhodes Scholar shipment—a man named Blodgett, a great red headed, red hairy giant. He was assigned to Wadham. The first night he was there he went up and banged a huge fist on the shoulder of some shrinking primrose and said, "My name's Blodgett. I'm from Missouri." The victim turned to a fellow standing by and said, "Oh, I say, how peculiah!" The gears between the cultures don't always mesh.[12]

One of the peculiar things about Sperry is that up until his return from Oxford the long-standing trans-Atlantic connections were found mostly through evangelical and revivalist circles.[13] Being neither an evangelical nor an Anglican meant that Sperry, as a New England Congregationalist, was a very unlikely conduit for Anglo-American theological exchanges. The recurring themes of Sperry's life and mind are contained within these complementary parts being fed by both British and American sources, which gave his version of liberal alternatives an added dimension. That Sperry had very little contact with German theological trends, except for Harnack, makes his case all the more special to study.

The double-facing of his ecclesiology also differentiates him from many other modernists. He was both a church insider and church outsider, depending on where, in his opinion, the best wisdom and most sincere expressions of the time could be found. He insisted that "an institution which is too dependent on its constituency for its support tends to follow the line of least resistance along the ways of opportunism. Theologies of accommodation... are not signs of spiritual life." Sperry asserted, in what surely is a note of dissent, that "the truth is that in America we spend altogether too much time and effort in simply keeping churches alive." Noting the consequences and, therefore, the priority of ideas, Sperry remained suspicious "that running a successful church may not be identical with spreading the Christian religion."[14]

Sperry's guiding principle was stated in the preface of his Hibbert Lectures for 1927, published as *The Paradox of Religion*. He wrote, "Often we have to look twice. When we look the second time we find that little happenings, which in other less perplexed years pass unnoticed, now take on a new meaning and value."[15] Sperry self-consciously developed a theological mind of second thought, probably dictated by the intellectual milieu which sustained him, the constant double-facing of his history looking before and after 1914, his divided Anglo-American identity, his dwelling between the two worlds of the university and the church, and his reflections upon Christianity in the first and twentieth centuries.

As a consequence of constant double-facing, two minds often were synthesized. Sperry struggled in the murky atmosphere of paradox, perhaps more than any other key figure representing the middle ground of liberalism. Harry Emerson Fosdick, according to his biographer, Robert Moats Miller, had little sense of paradox. In analyzing Fosdick's sermons, Miller concludes, "there is a certain irony in the observation that Fosdick's liberal, decent, humane, hope-and-love-filled certitudes were absolute certitudes as uninformed by ambiguity, irony or paradox as were the certitudes of the most unreconstructed fundamentalists."[16] In contrast, Sperry worked to get paradox into liberal sensibilities, even though its "inclusion and reconciliation provide constant difficulty for faith and conduct." He defended his practice of yoking opposed areas of concern within the framework of his books and sermons because "religion perpetually renews itself... by appealing from the emphasis that custom insures to the antithetical concern."[17]

Sperry is not only a field study for a mind meeting new boundaries in a period of rapid transition, he is also a test case to be measured against existing notions of what constituted liberal Protestantism in its various stages of development. Sperry, generally, belongs in the Christocentric liberal tradition, or, at least he starts there, as described by H. Shelton Smith.[18] He meets Smith's broad criteria. Like the Christocentric liberals from Bushnell to Fosdick, Sperry also accepted the principle of organic evolution, employed the historical method in his interpretation of the Bible, utilized the findings of psychology and sociology, appropriated the insights of modern philosophy, especially philosophical idealism and recognized vital moral values in a fully socialized democracy. But when Smith clarifies the nature of Christocentric liberalism in its major doctrines, Sperry, it seems, has drifted off center—he was not as convinced an immanentist as Borden Parker Bowne; he came to doubt the liberal view of human nature; he adjusted his Christology to allow for Schweitzer's eschatological corrections; and he had reservations about the realizable Kingdom of God.

Kenneth Cauthen has divided American Protestant liberals into two groups: evangelical and modernistic. The categories under these major divisions include on the evangelical side, personality-centered Christianity represented by Harry Emerson Fosdick, the Social Gospel, theological personalism and evolutionary theism. On the modernistic side are the categories of social Christianity, empirical theology and theological naturalism. Nowhere does there seem to be room for a theology sensitive to paradox in Cauthen's schema. Furthermore, as Jaroslav Pelikan says in his foreword to Cauthen's book, *The Impact of American Religious Liberalism* (1962), "Dr. Cauthen's researches suggest the extent to which liberalism of the 1920s was a product of its own time. Repeatedly he shows how uncritically the advocates of liberalism accepted the spirit of their time and incorporated it into their own theology." This is simply not the case. Willard L. Sperry was a very discerning critic of the "moralism and naive empiricism of the American liberals" of the 1920s.[19] As William R. Hutchison argues forcefully, Cauthen's differentiation was based too readily on the theological consequences of evangelical and modernistic liberalism, which is not helpful, ultimately, in grasping what they intended.[20]

Hutchison's book, *The Modernist Impulse in American Protestantism* (1976) becomes the next jumping off point for this discussion of Willard Sperry. In it he resuscitates Sperry as a potent critic within modern liberalism, but because of Hutchison's wide scope, important details about Sperry escape notice. Sperry fits in with Hutchison's sweeping metes and bounds of modernism, but not always comfortably, and at later times not at all. Just as recent critical biographies of Walter Rauschenbusch, Reinhold

Niebuhr and Harry Emerson Fosdick have appeared from the varieties of liberalism which Hutchison has advanced, so too a particularistic study of Willard Sperry seems warranted and timely.

Part of the problem in locating Sperry within liberalism is with liberalism itself. The ambiguities of the term "liberalism" or "liberal theology" are self-evident. Claude Welch in *Protestant Thought in the Nineteenth Century* (Volume 2, 1985) ponders the difficulty: "Does liberalism refer to a spirit of inquiry and affirmation? To a program? To a complex of ideas (immanentism, religious experience, revelation as discovery, evolutionary models and optimism, the primacy of the moral)?" Welch agrees with Hutchison that "modernism" and "liberalism" are interchangeable terms, but he also thinks Hutchison's attempt to put the modernist impulse within liberalism exclusively is not finally convincing, because liberalism was by its nature "all pervasive."[21] Surely, then, there can be more than one kind of modernist or one kind of liberal. Willard Sperry, for instance, cannot be classified by categories that have been thus far arranged. He is elusive and difficult to place, just as liberalism itself defies fixity, because he is in that neglected mid-range of liberals surviving on second thought not new theology.

One of the broader questions which lies behind this study and which must be stood against prevailing historical assumptions is: was there an identifiable middle ground within the Protestant liberalism of the 1920s and 1930s that has been largely ignored? How else does one account for the fact little or no scholarship has been produced on figures like Sperry? While the long range aim of this discussion is to describe and put into context the theological standing ground of an accessible Protestant thinker, the immediate goal is to trace his steps over a theological landscape that leads surprisingly far afield, extending from fair skies at the turn of the century, through the fog of the twenties and thirties, to storm clouds on the horizon as the middle ground of liberalism runs out of room and bumps up against neo-orthodoxy, short of breath in the forties.

This is not an exhaustive treatment of Sperry's thought, if only because of what it selectively omits. Not because they would prove or refute the thesis, but because they are non-essential to its discourse, topics relating to Sperry which are barely or never mentioned are his commitment to ecumenism, his contribution to the Revised Standard Version of the Bible as a consultant on English style and usage, his narrative history of American

religion or his views on bio-medical ethics. Except as background and
explanation, much of his personal life has been left out of these pages, and so,
too remarks about his work as a Dean and college chaplain are minimal.

In the first two chapters Sperry's intellectual roots are examined in
detail. These two sections become the family tree of his subsequent thought.
In chapter 3 Sperry is shown to make quick repair of a liberal theology
broken and battered in the aftermath of August 1914. He is conspicuous in
acquiring the capacity for second thoughts about social progress, God and
human nature. He discovers a correction in paradoxes. His relationship to
the church is the major reference point throughout his life, the center of
gravity around which his mind is ordered. He invests serious thought in
what should go on inside the church while relying extensively on the
thought occurring outside the church.

In chapter 4, "Inside the Church," an exposition is presented of how he
viewed the ministry, worship, and the function of prayer and preaching,
with particular notice given to the objective and subjective components
which, for Sperry, define the reality of worship. This was a signal departure
from the prevalent liberal attitude about the subjectivity of religious experience.

In chapter 5, "Outside the Church," Sperry's intellectual journey is
portrayed with a sense of irony. When addressing the deficiency of Protestant apologetics, Sperry proposed the model of the illiberal liberal, who
symbolized, in his view, a bell buoy telling Protestants they were at sea
theologically. By offering a conception of the illiberal liberal Sperry was able
to embrace the spirit of science, perhaps equivalent to a *Zeitgeist*. Seeing the
potential mystic in the scientist, yet unable to satisfy the soul of the poet
through modern science, Sperry reclaims William Wordsworth, the
epitome of the Romantic Age, as a kindred spirit to the Protestant liberal.
This is a rather surprising turn of mind, but part, no doubt, of some eternal
return in the cycles of liberalism. Sperry at this point takes up questions of
immortality intimated in Wordsworth.

In the late forties Sperry resumes his interest in Christological problems
to which he was first introduced while at Oxford in the twilight of pre-1914
luminescence. In this endeavor not to abandon the Jesus of history, he is
rebuffed and discouraged. Carrying the banner of an older, middling
liberalism, Sperry's final assault signaled the end of an era that extended
for a full half century, which is long past the usual date given for the decline

of the liberal theological position developed in the glow of nineteenth century promises. Historians have left the impression that by 1930 all that was left was "the post-liberal mind."[22] And yet, the themes governing Sperry's religious concern have not approached the vanishing point. The salient issue seems to be, instead, that the experience and thought of Willard L. Sperry will continue to provide more than a subtext for the present day. His second thoughts are very much a part of the American Protestant mind at the close of the century.

ॐ

Study, thought and writing are inseparable from obligation. For the years and hours at my desk, in libraries or in conversation, which are made tangible in these pages, I have accrued debts of gratitude that cannot be easily retired, only forgiven. For their kindnesses, efficiencies and capabilities to ease time pressured research, I would like to thank the staffs at the Andover-Harvard Library, Pusey Library and the Widener Library of Harvard University. Alan Seaburg, Curator of Manuscripts at Andover-Harvard, in particular, ran the extra mile and along the way became a Sperry disciple. The Congregational Library in Boston had stray material not found at Harvard which Harold Worthley located for me. The collection of Sperry's published works in the Sperry Conference Room at Memorial Church in the Harvard Yard is the only place I could find early sermons published by the Boston Monday Club. Access to those holdings came through the good offices of my friend and former instructor in homiletics at Harvard, Peter J. Gomes, a worthy Sperry successor at Memorial Church.

The library of Wesley Theological Seminary in Washington, D.C. was convenient and hospitable as a place to use periodical and reference works. Gracemary Snyder took especially good care of my borrowing and copying needs. The Library of Congress was not only accommodating in terms of rendering personal assistance, but was inspiring for its atmosphere. The libraries of American University and The George Washington University were useful in gathering select secondary material. The courtesies accorded me at both places are appreciated. On several family vacations the library at Wofford College in Spartanburg, South Carolina proved to be an inviting retreat. Because of this opportunity for fruitful thought at Wofford and because of limited space for luggage in the car, the golf clubs usually got bumped in favor of the brief case full of documents and notes.

Extensive conversations in the early going with Walter D. Kring, Ralph Lazzaro, Paul G. Kuntz, Dan H. Fenn and Seth R. Brooks convinced me that Sperry's thought was interesting enough to invite further exploration. Mason Hammond graciously consented to be interviewed and gave me in a single morning a lifetime of Harvard lore. Important to mention are the insights of Sperry's former student, Charles Forman, who claims that our appointment was on his mind only minutes before the anesthetic took effect as successful open heart surgery ensued.

I owe a profound note of gratitude to Lady Henrietta Sperry Wilson, the Dean's daughter. Lady Wilson cooperated with every request and never questioned the bounds of propriety which my eagerness must have, at times, tested. She shared an extraordinary store of personal reflections about her parents. My own impressions were deeply enhanced by the bits and pieces of family correspondence that she sent me from London. Of added value in this project was the occasion to meet Lady Wilson when she was in Washington, D.C. and to introduce her to our six week old daughter, Hallie. Lady Wilson's cousin, Mrs. R. H. Milbraith, kindly sent copies of family correspondence in her possession.

In the course of research the approbation of George H. Williams, C. Conrad Wright and William R. Hutchison, all of the Harvard faculty, is appreciated. Because of their casual suggestions this work gains weight.

My gratitude also extends beyond my prior Harvard associations to those responsible for my twice-born graduate school experience. For their ready qualities of critical thinking and historical dispassion in twentieth century American history, William R. Becker and Leo P. Ribuffo of The George Washington University history faculty are model readers. Their comments held me to their own high standards of scholarship, precision and mastery.

Heidi Burns of Peter Lang Publishing, Inc. has been exceptionally generous in offering advice that spared me many embarrassing textual problems.

From the outset, however, Dewey D. Wallace of The George Washington University Religion Department was everything one could desire in a teacher. His judicious criticism was invariably exacting, but always thoughtful. His command of bibliography outside his own specialty was remarkable and indispensable. Further, his encouragement was effusive, contagious, and most importantly, well timed. I owe him more than I can repay.

While many persons deserve credit for the form and manner this exercise has taken, in the end, I acknowledge that the responsibility for the outcome is mine alone. I have been at pains to avoid the dangers of being compromised by my own liberal Protestant roots and preferences. I have carefully tried to harness emotions not to partisanship, but to a desire for getting the story right.

Lastly, a word about my family is necessary. My parents have an avidity for books, my mother for mystery stories, my father for biography. Their influence is clearly present here. And in the case of my father, a retired academic, I have known firsthand the life of a scholar since I first "took up and read." Further, this book would have been inconceivable without the patience and humor of my wife, Lynn. Her faith in my work, expressed in ways so completely natural to her and, therefore, probably unknown to her, warrants my simple response which appears as this book's dedication.

William L. Fox
Claremont, California

Willard L. Sperry

CHAPTER 1

Early Intimations of Religious Thought

*"And he will turn the hearts of fathers to their children
and the hearts of children to their fathers."*
—Malachi 4:6

WILLIAM WORDSWORTH IN a striking tangent of matter-of-factness writes of the relationship between things that fit and things that are plainly out of place. He says that the best part of an interesting life lies in the perception of "similitude in dissimilitude and dissimilitude in similitude." In other words, life becomes tedious when it is all a matter of unrelieved monochromes and undeviating patterns. Life holds interest only when one meets in it the eternal riddle of likeness and unlikeness.

Any time one is introduced to a mind and personality that seems to balance the equation Wordsworth proposes for human interest, one is led to ask some obvious questions. How does that person resemble his own times? Is he typical? Is he exceptional? What makes him unlike his contemporaries? What are his society, his world of ideas, his cultural milieu and his personal history supposed to represent? And do they mesh? Does he speak to that time, or like an appealing anachronism, are his words meant best for some other, distant age? Why is he significant to the past? Finally, what importance can he possibly hold today?

Willard L. Sperry (1882-1954) lived an intriguing, versatile intellectual life which, as the poet's prose thesis suggests, warrants concentrated biographical attention and study. Sperry seems almost immediately to embody "similitude in dissimilitude and dissimilitude in similitude." He was typically American, middle class and, except for lacking patrician similitude, as Victorian as Clarence Day in his childhood. And yet, he entered the twentieth century completely open to modern ideas and was prepared to reject much of a near, familiar past. He was the product of New England Puritan stock, feeling the force and austerity of Calvinism

1

throughout his life. And yet, he arrived a long way from any "implacable transcript of the most pitiless Calvinism," which had been in decline from the time of his boyhood.[1]

Sperry was thoroughly American—simultaneously growing up in New England and the Midwest, a fact of obvious dissimilitude by itself. As an adult, he became an ardent Anglophile. He was most at home, it seems, living in English society and as such was something of a world citizen, perhaps unlike most other American Protestant liberals of his time. In addition, Sperry was, as Dean of the Harvard Divinity School, of the Church, but not in a particular church. Moreover, Sperry was a birthright Congregationalist, but was never a denominational chauvinist, and might easily have been Episcopalian or for that matter Unitarian.

Sperry was, furthermore, a man of imposing knowledge, but was not an academic scholar doing abstract work. He was not a systematic theologian, but one finds order, continuity and forcefulness in his mature theological thinking. The breadth of his learning and the various subjects of his writing were certainly atypical for his modernist genre, ranging non-specifically from American religious history to child development, from professional ethics to liturgical aesthetics, from literary biography to spiritual autobiograpy. The diversity of Sperry's work in the context of a major administrative responsibility alone points to dissimilitude in similitude.

What produced such natural contrasts in one life? What were its strengths? What or whom did it come to influence? Why was Sperry, knowing so much and giving so widely, known so little outside a Sanhedrin of twentieth century American Protestant luminaries?

❧

The poet also says that "the Child is father of the Man" and consequently, the answer to certain of these inquiries must begin with some formative boyhood impressions upon him. The Sperry family circle was largely centered in a mid-level New England culture and in the life of the Congregational church and manse as it stood in transition during the last quarter of the nineteenth century. Willard Learoyd Sperry was the first born in a family of three children. His parents had been married for three years when their only son was born, April 5, 1882. At the time of Sperry's birth, his father, Willard Gardner Sperry, only several years out of his deferred theological training, was minister of the South Congregational Church in Peabody, Massachusetts (1878-1885).

Willard Gardner Sperry (1847-1906) became a minister only after he had been a successful "school man" for nearly a decade. Born in Cambridgeport, Massachusetts to Henry and Mehitable Preston (née Berry) Sperry, August 10, 1847, he was educated at Phillips Academy, Andover and was a member of the Yale class of 1869. From Yale he went into teaching and eventually became principal of a secondary school in Beverley, Massachusetts. It was most probably in Beverley that he met his future wife, Henrietta Learoyd, also a school teacher. Before marrying, however, Henrietta Learoyd (after several years of teaching in Beverley) left for a new position at the Abbot Academy in Andover and for one year was the acting principal there.[2]

Meanwhile, Willard Gardner Sperry, at an age when most men's careers were already established, also left Beverley, but to cease school mastering and to prepare a theological course leading to the parish ministry. He returned to the Divinity School of his alma mater, but stayed at Yale for less than a year and a half. It is not clear what precipitated his departure, but he transferred to Andover Theological Seminary, nonetheless taking the appropriate degree one year later in 1878. It is possible that the advantages of an Andover education were less theologically than geographically desirable. First, Andover was familiar to Willard because he had prepared for college at The Phillips Academy, but second and of larger note, Andover probably had ultimate appeal because of Henrietta's presence in the town. The transfer may have been no more mysterious than for reasons of the heart. That summer he was ordained to the Congregational ministry in Peabody, Massachusetts.[3] The following new year (January 2), perhaps being sufficiently settled and promising in his thirty-second year, Sperry married Henrietta Learoyd, daughter of John A. and Sarah Stacy (née Silvester) Learoyd. They made their home in Peabody for the next six years and welcomed into the world two of their three children.

When it came time to accept a call to Manchester, New Hampshire, the boy Willard was three years old and his sister, Pauline, was a babe in arms. The third child, Henrietta, would be born four years later, just when her older brother's most vivid childhood memories were being fashioned and firmed up. The family was, no doubt, rather typical in its composition for middle-class Victorian America. The father was forty-two when his last child was born, perhaps the only notable fact thus far in an unexceptional family sketch of origins and status.

The Sperrys lived in the small city of Manchester, New Hampshire, from 1885 to 1893; it was an industrious community, making up in wholesomeness for what it lacked in sophistication, but was not so far from occasional contact with Boston to be considered a solitary place without cultural stimulation. Manchester was somewhere between the settled farm and the far city. During the eight years of the Manchester pastorate, a total salary of thirty-three hundred dollars was paid to the Reverend Mr. Sperry, an average of a little more than four hundred dollars per year.[4] That was rather standard clergy pay for those days, which required of them regular habits of thrift, even if the succeeding generation asked of life margins of financial security which an earlier generation did not demand. One must bear in mind also that the situation for clergy on the average was then not on the incline of improvement. Thirty years later the average pastoral income was less than a thousand dollars per annum. Many skilled workers, such as masons, plumbers and bricklayers, were by 1920 earning wages higher than the clergy.

Shortly after the birth of Pauline, the Sperrys managed to purchase a cottage on the southern coast of Maine in 1885, for two thousand dollars. The family regarded the acquisition of vacation property as one of the more sensible things the father ever did with money. In this regard there was a large measure of return over many years. He was not, however, always successful in dabbling with other real estate investments. On separate occasions the father of the young Sperry family tried to improve their financial estate with some land speculations. He bought shares, probably as a limited partner, in a copper mining operation located in the Upper Peninsula of Michigan. The younger Willard would reflect back on the venture with amusement. About his father's investment efforts he says, "There undoubtedly was copper in the Upper Peninsula, but it certainly was not where father's stock certificate said."[5]

There was, in addition, a befuddled attempt at riches out west when lots were purchased in the path of growth and expansion in burgeoning Denver. Again, the younger Sperry remarks sardonically, "there indubitably was land in Denver, for after father's death we periodically had his located and verified." The story continues, however, in an easily predictable, downward spiral. "When it became clear that Denver had not developed according to the original prospectus, and that our Colorado estate bordered on the city dump, we were glad to unload for the taxes."[6]

As the family established a pattern of deliberate, unhurried itinerancy, moving from parsonage to parsonage and eventually into the academic equivalent, a college residence, the cottage at York Beach, Maine became more and more the family home and anchor. Looking back upon the tie to one familiar, unchanging place, Sperry expressed a sentiment retained in the tranquillity of a mature man who realized, "our tether was sometimes a hundred miles long, sometimes a thousand, at times three thousand, but for nearly fifty years the cottage was ours—known, accepted with uncritical affection, patched, painted and reaffirmed."[7]

In 1893 Willard *Gardner* Sperry was called to the presidency of Olivet College, a small replication of Oberlin, out in the heartland of Michigan. As a Congregational college it was not unusual in those days that a parish minister, and not a professional educator, would attain the office of its president. What is less obvious about the move are some of the financial incentives warranting another change for the family. He accepted the job for twenty-five hundred dollars annually which was a substantial increase over his pay in Manchester. But alas the family of five still struggled to make a decent home for themselves, particularly after 1897 when national price levels rose drastically. There was no chance of sending the son to board at a New England preparatory school. As for college the first born also had to stay at home and attend Olivet, one assumes without fee for tuition. The two daughters, coming along a few years later, had opportunities to study at Smith College, a much happier prospect than staying home. The son recalled his teenaged years with some degree of marvel at how they survived various economic set-backs: "Certainly my father had no sense of money, and I suspect it was the familiar story of the mother of the family being a good manager."[8]

Having settled in the Middle West, a family custom of reverse transmigration was created in order to preserve its Yankee continuity. Every summer in the 1890s the family made its annnual trek east to its one abiding reference point, the cottage at York. The New England connections were very real and deep to the Sperrys, and such dislocations were not to be taken naturally or comfortably by them. Although there were already at that time distant Sperry relatives in California, the branch of the family represented by Willard G. and Henrietta L. Sperry and their offspring could not be long separated in spirit or in fact from the land of their Puritan ancestors.

They were directly descended from Richard Sperry, a farmer, who appeared on the American scene near the end of the founding of New Haven (1637-1643). At the time of the Restoration under Charles II (1660-1661) the New England colonies were in a delicate position as the Puritan clergy and magistrates were, for the most part, generally sympathetic with the cause of the Commmonwealth. New Haven harbored the fugitive Regicide judges, Edward Whalley and William Goffe. It was the courageous yeoman, Richard Sperry, who was, it turned out, a faithful friend and protector of the Regicides. He sheltered and fed them in "The Judges' Cave" on his farm.[9] Willard Learoyd Sperry was nine generations removed from this heroic, hard-working grandfather of the seventeenth century.

As family-minded people naturally seek their deeper beginnings, which is often problematic, the initial effort consists of bringing back into focus, if possible, the starting point against the depth of field that also pictures the rising and passing generations. Where the ultimate origin of the Sperry family lies is, like the case of many Americans, in the realm of speculation. Pushed to phonetic suppositions, "Sperry" has a Gallic ring to it. That was, at least, the operative and revisionist theory of some later geneaological research the family had done. Willard merrily reports the development to his sister, Pauline. While attending a funeral service for some obscure "Aunt Hitty, Marion's mother," he says, "I learned to my great joy that the Sperrys are not as I had been led to suppose an ancient Welsh family which fled to New Haven circ. 1640 because of certain encroachments on the decalogue, but FRENCH. The California branch have looked the matter up. They have metaphorically speaking shinned down the ancestral tree, to chere Paree or thereabouts. You wouldn't hardly notice would you?"

Sperry's proper indifference to aspects of family history thence degenerates into parody:

> I sometimes look at myself in the glass and wonder if it is really so. *Sed quantum mutatus ab illo* as Horace or his ilk hath it, from that early Carlovingian King, or ancient Bourbon knight who laid the foundations of our clan. So that when you and I wish to keep old home week, we don't turn our aching hearts from alien corn back to the dear old streets of Llangranooghiewid slumbering at the foot of grand Tranwfynddidloh, by the loved stream of Rhadalldryyn Gwwy—not a bit of it, we buy $500 of American Express money and bolt for the Champs Elysees.[10]

New England, nonetheless, held firm the Sperry family sense of place more than any other region occupying its composite memory. Getting back to New England in the 1890s opened to them, as Walt Whitman expressed it, "the large unconscious scenery of my land."[11] There is, as any vacationer discovers, something eternally fresh about the seacoast, unconscious of itself as it were, which made a powerful appeal to these Sperry children whose happiest memories gave them "comradeship to those who follow in the Arabella's wake."[12]

Traveling each summer to Maine from their outpost in Michigan and contending with an austerity budget in the process meant that the difficult journey would in retrospect serve as a large boulder of impression. Would it not also seem in the eye of a child's mind to resemble a family's religious pilgrimage, in effect reenacting the annual visit to Jerusalem for the Paschal Feast? Managing the train fares back and forth for a family of five must have required a combination of enormous sacrifice, attention to economy and intense desire to get there. Sperry recalls, "we never aspired to a *bona fide* Pullman. In better years we afforded a tourist sleeper; in lean years we 'sat up all night' in a day coach."[13]

This particular nocturnal vigil may have signalled initially some of young Sperry's nascent sensitivities to religion. He was, in mythopoetic terms, riding a train hauling spiritual freight for its young passenger. In the memoir of his boyhood, *Summer Yesterdays in Maine*, Sperry remembers "certain exciting compensations" in the overland rail route. He writes, "it allowed us either to peer out into the darkness of the night [or] to await the still blacker darkness of the Hoosac Tunnel, or to watch for the lattice-like framework of the St. Lawrence River bridge at Montreal. The Stygian night of the tunnel or the shuttling slats of the bridge as they passed the car window, with the ominous hollow rumble from either tunnel or bridge, were intimations of mystery to which no child could be insensible."[14]

Sperry explains that his father, once free of his academic obligations at Olivet, would arrange to get pulpit supply work during the summer at churches in and around Boston. He would work out the preaching schedule and cross-country rail fares in order to break even at two hundred and fifty dollars a year. This meant that the father's vacation was interrupted constantly to obtain the extra fees off-setting the family expense of summer travel. It was a hardship he bore with transparent discontent. "He was a man who could ill conceal his feelings, and as Saturday noon came around,

gloom settled over him as he dressed and packed to go away. . . sunk in a
mood of ascetic resignation." Getting home by return train the following
Monday, "he stepped off the train like a ten year old, looked at the sky, wet
his finger, held it up to feel which way the wind was blowing, and plunged
at once into discussion of the possibility of getting a couple of hours sailing
before the breeze died out."[15]

Sperry gives still other personal reminscence about there being the
residue of a rugged Maine summer on his father's hands which always
outlasted the vacation period and carried over into the restored routine of
autumn. The father had pulled so many cod lines in July and August that
his hands had been toughened and inflexibly calloused. Apparently, in the
pulpit his forefinger, like cracked leather in need of neetsfoot oil, could get
no grip on the pages of his sermon manuscript. His sermon paper had holes
punched in the left-hand margin, and the pages were tied loosely with pink
kitchen twine. His habit, therefore, was to turn pages instead of sliding
them loosely to another place on the pulpit desk. As the son recalls of the
father, there was no way to avoid giving his right forefinger a swift,
unconcealed lick with his tongue when a page required turning. The son
would one day look back on the vision in winsomeness because that
"gesture horrified my mother, and is not, I must admit, included in any of
the manuals for effective public speech which have come to my notice."[16]

Throughout Sperry's boyhood the severe ethic of duty above pleasure
guided the father through his summer weekends of work. The supplemen-
tal pay made possible a family headquarters and hub around which they
happily orbited for many ensuing years. How much the father's uneven
attitude toward his professional life influenced the future decision of his
son to follow him is a question worth exploring, if only to dig around some
of those early and delicate intellectual roots. The elder Sperry was a man of
realism and great discipline, "but there was enough of the uncorrupted boy
left in him to rebel at having to get out of a flannel shirt on Saturday
afternoons and into a boiled shirt, and off on a dusty train to Boston."[17]
Sperry admired this whimsy in his father and its subtle suggestiveness
perhaps made the ministry a vocational option with fewer psychological
impediments and intimidating imperatives than otherwise assumed by the
uninitiated. The son of such a minister saw a life fairly balanced between
work and recreation, but whatever puerile resistance the father put against

the costly personal time away from lazy summer Sundays, was not the whole story of his ministerial example.

Sperry alludes to a more serious message of protest from his father just as the son embarked on graduate theological study. After all, the generation of the father had experienced unprecedented intellectual upheaval deposing finally the older New England theology from its prominent sphere of influence. The shock waves of evolutionary theory, the cascades of higher Biblical criticism and the hammer of the Social Gospel hit the father's generation with full impact. The *fin de siècle* mood had left much fall-out and its survivors remained in a state of shaken confidence. Thirty years later Sperry reveals, at another poignant moment of ministerial defensiveness (the 1930s), his father's enlarged uncertainty: "I remember that when in 1904 I decided to enter the ministry, my father said, 'I do not know whether, if I were your age now, I should have the courage to make that choice a second time'."[18]

There were many reasons for feeling that way, other than the fear of domestic hardship and the struggle to maintain consistent financial security in the depressed 1890s. Clergy families have usually been somewhat resilient to those issues about relative prosperity, decency, comfort and occasional luxuries. Sperry writes, "I do not mean to suggest that my father sinned the sin of simony, or that he did not enjoy life as a minister; he did, and was beloved as a preacher and a pastor."[19]

The chief problem for the older Sperry was rather that of seeing a sentimental cause irrevocably altered and in some minds finally lost. As a student at Andover Seminary in the late 1870s he belonged to the generation which was casting off the last remnants of the hereditary Calvinism of New England Congregationalism. The presence of cumulative internal strains would be expected, let alone the obvious outside and downward pressures upon a diminished clergy social influence, which come to bedevil any one wrestling with the first raptures of progress and the new order. It is plausible to suppose that while his son and daughters were growing up, the elder Sperry had become quite relaxed in his theological thinking over the two and a half decades of constant accommodation to cultural developments. He wisely gave his children wide theological berth, never preaching at them or trying to indoctrinate them in any way. As adults his daughters would be blithely indifferent to church-going, though Pauline's interest was revived in her late middle age. The father's interests were projected as being warmly human and "he had a genius for friendship."[20] Systematic theology and the development of doctrine mattered little to him, especially in his role as a father.

Sperry noted the quality of openness in his father, in contrast to his mother's exacting standards, on the occasion when a new minister arrived at the village church in Olivet, Michigan. The young man had recently graduated from Union Theological Seminary of New York City, so was naturally held under some doctrinal clouds of suspicion in that less advanced rural setting of his call. The rumor circulated that this fledgling preacher did not believe in the Virgin Birth. This was particularly disturbing to mother Sperry who brought the matter to the front in the form of dinner conversation. The father and chief justice of the family patiently listened, but was non-plussed by the weight of his wife's scruples in the matter of pure dogma. Sperry came to believe in later life that such incidents and overheard discussions of this sort familiarized him as a boy with "the fact that the letter of the faith once delivered to the saints was in process of change." By the time Sperry began to study the issues of historic theology for himself there were no corresponding shocks about myths being exploded, a typically jolting effect that is so often experienced in college and seminary years by more naive students. Sperry shared something of his father's disposition all his life:

> I knew that damnable errors and heresies were abroad in the land, and never was thrown into any panic by that awareness. Indeed, I am inclined to think that the memory of those earlier years persuaded me that if there is a theological skeleton in the closet, it is no use to lock the doors and throw the key down the well; it is much better to open the door and have a look at the brute. [21]

The attitude posed by both Sperrys in some way resembles the insistence of Charles G. Finney (1792-1875) that places "schooling before theology." Finney, in fact, rebelled vigorously against any methodological or theological rigidity. Combined with his subjective and pragmatic standard of spiritual values, the American evangelist was disposed positively toward strands of the new theology. That theology reflects a complicated, but immensely important man in mid-nineteenth-century America and the American Reformed tradition. Moreover, Finney's revivals were catalytic agents in the rising abolitionist crusade and in the development of urban evangelism. A rival of Lyman Beecher and later an ally, Finney at first represented an aggressive departure from the evangelical "united front" that can be traced to the Great Awakening and Beecher's campaigns against Boston Unitarianism. Finney, like Beecher a licensed Presbyterian preacher, went beyond even Beecher's modifications of the Westminster Confession. In Finney's theology, for example, sin was a voluntary act and hypothetically avoidable, hence holiness was a human possibility. This bold proclamation, "even from the liberated ground of Taylorism," was an extreme departure from earlier Calvinistic emphases.

In part, therefore, Finney's legacy was liberalism since his "anthropology" seemed "higher" than Beecher's. But he was not himself disposed towards anything like the liberalism about the Bible that one might associate with later times or even with Horace Bushnell. The connection is there, but needs handling with precision to be found. It is visible, most obviously perhaps, in Finney's demand that some kind of germane social action follow the sinner's conversion—hence, his tie to "liberal" reform movements with attending evangelical fervor. It is also the case that Finney is significant as a Fundamentalist forerunner too, as George Marsden argues successfully in his book on the New School Presbyterians.

Furthermore, it is significant that the Sperrys are probable, though probably unconscious, followers of Finney because Olivet College was established in 1844 by adherents to Finney's point of view. In the half century that preceded the Sperrys' time there, the Finney influence was not likely to have diminished very much. Olivet originally drew people away from Oberlin to found "a Christian community" on the frontier along the Grand River with just a few settlers in cabins built on the high ground. The Reverend John Jay Shipherd, the principle founder of Olivet, was an enthusiastic follower of the Finneyite movement. Shipherd's intention in going to Michigan was clearly to put in place an Oberlin satellite.

The centennial history (published in 1944) of the college and village traces the early years of struggle, followed by a decimated student population attributable to the Civil War. For lack of men the graduating classes during those years were entirely comprised of women, in keeping with the progressive ideas of education inherent to Congregationalism. The college, however, did not lack for continuity in those disruptive years. Notably, in the commemorative volume celebrating the first hundred years of corporate existence, there is hardly any mention of The Reverend Willard G. Sperry whose presidency at Olivet for thirteen years must have counted for a most crucial phase of its development. Rather, the entry for 1893, the year President Sperry began his term of leadership, reports the death in December of Professor Oramel Hosford, who had retired in 1890, after teaching in the college since 1844. It was generally assumed that Professor Hosford taught the first class that ever met in the college.[22]

The curious and slighting juxtaposition of condensed news tells much by what is left unspoken. The saving remnant of the Finneyite impulse was not only still flourishing when the Sperry family moved from the manse to the campus, it was in Olivet esteemed, embraced and beloved. One can only surmise that to survive in that climate of tradition, there must have been by even the new arrivals in 1893 some built-in sympathy for the prevailing holy winds of long ago. In terms of the college's collective memory, President Sperry was only a generation removed from Finney, and perhaps to the Olivet community represented a mere continuation of that influence. There is no record of any theological rows or heretical challenges to indicate it might have been otherwise.

What the younger Sperry reports of his father bears some likeness to the well known account Finney provided of his post-conversion dismissal of an older, dated article of faith. In his memoir Finney takes great exception to a Protestant scholasticism that no longer speaks to the condition of common humanity as he understands it to be:

> Soon after I was converted I called on my pastor, and had a long conversation with him on atonement. He was a Princeton student and of course held the limited view of the atonement—that it was made for the elect and available to none else. Our conversation lasted nearly half a day. He held that Jesus suffered for the elect the literal penalty of the Divine law. . . I objected that this was absurd; as in that case he suffered the equivalent of endless misery multiplied by the whole number of the elect. . . On the contrary it seemed to me that Jesus only satisfied public justice, and that that was all that the government could require. . . . I thought he did not sustain his views from the Bible, and told him so. I thought he had evidently interpreted those texts in conformity with an established theory. . .[23]

To the extent of tracing inductive religious thinking at all, the Sperrys, father and son, are kindred spirits to that line of intuition suggested by Finney's subjective simplification and common sense judgement of religion. One of Willard Sperry's favorite stories, which he often repeated, pricks the reputation of a too tidy doctrine inflated with puffery. Dwight L. Moody was a surprising protagonist of an anecdote told by the Dean of the "corpse cold" Divinity School at Harvard. Sperry, nonetheless, admired Moody, Finney's popular successor in American revivalism. No one questioned Moody's sincerity, though, as Sperry points out, there have been many sophisticated jabs at the evangelist's sense of propriety. After one of Moody's sermons a certain linguistic Pharisee taunted, "Mr. Moody, I noted fifteen mistakes in grammar in your sermon." To which Moody replied, "I am using all the grammar I have for God, what are you doing with your grammar?"

Sperry used the Moody story to illustrate the necessity of testing religion for its purity of motives instead of applying such intense scrutiny for the mere precision of argument. Interpreting texts, therefore, "in conformity with an established theory" went against the family grain of conscience. Sperry makes the further disclaimer, however, that after Moody's time "the professional breed [of revivalist] began to disimprove."[24]

The Sperry family was too demure, too cerebral and too traditional ever to be more than tepid about their long-term confidence in popular evangelism. Sperry became a student secretary in the Y.M.C.A. the first year out of college (the fall of 1903), circuit riding in Kansas, Oklahoma and parts west. He detested the experience. It was, in his words, "too desultory." He found that the theological dogmatism of the Y.M.C.A. at the time, and more particularly its rather superheated emotionalism were not suitable to him at all.[25]

Sperry came down very hard against the subsequent line of Finney and Moody spiritual heirs in the twentieth century. He tangled with the Billy Sunday traveling crusade while serving as the Minister of Central Congregational Church in Boston, and years later commented that, in his opinion, "the final degeneration of what had been one of our major religious institutions" was represented in Billy Sunday. The theology was too crude, the methods too theatrical, the commercial demands too calculated and the psychology too manipulative to command the moral confidence of people like Sperry. For him Billy Sunday "defeated his own ends, and discredited the tradition in which he stood."[26]

Writing in subsequent years to an English audience inspirited with the upper class fervor of Buchmanism (the Oxford Group Movement, otherwise called Moral Rearmament), Sperry said that the American scene has been so often "burnt over" by revivals "that there is little standing timber or dry grass left among us to kindle in precisely this way." He tells his English readers that "even though the techniques of Buchmanism were addressed to upper social classes—the Salvation Army in dinner jacket" the distinguishing signs of revivalism are unmistakable in any guise. Sperry had seen all the old tricks before and what swept the Oxford community in the 1930s was little else than the mostly "spent force" of American revivalist techniques. He summarizes the old story of revivals for any neophyte enthusiast, assuming by mistake it was something fresh:

> Their theology was often incredible; their applied psychology was filled with emotional dangers; their influence was too ephemeral; their permanent residue was too meagre; their mechanism too obvious, too well oiled; and their commercial instinct too highly developed.[27]

In so far as Sperry has childhood surface roots in Finneyite Congregationalism the evidence suggests that he agreed selectively and only in principle with that subjectivist tradition, which is the validity and priority of private religious experience and individual interpretation. For him doctrine was never absolutely binding, or else the primacy of personal feelings would not be genuinely ratified. It must be noted, however, that Sperry was not in his mature religious thinking an absolute subjectivist, nor did he emerge from a background where much Biblical literalism predominated. In the future Sperry would argue cogently for the necessity of some religious objectivity, of looking outside the self for genuine religious feelings to be ponderable. His book, *Reality in Worship*, explores and develops his departure from Finneyite revisions having to do with the beginning and end of religious experience, especially in the corporate context.

The Sperrys lived mentally at the incipience of Finney's principles, and never near the center and conclusion of Finneyite practices. They were, no doubt, sympathetic to other causes Finney represented, if only because Olivet brought forward that special brand of progressive mid-western Congregationalism into the 1890s. Olivet was known from its inception as a place in the woods "tainted with abolitionism and kindred heresies," much like its parent, Oberlin.[28]

There were other childhood and formative influences which served to shape Willard Sperry's peculiar twentieth-century liberalism, a cast of mind that cut across the usual boundaries of theological division. Foremost in the making of a minister was the unspoken reassurance absorbed from a father's quiet example, an influence exerted upon an adolescent in largely an unconscious and unplanned manner, completely unrealized by the son until later in life. It will be useful in tracking continuities from his youth forward in time and from his maturity backward in time to locate the father on the theological map of his son's impressionable early days. One of the specific landmarks upon the shifting scene of ministerial roles in general and Congregationalist strategy in particular for that generation is found in the area of foreign missions. Sperry's eventual ambivalence toward the efficacy of the social gospel probably reflects his father's earlier position which did place him on the back edge (as opposed to the cutting edge) of modernism with respect to missionary attitudes.

In the autumn of 1903, with his son fresh out of college and on the western Y.M.C.A. circuit, Willard Gardner Sperry went east to attend the annual meeting of the American Board of Commissioners for Foreign Missions (ABCFM). He had been invited that year to preach the sermon, an extrememly high honor, given the list of pulpiteers who had preceded him, including the eminent minister of Old South in Boston, George A. Gordon. For Sperry the trip would be a sentimental journey as the meetings were held in Manchester, New Hampshire, the place of his last pastorate before moving to the presidency at Olivet.

The ABCFM had not lacked for controversy in the twenty-five years since Sperry's ordination to the ministry. Its obvious responsibility for the support of Christian missionary endeavors was coupled with a secondary purpose of major consequence. The ABCFM had developed into a kind of ecclesial experimental station out in the field. It was something like a weather vane and lightning rod atop the New England Congregational Church, catching the winds and static from the academic storm center before the same force and change could ever be felt in the pulpit and the pews. The test case for the Old Theology of New England was tried and blasted in various meetings of the ABCFM. The theological signs of the times were perhaps easiest to read by watching the weather gathering over the annual deliberations of the ABCFM. There seemed to be in that setting, like none other, the greatest opportunity to air thoroughly the issues of a vague modernism without threatening established church structures and foundations. By exposing there the immediate concerns and past glories in utter nakedness, it was improbable that any comparable challenges to doctrine would reach the local church any sooner. If anything, the typical parish minister would see to it, at all costs, such vehemence be kept out of the business of the congregation.

The ABCFM provided the context for reworking the distinctiveness of the Christian message which was becoming obscure as the old Calvinist system was replaced. The very notion of divine selectivity, for instance, posed a serious moral conflict within the cross purposes of exporting western ideas to foreign cultures. George A. Gordon was perhaps the best known spokesman of the New Theology. Gordon is, in various ways, associated with the "Christocentric liberal" tradition which included Horace Bushnell, Newman Smyth, Washington Gladden, Arthur Cushman McGiffert and William Newton Clarke. These prominent figures were, of course, directly or peripherally involved with the liberal theologians of Andover Theological Seminary. Newman Smyth, for example, stood courageously opposed as a young man to the dominant Edwards A. Park of Andover because of Park's "orthodox rationalism."

Gordon's thought and career obviously intersected the paths of both Sperrys and, at one of these cross-roads, a closer, though not even a semi-filial relationship began between Gordon and the younger Sperry from 1914 to 1922 as they were, during those years, ministerial colleagues in the Back Bay. Gordon, therefore, was not only a representative of broad currents of thought within American Congregationalism, he was also, in the case of the Sperrys, a household name and a tangible person.

Gordon had entered the fray of the missionary question in the late 1880s by attending the ABCFM session in Springfield, Massachusetts. Gordon was a modern thinker, finely tuned to the nuances of the Harvard Department of Philosophy. As a person trained in philosophical discourse, Gordon aniticipated correctly that the issue of future probation would be the final battlefield between two conflicting theological worlds within the New England mind. Here the older New England theology would take its last stand.

Future probation was a controversial article of New England doctrine which also signalled a major denouement in the Andover drama that led finally to the passing of the New England theology. How the controversy ensued centers on the old problem of how missionaries address the question, "What shall Christians think about the fate of those who die without saving repentance? Are they condemned to everlasting punishment?" And to be sure, the problem of the unsaved persists in evangelical and Fundamentalist theology. It is not only the wounded head of a universalist challenge to orthodoxy picking itself up again to declare all are saved; it is an issue that conflicts with a belief in a merciful God. The line of questions for the American missionary runs into speculation: since so many people die without hearing the gospel, are they all lost or is the gospel absolutely necessary to salvation?

By the time Gordon came to the ABCFM meeting of 1887 he was traveling in a new and decidedly liberal direction. The debate about eternal punishment had thus become a yearly event on the ABCFM agenda. Gordon witnessed the heated colloquy in a mood of combined laughter and disbelief. Worse than residual adiaphora, Gordon found the whole business "preposterous, such a mere matter of miserable detail," like worrying about the number of angels dancing on the head of a pin.

Gordon had risen to the role of point man in the assault to claim the higher ground of the modern missionary. "It was here," he said, "that a sense of mission to my generation came to possess me." Gordon carefully reasoned that "under the Calvinistic scheme... the good was not true and the truth was not good. At the heart of the whole business this was the fatal contradiction in our inherited faith." Gordon could not imagine a divided humanity as having anything to do with divine will. It was impossible to conceive of humanity as mere sheep and goats, separated by election and damnation. How can God simultaneously will for some their highest good and for others their eternal misery? "If this is the truth," he warns, "it cannot be good; if the good be the vision of God as the lover of every soul... its home and infinite peace, the good is not true."[29]

What, then, were the irreducible realities for modern Congregationalism? Gordon listed personality, humanity, optimism, the moral order and God as the articles of the new creed necessary for Christianity not only in the modern world, but to the world inhabited by those prospects whom the Christian missionary sought to convert.[30]

Gordon's prescription by 1895 presented some subtle difficulties, but for its fresh enthusiasm and renewed optimism a general degree of liberal self-confidence resulted. When it came time for Willard G. Sperry to address the same body eight years later the finer distinctions which Gordon drew with facile and delicate lines were, in 1903, blurred marks of new territory. Against a background of previous controversy and a new arrangement of ideas, the Olivet president was given the privilege of following Gordon before the same body. How he was chosen to be invited remains in question. Whether he was in the Gordon camp or an old-fashioned moderate may be easier to ascertain. For instance, in the sermon preached, how much in keeping with Gordon's ideas did Sperry obtain? What of the older Sperry's sense of the New England tradition, whether refuted, revised or reaffirmed can be ascertained? What was President Sperry's world view and did it comply and fit with the picture Gordon drew in 1895?

The fact that the younger Sperry's father was part of a clergy generation undergoing rapid rearrangement in a time of perceived "change and decay" makes the little patch of common ground with contemporary figures and organizations significant. At a critical juncture in the life of the son, the father had an important moment of public recognition. Whatever bearing all this had on the son can, it seems, be determined best in the larger context of upheaval and adjustment which the ABCFM, acting as a weather vane, symbolized to the first generation of liberals in the twentieth century that included Congregationalists such as George A. Gordon and Willard G. Sperry. Finally, what one seeks are the theological atmospherics, the barometric pressure of the time before the youthful Willard L. Sperry went up to Oxford to read theology. And in arriving at Queens College in the autumn of 1904, one must ask, what pre-conceived ideas did he bring with him and would they continue with him in later life?

The last quarter of the nineteenth century has been called a watershed period in American religion, particularly for the Protestant mainline. Richard Hofstadter in a seminal work (*The Age of Reform*) argued that the late nineteenth-century clergy were "probably the conspicuous losers from the status revolution." Hofstadter has some justification in saying that "the increasingly vigorous interest in the social gospel, so clearly manifested by the clergy after 1890, was in many respects an attempt to restore through secular leadership some of the spiritual influence and authority and social prestige that clergy had lost." There have been any number of responses made that qualify, temper or flatly refute Hofstadter's premise that the church and clergy were losing their position on the top rung at the turn of the century.[31] It is hard not to see the obvious, however, that role declension struck clergy unusually hard. One may even sustain the defense that such social alienation oddly and inadvertently compensated the once leading professionals. As Robert T. Handy demonstrates persuasively, the resurgence of missionary activity was rising "as the century drew to a close by a growing feeling that Protestant Christianity was rapidly becoming the most important religious force in the world." Handy quotes a Congregational theologian who boasted that "today Christianity is the power which is moulding the destinies of the world. The Christian nations are in the ascendant."[32]

It was, ironically, a time of self-congratulatory optimism and of religious superiority with imperialistic ambitions, while most of the perceived moral triumph abroad was not particularly warranted by realities at home. There was, to be sure, a sense among church leaders of decline and of social displacement in the context of all this inflated self-assurance. While "the achievement of the missionary movement, in which American Protestantism had become so deeply involved, was a major event in Christian history," there were hidden costs to be reckoned when the piper came to collect his pay for this false jubilation.[33]

Much of the missionary expansion was a compensation for the growing sense that the church was losing its equilibrium of moral and intellectual leadership. Meanwhile, other institutions were beginning to prosper and encroach upon old church boundaries. Churches, for example, were not able to endow libraries (per the Carnegie model) and so were looking for new venues to reclaim an always tenuous community position. Sydney Ahlstrom explains how the crisis was building into "an unexpected tempest" as it was becoming obvious "that the foreign missions revival may well have arisen as a half-subconscious effort to divert Protestants from intellectual problems and internal dissensions by engaging them in great moral and spiritual tasks—only to have deeper problems and moral dissension reappear."[34]

Willard G. Sperry may have foreseen many of these deferred intellectual problems in his sermon, "The Vision of the Kingdom," preached eloquently to the ABCFM in 1903. It was generally a message inspiring hope, but with an exceptionally strong note of caution which disputes the prevailing trends of corporate theory and the social gospel sweeping through anxious Protestant minds of the day. His skillful exegesis of the text from Revelation (14:1) traces the mood of Pentecostal joyfulness back to the Acts of the Apostles. What follows thence "down to the last of the epistles" is "a sobering change." He enjoins his listeners to "read the beginnings of this great story, when the church won her first magnificent triumphs and your heart is stirred by the reverbative sense of power and victory." As one's reading proceeds, however, he yields to "the sadness of inevitable conflict yet to be prolonged, and of temporary defeat." In considering the epistles it is quickly apparent that "their note is one of warning, not of victory. You hear not a paean but a miserere. . . Faith has declined. . . Love is replaced by selfish worldliness."[35] Is there not some self-conscious chiasm in the rhetoric? Is the glory day of the early patristic period not unlike the height of Calvinist power in New England? And then, after initial euphoria there is parallel decline.

Sperry adeptly reverses the mood of despair, but not at the cost of reality. He says it is fortunate that the New Testament does not end in a contentious state with Jude's epistle. This is not to be the last word. "In the revelation (Revelation 14:1) we leave much of the story of the past behind us, and we turn to the vision of things yet to be." Sperry posits the liberal construct of heaven as "an individual life, exalted, inspired, perfected and precious; and it is also a redeemed society, in whose choruses and ranks and companies the personal worth of each life is not lost but found, and is found to be a thing of indestructible worth and of worth beyond all price." While this vaguely sounds like universalism, most liberals, including Gordon, assumed that many would hear the gospel but reject it. There is no reason to believe Sperry would push his vision of "the personal worth of each life" beyond the implicit assumptions of even a diluted Calvinism requiring the condition of human choice to merit salvation.

The hope of the New Jerusalem is set beside the countervailing gloom of Jude. Sperry describes the vivid apocalyptic imagery—the Lamb sits on a mount surveying a highly organized human society, a "unified army of the redeemed." There is precision, not anarchy in this multitude of 144,000. It is somewhat representative of a kind of utopian society some would imagine for the twentieth century. And therefore, the vision, according to Sperry, invites the thought about the compatibility of a redeemed personal life with a redeemed society. Do the interests of the individual and of society clash? It is an issue as old as Plato. After all, there is the recurrent problem about "how imperfect have been the best attainments of the best social order in the world about us." The antagonism between the individual and society has at various times made it seem "that society is not the cradle of the personal life, but the grave of personality."[36] Which is to give way and what bearing does it have on the Protestant sense of mission?

Sperry's preference is more than rhetorical. Too often organizations "went far to convince the world that the church itself was everything and the individual nothing." Sperry is bold to claim that the impersonality of social theory, and particularly that brand of it which had enraptured many progressive churchmen of his day, was at variance with the good of the individual. He rings down the mistakes of subjugating individuality to impersonality which threatens to infect the church trying to expand at the wrong time:

> They have been unable to make real, often they could not imagine a social life in which a man should come to know himself, his capacities, his duties, a society so spontaneous, so free from dull formalities, and so full of divine impulse, that it could cultivate the life of the individual, who of us has seen it? Who dares dream of it? No doubt one part of the unrest with which the twentieth century begins is the feeling that society, however organized, fails to hold sacred and precious the life of the individual.[37]

Sperry, in de-emphasizing organization (in particular church missionary infrastructure) and by exalting the individual is drawing from an up-dated antinomian liberalism that is also given to a heightened anthropology. One can infer from Sperry's sermon that the worst thing that could happen is a conformity whereby people "set a low value of themselves. . . a life of selfish expediency in the midst of a society which had no spontaneous power. . ."[38] It is, accordingly, impractical to transform whole societies without first generating specific opportunity for individual freedom. This was and still is the major crossroads redirecting dissension within the liberal ranks. Sperry invokes verbatim Horace Bushnell's notion of divine immanence, that "the grandest things that ever come into us are commanded in." The vision of the kingdom is inner-directed, an inner reality, and cannot be effective ultimately by any prior, outer social imperative. Form follows function or in religious terms, where your heart is there also is your treasure.

Sperry applies his argument to the situation of the Protestant foreign missions. His fear is that the missionary impulse has changed for the worse from personal to social labor. Sperry is here, it seems, resisting the natural attempts to socialize the gospel as a strategy for holding the line on Protestant status. Sperry saw much that would be lost if "personal ministries to individual souls" were forsaken for a broader program. This dates one aspect of the Protestant dilemma a few years sooner than Sydney Ahlstrom puts the approaching controversy. He says, "As early as 1911, Joseph E. McAfee, a Presbyterian. . . defined the crisis: 'If the missionary maintains that the individualistic method is ultimate and represents an individualistic scheme of salvation as final . . . he runs counter to approved world tendencies and repudiates a social theory which schools of thought in all civilized lands are successfully establishing'."[39]

It is most unlikely that Sperry would take any exception whatsoever to the theological sentiments implied by McAfee in 1911. The distinction which Sperry sketches in the autumn of 1903 is that in disposing of the exhausted and narrow conditions of personal salvation (i.e., the strict acceptance of soteriological and Christological suppositions of historic doctrine)—a theological non-issue for liberals as McAfee says—there is danger in throwing out the proverbial baby with the bath water, namely the personal care of souls. To socialize the gospel does not necessarily make a socialized ministry valid. Sperry concludes his sermon, "If, then, afterward, we find a large place for Christian Socialism, and we learn that all things are unchristian which are unsocial, may we be reminded that better institutions ... will not redeem the world ... [but] in the wider views of evangelism which belongs to these last days may we recognize the workings of that one and self same spirit, dividing every man severally as he will."[40]

One line in the sermon which is striking for the way it reemerges in the son's life of the mind reads, "The twentieth century which has made infinite progress along some lines seems sometimes far too much like the first Christian century. At any rate it has shown its own tremendous problems which, if we are to judge, should have been left behind us centuries ago. . ."[41] The son very often drew parallels between the two centuries, the deficient ends of the past, the unimproved means of the present: "Our modern apocalypses, therefore, do not bid fair to be more accurate than were the ancient apocalypses, though by their overstatement they may serve to waken us to the nature of the drastic changes through which we are now passing."[42] We can see in other ways, too, the impact which the sermon by the elder Sperry had on the younger. In his provocative first book dedicated to the memory of his parents, Sperry takes up the chicken and egg issue all over again where his father had left it—the personal comes ahead of the social. "From this social outreaching of the individual who in his solitude knows both the catholicity of his most personal and private transaction with God and his need of comrades that his joy may be made perfect, churches spring."[43]The sequence of religious experience, identical to that depicted in the father's message to the ABCFM, follows that the collective spirit cannot precede the personal reality of an inner vision. First the blade, then the ear, then the full grain in the ear.

And yet, the younger Sperry, not soon before the guns of August 1914 roared, preached for the ABCFM in Boston a sermon entitled, "The Case for Foreign Missions." He set forth several reasons in keeping with the father's general endorsement in which both deplored American nativism or ecclesiastical chauvinism. The potential for doing good on an individual basis still resides within the charge of foreign missions, claimed Sperry, so long as social consequences are secondary considerations and the individual work primary. As Sperry analyzed the situation, the missionary must avoid the attitude that "what I am doing is for your own good" because that leads to the undesirable scenario of imperialism.

Sperry believed in foreign missions for three reasons: they make for peace; as the world "is fast becoming one world ... the interchange of ideas is also inevitable;" and they offer an opportunity to test the spiritual austerity and mettle of Christianity against any self-seeking motives for material return. Sperry's first ideal about peace-making was derived from the Rhodes Scholar program as a model which in both purpose and form is cooperative and not competitive. His enthusiasm for what an international experience meant to individuals, apart from such an experience between governments, was vague anticipation of the American Peace Corps.

Secondly, once there in a foreign land, the missionary must not be "impudent and interfering" with the indigent culture. The missionary's "task is not to supplant but to supplement the religious findings of non-Christian faiths, to build upon the foundations already laid by common religious consciousness." Sperry also believed in foreign missions on the eve of the Great War because in the interchange between cultures "the Christianity of twentieth century America will be brought to new self-criticism and a fresh self-consciousness." He elaborated his rationale for the use of missions as a test case by explaining that "missions remind us, to our perpetual humiliation, that all of the world religions are eastern religions, that Christianity is an eastern religion, that the genius of the West has been turned into other channels, that we have been perpetrators and interpreters in religion, rather than creators."

Thirdly, missions afforded the Church the opportunity to do more than just talk about the ideal of "hoping for nothing in return" while the other side of the mouth uttered platitudes of American middle class prosperity. Missions reduce the measures of profit and self-seeking to a minimum when they are genuine to the tenets of Jesus which, in turn, will "offer the Church her supreme opportunity to test her faith and practice."[44] These general ideas which Sperry outlined in sermon form in 1914 were on the same trajectory as the later reforms proposed by the eminent philosopher and Congregationalist layman, William Ernest Hocking in the 1930s, whose notion of "ambassadorship" was found in "world understanding on the spiritual level." Sperry, at least, foresaw the revisions in theory and practice of the Protestant "errand to the world," even though his prior interest in that field of Christian service never again materialized after 1914.[45]

❦

At the time Sperry's father was preaching before the august national body of the ABCFM Sperry himself was writing home from the Y.M.C.A. outpost in Fort Riley, Kansas, working out of "a small private tent just at the foot of the bluff." It was a lonely time for the oldest sibling whom the family had nicknamed "Roy" as indicated by his letters soliciting news and trivia from Pauline. She supplied him with some campus gossip and an occasional recapitulation of a college football game. Writing a couple of weeks after the sermon was delivered, "Roy," a little behind on the news, seeks current information. "I heard of father's going east and Mrs. W.G. [mother] also, was glad to know of that . . . but further than that nothing. If they have not already done so I hope they will send me some sort of report of the Board meeting [of the ABCFM], especially the sermon."[46]

The eagerness of a son to share in the father's shining moment is a broad hint that, far from filial indifference, there was instead deep devotion between the two men. Less than three years later Sperry's father died and one can safely assume that his early death (at the age of 59 from Bright's Disease) gave "Roy" the partial impetus to complete the father's unfinished work in the ministry. The dim half-miracle and early patterns of family life can be discerned many times over in the later sensibilities expressed by the son. It is by either Baconian or discursive reasoning wise to work back to the barely visible strands of evidence about parental influences. As historian Philip Greven makes abundantly clear:

Childhood was the matrix which the sense of self, shaping consciousness and convictions, was being formed, not only because many parents set about to ensure the inculcation of particular modes of behavior, values and beliefs, but also because the accumulation of personal experiences in the earliest years of life had an enduring influence upon the development of the temperaments and religious experience of people in adulthood.[47]

In the relative terms of social and educational background, the Sperry family closely resembles the general profile of prominent Protestant ministers for 1875-1915, compiled by William R. Hutchison using his innovative method of "controlled group biography" (that is controlled in the sense of data, but also in not rushing to hasty conclusions from computer regression analysis).[48] The period of this study is pertinent here because the years by which it is framed include two generations in one ministerial family, thus giving double validity. While the family disposition may not have been thoroughly advanced in all liberal causes, there is no evidence to suggest that the liberalism of "Roy" Sperry was a radical departure from his childhood faith. To the contrary, it was a continuation of family habits already established in a disciplined, yet not overly aggressive Victorian environment.

Sperry speaks of his mother's strong influence and makes of it a more direct religious force in his life than his father's moral authority. His filial respect for his mother is transparent, because she was the family theologian, taking a keen interest in matters of Biblical criticism all her life. "She had," writes Sperry "something of Newman's dread of liberalism," looking with apprehension at the judgements of the higher critics. She "often spoke with distaste of the works of a German gentleman whom she insisted on calling 'Karnack'." She uttered his name with the same disdain which Churchill used to put into his references to the "Nazzys."

The Sperry home was organized around a Puritan culture still in force. The expected tabus against wicked indulgence were strictly pressed; the sabbath was scrupulously observed. To both parents matters of conscience were all important and the test of integrity was set against the lie, the one unforgiveable sin in the eyes of Willard and Henrietta Sperry. Their son, however, came to believe "that discipline persuaded me that sincerity is a cardinal religious virtue, whatever the price for its observance or penalty for its abuse."[49]

Henrietta Learoyd Sperry was, no doubt, a forceful personality. In the words of her granddaughter, she "was a small spare woman, not given to displays of emotion, mentally alert, very New England. Though she was undemonstrative she always seemed to have time for a small girl."[50]

"Roy" Sperry was at home during his school and college years. Whatever power Olivet College had exerted upon him, it cannot be characterized in any equivalent terms as the major impact that his parents and, later, Oxford had on him. Olivet "was at that time unequivocally denominational." One of the required courses in the curriculum was titled "Christian Evidences"; it was taught by "a hard, doctrinaire old gentleman whose rigid mood and dull lectures were guaranteed to discourage any possible interest in religion. His nature and character were anything but an evidence of that which he professed."[51]

It is worth noting, however, that a course on "Christian evidences" was the center of the old Finneyite, "common sense" and evangelical curriculum. While many of Finney's critics often felt he overlooked the importance of instruction in concentrating his efforts to bring about the moment of conversion, this charge turns out to be an oversimplification. The tradition of "affections" and intellect being blended was as old as Jonathan Edwards, and though at times divided from Finney's priorities, was manifested eventually in Archibald Alexander's widely distributed *A Brief Outline of the Evidences of the Christian Religion* (1825). Alexander made his case out of prolonged pedagogy, whereas Finney stressed "the most arresting and persuasive presentation of the gospel at the moment of appeal."

Drawn from the apologetic writings of Anglican Latitudinarians Samuel Clarke (1675-1729) and William Paley (1743-1805), Alexander's strategy followed closely the central lines of eighteenth-century antideistical writers who argued first for "external" evidences of miracle and fulfilled prophesy to prove that the Bible contains divine revelation. In addition, the "internal" evidences, making a subjective appeal to the individual's moral and religious sensibilities, became Alexander's surest foundation for an intellectual defense of Christianity, thus approximating the positions of Edwards and Finney. Sperry's youthful ambivalence toward Christian apologetics later flowered into a serious attack against its bankruptcy (see chapter 5). Sperry would likely have chortled at the quip of the deist Anthony Collins that no one doubted the existence of God until the apologist Samuel Clarke undertook to demonstrate it.[52]

Two things at Olivet were significant in Sperry's general education at a small provincial college of liberal arts. He was first introduced there to the joys of serious English literature, in particular Carlyle, Tennyson and Browning. *Sartor Resartus* was a rare, transforming event. By depending on *Sartor Resartus* as a paradigm for the getting of religion in a scientific age, Sperry naturally turned in a direction that had already had enormous precedent in the nineteenth century. *Sartor Resartus* has been correctly judged as a focal point for the romantic religion of several generations, the last of which managed to reach Sperry via a nineteenth-century college curriculum. This is a key book, it seems, for the overcoming of religious doubt by vague affirmations, written as a response to "the disappearance of God" in Victorian literature and culture.

Carlyle, unlike Matthew Arnold, did not spend his time lamenting the fact of God's apparent absence. Rather, he took the offensive and tried to re-establish a secure life of the mind and a rationale for human action in the face of God's "reticence." *Sartor Resartus*, in contrast to Nietzsche's *Thus Spake Zarathustra*, ends optimistically, setting up an interpretation of existence that makes life essentially mysterious, indefinable, yet hopeful. Typically for nineteenth-century readers, the climactic experience of three particular chapters of *Sartor Resartus*, the "Everlasting NO," the "Centre of Indifference," and the "Everlasting YEA," were the most important sections, not only because of what they reveal in the way of an autobiographical transition, but also for how they capture in the imagery of conflict and resolution a self-realization.

The memorable description of the machine universe, at the heart of the "Everlasting NO," is a justly famous passage of anxiety prose. "O, the vast, gloomy, solitary Golgotha and Mill of Death! Why were the living banished thither companionless, conscious?" The loneliness is constant, as the realization is of a world without a clear plan or direction, when faith in an omnipotent God is lost. The remaining belief is merely a mechanical process without Divine authority, without apparent intention. Then Carlyle's instincts take over in romantic rebellion.

At this crucial moment in the "Everlasting NO," Carlyle emerged from a pessimism generated from an overly materialistic view of life—the universe as "one huge, dead, immeasurable Steam-engine, rolling on, in its dead indifference"—to a defiant stand against mere pessimism. He uses this newly discovered confidence not only as a means of defense, but as a stand which is transformed eventually, through the "Centre of Indifference", to the "Everlasting YEA" which comprehends at its essence that there is a deeper obligation in life, a religious impulse which cannot be denied to participate and not merely withdraw in fear and trembling from a threatening universe. From "a feeble unit in the middle of threatening Infinitude," Carlyle is liberated, gaining critical powers of analysis over his situation in order to proclaim a positive message. Instead of throwing away a seemingly defunct Christian message, Carlyle turns to redefining it.[53]

This major element of romantic optimism permeates the sense of religious struggle from Henry Adams's "The Dynamo and the Virgin" to Alfred N. Whitehead's model of transition which begins with God the void and moves to God the enemy, thence from God the enemy to God the companion. Needless to say, Sperry heard his own voice in Carlyle's depiction of a rational believer confronting a modern world, and therein found reassurance.

Along with Carlyle, the works of Tennyson and Browning, especially the latter, were subsequently committed to a store of wisdom for a lifetime, having "passed miraculously inside to take up their permanent lodgement" at a time and a place which otherwise might have utterly neglected to notice what they offered. And the second formative experience in college came with scientific study. Sperry had planned to enter medicine through his college course until a close boyhood friend suddenly died in his senior year. The tragedy shifted his interest from natural science to reflective religion, but not before he had become well acquainted in college with the scientific method and how it really functions in the context of theory.

When his fiftieth class reunion appeared on the near horizon Sperry was invited back to Olivet. He could return a conquering hero, one of Olivet's proudest sons giving the commencement address as a noted university figure of national prominence. He chose not to go, as little sentiment was held for a place he had outgrown years before. If half of literary and creative America is trying to escape the small town and the other half of the talent is trying to find the village life, Sperry was among those who wondered if the latter group ought not give the prospect some second thought. He replied to an old friend with just a trace of pain in his memory:

> My feelings about Olivet since graduation have been curiously mixed. When my father went there in 1893 he was assured by the trustees that he would have no responsibility whatsoever for finances. Nothing could have been farther from the fact—all the responsibilities were dumped on his

shoulders and he died . . . worn out by the heartbreaking task of paying the bills year by year.[54]

The frontier did not play an especially critical role in the shaping of Sperry's mind. He looked east and beyond. Oxford was the place of his first intellectual loyalties. One of Sperry's almost exact contemporaries was the renowned historian, William Warren Sweet (1881-1959). Of Sweet a biographer writes that his "historical portrait of American religion was a historical reification of his childhood world, almost Baldwin City [Kansas] writ large. Both its strengths and its weaknesses, its genius and its limitations, ultimately derive from this fact."[55] Sperry, once again, represents dissimilitude in similitude. His intellectual roots were never very deep in the Congregationalism of the midwest and for that matter the thin soil of New England did not hold his sense of tradition in the way geography defined other Protestant minds. Sperry does not fit any particular category that can be writ large for the rest of his career. The intellectual sources which informed his mature thinking were not of authentic American stock, though it could be argued that while his theology did not finally derive from American sources, it returned to be fed by an American experience. In this sense the background of the midwest and of New England becomes here significant. Further, he is by comparative measure in dissimilitude by being born between two worlds, the one dead to the past—the world of his parents—and the other, of course, powerless to be born, namely where he made his home in a deficient twentieth-century liberalism.

Once Sperry got away from Olivet there was no looking homeward in that direction. While the Y.M.C.A. stint may have prolonged his restless phase of prairie captivity, "Roy" could at the time write home cheerfully, knowing it would not likely last and he would not remain long "out here where they don't wear their trousers big as meal bags but where they make up for every other deficiency by the brim of their hat [just because] one can't keep up to date."[56] Later in life "Roy" would fix in his mind those formative years at York Beach (Maine), Olivet (Michigan) and the wide open spaces of Kansas as the first great divide of emotion recollected, for "it is a strange thing to remember," he tells Pauline in 1950, a few years before he died, "that in say 1895 the Civil War was nearer to us than the First World War is to us today."[57]

CHAPTER 2

OXFORD: The Central Stream

Below the surface stream, shallow and light,
Of what we say we feel—below the stream,
As light, of what we think we feel—there flows
With noiseless current strong, obscure and deep,
The central stream of what we feel indeed.
　　　　　　　　　　—Matthew Arnold[1]

DURING THE RUSTICATION of his Y.M.C.A. appointment (1903-1904), a restless interlude of wanderings across the short grass country of Kansas, Sperry received a letter from his father, saying that a committee of three college presidents in Michigan had been formed to select the first Rhodes Scholar from that state. President Sperry of Olivet was one of the three men appointed. As a gesture of fatherly encouragement, Willard G. Sperry enclosed with his letter some of the leaflets that Oxford was distributing in the way of advanced publicity. He thought that his son, not entirely content with the Y.M.C.A. experience, might like to consider the prospects of a scholarship to Oxford.[2]

The Young Men's Christian Association, though traceable to eighteenth-century organizations in Germany, came to the United States through British sources in the 1850s. Emphasizing Christianity in practical work, it proposed four major fields of service and operation: physical, educational, social and religious. In its religious endeavors, coordinated with its recreational purposes, the Y.M.C.A. was a powerful force that became more than an ecumenical service agency, it functioned virtually as a church with an evangelical focus through its Bible classes, publications and lectures. Y.M.C.A. secretaries were the agents of athletic ideals who usually touted a muscular Christianity to their fellow youths or the benefits of what William James called "the strenuous life." Dwight L. Moody (1837-1899), a symbol of Y.M.C.A. values and methods, launched his remarkable public ministry as an evangelist (in the Finney tradition) from a high position in the Chicago Y.M.C.A.

The source of young Sperry's post-college dissatisfaction lay in the conditions he found in itinerant life. The hard work, the rough quarters and the pious excesses of the Y.M.C.A., combined with his own false enthusiasm, were tolerated grudgingly. He was no private school snob, but was accustomed, in the home of a minister and college president, to a modest level of Victorian learning and refinement. Instead, he was visiting towns where "the wind drives dust, papers, and pedestrians all around the streets, a lot of snarling dogs infest the gutters, gaunt farmers, with long mustaches, who look like 'forlorn hope lost in fog' are always lounging in the corner praying for rain, and in the midst of all towns the sumptious hotel, where they dispense cold rooms and 'salid' as my menu said today, for 2 [bucks?] per day."[3]

Most of the young man's complaints were made in good humor, though in a frame of mind that could not long stand what the turn of the century prairie offered. During his peregrinations Sperry encountered such diversions as the American army, and this contact led to rather colorful descriptions of the training camps filled with soldiers. In all his mission work that year, dining with the regular army and militia while trying to "put any religion into" those soldiers that might be received, was the most repulsive. He wrote home about one stretch of days near Fort Riley, Kansas:

> Really I don't think I should care much for the army life 365 days in the year. This play war is all right for ten days, but it would be solemn year in and year out. We have been eating at a commissary lunch counter and though I have had the honor of eating in a good many dirty places, I never struck anything quite so bad. "Ham and eggs," & "pie" constitute the menu. The tables are rough pine boards, strewn with sugar, flies, half-eaten pies, bottles, dirty dishes stacked a foot or so high, scraps of meat and bread, everything swimming in black coffee, which has been spilt over. When they clean off the tables they do it with a broom, "and great is the fall thereof." And yet they talk about the extravagance and "graft" in the army.

The alternative to the commissary diet was the soldiers' mess which held its own hygienic advantages as the lesser of two evils: "What you do is to take your tin plate and cup and go up to the cook and get your allotment of beans and potato, meat and coffee and then go."[4]

It is easy to imagine why, then, the remote possibilities of study overseas held for Sperry instant appeal. The contrast between an envisioned opportunity and visible slovenry was posed like the Shakespearean "Hyperion to a satyr." He did not hestiate for a moment to try for a Rhodes Scholarship upon learning of its existence from his father. "I am rather surprised at myself," he told his sister, "that I have jumped into this so quickly, but it is well to be ready and then if I do not want to try it finally, I can drop out."[5] When the father learned of his son's intention to compete for the scholarship, he resigned his position on the selection committee to avoid the obvious conflict of interest.

Sperry's initial fervor toward the scholarship was not easily sustained once the review for comprehensive examinations was underway. The Rhodes Scholars are today selected by other criteria and means than from a common body of general knowledge and ancient languages, but in 1903 there were apparently uniform entrance examinations which Oxford University itself administered. After careful consideration of the requirements, Sperry announced to his middle sister, Pauline, that on the whole he felt confident to "make the examinations. The Arithmetic is not bad, the Algebra goes through simple equations and I have gone over all that ground. . . and can handle that all right." What gave him the most concern was the inflexible rule that adequate competency be demonstrated in ancient languages. "The Latin and Greek translation is a fair test, but the grammar is 'fierce'. That is really very hard as the exam is not on general work but is at least half catch questions on fine points, such as irregular verbs and nouns, exceptions to exceptions in gender and so on."[6]

Sperry instructed the family to send him his Goodwin's Greek Grammar that he had left in the hall bookcase and also asked that a Caesar and an *Anabasis* be shipped at once. Because of the dual time demands upon him, the Y.M.C.A. fieldwork, and the necessary preparation for the Oxford entrance exams, Sperry would not make it home for Christmas that year. He hated "the idea of hanging around Topeka," but realized it was a prudent decision in order to give full attention to his Greek and Latin vocabulary and syntax.

Sperry found himself mirrored, at least in mythic parallel, by the incipient hopes of Jude Fawley in Thomas Hardy's tragic novel, *Jude the Obscure*. In mature reflection, he even saw himself as something of a Jude figure. Here a young man had had a glimpse of a possible, and otherwise unlikely academic career at Oxford. Jude was a prisoner of hope, encumbered by a joyless lot in life. Jude, like Sperry, had already in his head pictured himself there, practically in academicals, but once the autodidactic

discipline of Latin and Greek began, the mood shifted. When it was discovered that so very much had to be "committed to memory at the cost of
years of plodding"

> Jude flung down the books, lay backward along the broad trunk of the elm,
> and was an utterly miserable boy for the space of a quarter of an hour.
> This was Latin and Greek, then, was it, this grand delusion! The charm he
> had supposed in store for him was really a labour like that of Israel in
> Egypt.[7]

Although he stood a much better chance for achieving the Oxford
dream than the fictional Jude from Wessex in Hardy's novel (the complicated impingements in Jude's life reflect rigid class status at keen variance
with middle-class America), Sperry nonetheless showed his own composite
Jude-like posture and frustration:

> I wish these exams would come and be over with, I am getting sick of
> keeping on the anxious seat so long and if I don't get a chance to ease off
> some spare steam [soon] something will "bust." Begins to look as though
> we weren't going to have any exams at all, and after I have learned so
> much. Even money I have learned everything but just what I shall need.[8]

After months of tortuous waiting and uncertainty, the younger Sperry
finally received word in July from the President of the University of
Michigan that he was being awarded a Rhodes Scholarship in its inaugural
year, 1904.[9] Only in a vague way did Sperry know that he wanted to read
theology at Oxford. He had had it in mind up until the end of college to
prepare a scientific career as one of his Olivet professors had strongly urged.
Professor Clark, a biologist, encouraged Sperry as a protégé and continued
the gentle pressure in that direction during the first year after graduation.
Sperry had done some original research with Clark and the professor was
eagerly pursuing publication of these minor works on Sperry's behalf.

Such close exposure to the scientific method proved invaluable later in life.
Sperry had confided to his sister the great admiration he held for Dr. Clark
who had written long newsy letters to an occasionally home-sick Y.M.C.A.
secretary: "He says more to the square inch than any correspondent I ever had
and it is in that calm scientific manner which is very attractive."[10] Sperry's
lifelong fascination with science and religion as complementary disciplines is
derived in part from this first and positive association with the "calm scientific
manner." The role of the scientist in religion and culture is one Sperry carefully
examined and, at times, promoted throughout his productive years of

preaching and writing. He interpreted religion in such a way that it did not preclude the scientific view. Importantly, he described this dual nature of religion as being both rational and emotional in an autobiographical essay written near the end of his life: "My religious experience has never been a matter of mere subjectivity. Objective realities have come and laid their claim on me, and I have had no option but to consent."[11]

Cool scientific objectivity was not incompatible with Sperry's religious thinking as it developed and extended from his youthful departure from science. Going against the grain of first vocational preferences did not, as might be expected, issue into an equal and opposite contempt for that preference. Rather than an acid antipathy toward scientific skepticism, Sperry instead had deeply benefited from the scientific approach and method which he readily adopted in temperament (though not in abstract or systematic thinking) to make religion more comprehensible in both its subjective and objective expressions. At his vocational crossroads in 1904, he chose a way that seemed to diverge sharply from his biology mentor's fieldwork, but Sperry, nonetheless, carried with him always a sense of where the other road was going. Unlike many, if not most, of the Protestant thinkers of his day, Sperry possessed firsthand knowledge of how scientific research is conducted and what scientific discovery feels like to the explorer. For Sperry the revelations of science were akin to the heights of mysticism.

Meanwhile, Sperry wrote the Rhodes Secretary, Francis Wylie, to say he was planning to enter the "Non-Conformist" ministry (thus bowing to British usage when the American equivalent was "Congregationalist") and asked him to choose an appropriate college suitable for that purpose. Sperry's criterion was that the college be "on the whole liberal and low church rather than ultra conservative and high church." Queens College was selected "and no choice could have been happier or more fortunate."[12] Sperry entered Queens College in October 1904 and remained there until 1907, although "belonging" to an Oxford college is generally a lifetime perquisite of close association which Sperry sustained and proved by habit and repute. He received the Oxford M.A. with first class honors in theology, reinforced a year later by a "modest" M.A. from Yale.

Introduction to a Serious Theological Life

Sperry landed in England just at the time that Canon Burnett Hillman Streeter (1874-1937) was appointed the Dean and Theological Tutor of

Queens College. B. H. Streeter became a seminal and then dominant influence in the intellectual and spiritual life of Willard L. Sperry and the
rapport that grew between them went considerably beyond weekly recita-
tions and cream teas. Streeter's career was that of a typical Oxford don in
that he went up to Oxford in 1893 with a classical scholarship at Queens,
the single college claiming the greatest portion of his academic loyalty, the
exception being a brief period of study at Pembroke College. His work in
the 1890s was nothing less than brilliant, with a first class in classical
moderations and various theological prizes and scholarships. Streeter was
only eight years older than Sperry, but was at the time of their first meeting
a quantum measure ahead of him in scholarly sophistication and critical
equipment. Streeter was already well on his way to becoming a world class
scholar in New Testament criticism and the philosophy of religion. While
he opened a whole new world and culture to Sperry, it is significant in itself
to consider what that world was like and how it introduced one American
liberal to a set of theological issues that were couched in uniquely British
expressions, particulary in contrast to the prevailing German sources of
American Protestant thought.

The year 1907 in British intellectual history, Sperry's final year at
Oxford, has been called "the stormiest year of the century, theologically
speaking."[13] Sperry's personal sunny interval of adult life, his entire student career at Oxford, came during a volatile period when at least three
major topics were causing sufficient atmospheric static to bring rolling
thunder into the long theological conversation of university and ecclesiastical life. That any one of these three thundersqualls should rumble while
in the course of one's study would naturally provide that individual
enormous intellectual stimulation for many years. In Sperry's case, however, there converged a harbinger of thunderheads like molten pewter on
the horizon. This formation signalled a new front of theological subjects
that also represented aspects of a foreshadowing departure from the immediate past. It was highly unusual that a student could possibly be present
in so short a residency for so much to happen.

Sperry stood precisely on one of the great theological meridians drawn
in the twentieth century, enabling him to observe and feel a crucial moment
in Anglo-American thought. He was at Oxford when the synoptic problem
was culminating, the Modernist Controversy was at its zenith (involving
the notorious challenge to Roman Catholic authority proposed by George

Tyrrell, but not in a totally unrelated sense pertaining also to the Non-Con-formist, R. J. Campbell who was at the same time flourishing), and the Christological crisis was about to explode.

What soon followed in famous published works was a product of all that had been brewing so vigorously during Sperry's formative season abroad. Tyrrell's *Christianity at the Cross-Roads* (a work to which Sperry made frequent reference and of which he made liberal use through much subsequent theological discourse) was published in 1909, only a few months before the English edition of Albert Schweitzer's *The Quest of the Historical Jesus* (in German, 1906, in English, 1910). *Oxford Studies in the Synoptic Problem*, edited by William Sanday, came off the press in 1911. Streeter was one of the primary contributors to the latter work which attracted worldwide attention. The following year, 1912, a remarkable and important book was published in England, edited by Streeter and entitled, *Foundations: A Statement of Christian Belief in Terms of Modern Thought by Seven Oxford Men*. Canon Streeter's essay therein on "The Historic Christ" was probably the most provocative bolt of lightning that flashed from the composite authorship of *Foundations* because it struck upon the sensitive issue of the resurrection. Streeter's boldness was not in denying the or-thodox point of view of the reality of the physical resurrection, but in denying also the modern perspective of resurrection as a "subjected vision." Streeter argued in *Foundations* for an "objective vision" theory whereby historic events and the interpretation of those events were to be attended with all the objectivity required of theological assurance and thus submitted to nuance for expression.

Streeter's underlying presupposition was that of the primacy of religious experience, but he articulated this view in his essay with more care, balance and subtlety than many others. Constantly aware of the work of Johannes Weiss and Albert Schweitzer, Streeter was convinced that if one remained faithful to the gospel account, then both the present (realized) and the future (expected) dimensions would not stand in conflict with each other. Typical of British philosophic judiciousness, or its capacity for mud-dling compromise, Streeter probed the interconnections between objective-ly given historical events and the subjective response to those facts by a sensitive reader. He gauges his opinion with precise calibration: "I feel I am on firmer ground than if I were to rest all on a view of miracle which the lapse of time and the growth of knowledge seems ever to be making less secure, and which in the last resort appears to mean that God did things in Palestine nineteen hundred years ago which He will not or cannot do for us to-day, and that Christ was raised from the dead in a way we shall not be."[14] In other words, Streeter places the issue in the context of "both/and" (paradox) and not of "either/or" (absolutes).

The stated purpose of *Foundations*, perhaps a single good clue to the atmosphere which immediately preceded its publication, was one "of combining continuity and progress" in the Anglican tradition of finding the mean between the extremes. Streeter explains the British theological habit of adaptive traditionalism (distinct from German-influenced modernism which was characteristically adaptive, but not so traditional) by defending "the special duty of the younger generation" because "our responsibility is of a different kind. It is the responsibility of making experiments."[15]

Streeter's "youthful" manifesto (he was then 38 years of age), declaring a mix of theological restlessness and caution, nonetheless, documents one of Virginia Woolf's convictions that "on or about December 1910 human character changed. All human relations have shifted—those between masters and servants, husbands and wives, parents and children. And when human relations change there is at the same time a change in religion, conduct, politics and literature."[16] This assault on authoritative tradition had its several representatives in theology, and though Streeter is regarded as a minor player, he was among those who are known to have been on the cutting edge of English ideas in the transition of pre-war society.

Of the three major intellectual events in theology transpiring through the narrow window of time before 1914—the synoptic problem, the rise and abrupt fall of Roman Catholic Modernism and the Christological crisis, dividing the historical Jesus from the eschatological one—Streeter was most intimately involved with the question about the gospel sources, and we can assume the same for any of his protégés. Because Sperry's most direct point of contact with the Oxford liberal climate came by Streeter, it is wisest to seek first the context and meaning of that particular pedagogical development involving Streeter which the educable Rhodes Scholar obviously followed. Next in importance for Sperry was the deep impression left on him by the work of Tyrrell and the Catholic modernists. Although Sperry "followed him afar off," he became in a strange way Tyrrell's apostle to the Gentiles (i.e., American Protestants). Finally, the event that probably touched Sperry the least at the time, because it centered on German and French traditions of scholarship almost exclusively, was the continental crisis in Christology which Albert Schweitzer brilliantly, though often it seems only temporarily, remedied. While still at Harvard in the late forties Sperry not only met the inspiring Schweitzer, but took up again in published form the question of the historical Jesus (*Jesus Then and Now*, 1949). Sperry anticipated a renewed quest for the historical Jesus despite the regnant assumptions of the neo-orthodox school of New Testament critics who thought the matter beaten and buried.[17]

The Synoptic Problem

The challenge and the threat of Biblical criticism investigating the human origins of scripture in the late nineteenth century posed many problems for the church and university scholar, often one and the same person. Because of the potential damage to authoritative doctrine based on the Bible, the up-shot of higher criticism had been controversy, denunciation and even legal prosecution. While general indignation and fear finally subsided, faith was not necessarily the victim of battle, but the survivor. And while faculties like those at Oxford maintained many clerics, their first loyalties were not always secured to either church or college, but to the historical truth. In that detached spirit faith would have to stand or fall on its own. Sperry characterized the Oxford system "as absolutely 'neutral' and wholly scientific. Of the catholicity of spirit, the candor of mind, the breadth of outlook and the tolerance of opinion of those who teach Theology at Oxford too much cannot be said."[18] Biblical study and investigation at Oxford reached its apogee in the pre-war years by moving sharply away from traditional church viewpoints about how the gospels—especially the words of Jesus, *ipsissima verba*—were recorded.

The historical method of Biblical scholarship that Sperry learned and absorbed dated to a prior Oxford generation represented in the intellectual disposition of the doleful Benjamin Jowett, who was the solemn master of Balliol from 1870 to 1893. It is said that Jowett wanted to "innoculate England with Balliol." Whether or not that happened, it is safe to say that Oxford was unmistakably injected with Jowett, as if to improve its immunities against obscurantism. Interpret the Scripture, Jowett had said, like any other book, and at Oxford the task of doing so was gradually accomplished, if with reserve and sobriety.

Emblematic of the tensions brought to the Victorian academic setting is the quip of Jowett who once imparted to Margot Asquith the advice, "You must believe in God, my child, despite what the clergymen tell you."[19]

The New Testament scholarship at Oxford did not intend to confront directly the issues of doctrine because its primary interest was simply that of objective historical inquiry. Meanwhile, its consideration of the human conditions and setting under which divine revelation had been received naturally suggested misgivings about the extent to which the divine word (inadvertently transformed by the critics' own investigation) might be discovered as being all too human. The interpretive transition managed by English Protestantism could have been easily reversed at the turn of the century and turned back into high church, anti-modernist obscurantism. Instead, the thinking of the leading, mature theological scholars came to quick terms with the new criticism because inspiration did not have to be sacrificed by the revelation of new light on old texts. This is not to say that liberal trends in theology were inconsequential. To the contrary, the high cost paid for intellectual integrity was, of course, some loss of confidence in traditional expressions of religious faith.

Into this highly charged and rarefied atmosphere Willard Sperry arrived at Oxford. Once there he became acquainted with William Sanday and the future Archbishop of Canterbury, William Temple (a Fellow of Queens College, 1904-1910) and, of course, his tutor and academic mentor, B. H. Streeter who was directly connected to all that had gone immediately before him in the chain of Biblical scholarship. The English colloquy that Sperry witnessed close at hand was mainly bibliographic, though he was in frequent, personal conversation and contact with several key participants, and in a short time developed an on-going friendship with Streeter that outlasted by more than twenty-five years the terms of the Rhodes Scholarship.

The inspiration of Oxford at a time of theological ferment had immediate effect upon Sperry, but also, like pungent vapors, it penetrated deep within him to a mental place of durable reserve. The steady, on-going supply of those Oxford years served him throughout the contentious period of American theology between the world wars. Sperry's Oxford roots are essential to follow and to explain because most American theologians of

Sperry's generation (except for Episcopalians) were still going to Germany for their foreign study. Charles Cashdollar points to a trend in the middle of the nineteenth century which was still in force by the end of the period that when "Reformed clergy crossed the Atlantic to study or tour, they passed through London but headed to the Continent."[20]

Secondly, these intellectual sources and connections gave Sperry a very different kind of voice, an independent part, to be commingled in the mix of Protestant opinion during the cultural upheaval of the post-war years in America.

Sperry's experience at Oxford was an anomaly for other reasons, too. There were three parallel strands of Modernism being woven into the broad cloth of English church life at the turn of the century, each one largely reflecting sectarian preferences and emphases. Anglican, Roman Catholic, and Non-Conformist Modernists overlapped in their concerns, but never deviated far from individual loyalties defined by polity and specific pietistic tradition. Ironically, the most important single influence upon English theology at that time, an influence felt equally and concurrently by Anglican and Nonconformist constituencies, was projected by a Roman Catholic, Baron Friedrich von Hügel.[21] This may explain why an American Congregationalist would not necessarily discover his closest religious affinities with English Non-Conformists. Some of those distinctions within the Modernist Controversy, so important now for historians to draw and comprehend, may have, nonetheless, then possessed typical English subtlety in theology so that the deeper lines of thought, below the surface of piety and tradition, were almost deliberately blurred. In the case of Sperry one would expect his American Calvinist background to be transferred naturally to an English Nonconformist foreground.

There were circulating within Sperry's reach high-powered theologians of that more familiar stamp, making significant contributions which, one may suppose, an American Congregationalist would find attractive. R. J. Campbell, P. T. Forsyth and John Oman would have been very accessible to Sperry. Although in the case of P. T. Forsyth, it is unlikely he assuaged many liberals at all. One instance of modernism crossing sectarian loyalties is found between Campbell and the Jesuit Tyrrell, otherwise at variance, *vis-à-vis* ecclesiastical boundaries. They shared, however, an important theological tenet, refuting doctrines of transcendence and embracing an extreme immanentism. The modernist impulse in American theology has been carefully delineated by William R. Hutchison to show that immanentism is one of three clear intimations of the liberal Protestant mind (the other two being cultural accommodation and a realizable Kingdom of God).

If everything were on the same footing, it would seem most plausible for Sperry to be drawn to the English equivalents of himself. And yet, there is no evidence from the Oxford years or in subsequent works that are obviously derived from those years, that Sperry followed any of the contemporary Non-Conformist theologians. As an American "Non-Conformist" his preferences surprisingly pointed to Anglican and Roman Catholic Modernists. The choice may not have been initially his to make, but one determined by the circumstance of his being at a particular Oxford college with Canon Streeter (instead of the Congregationalist Manchester College). Sperry records his second thoughts, later a guiding wisdom, about the role of "grace" in his personal experience: "None of the really important happenings in life have been of my own planning." The rather unanticipated, almost inconceivable associations formed at Oxford were on his part "a matter of yielding to sudden and wholly unexpected imperatives served on me by the outside world."[22]

Canon Streeter was a man of thin physique with unusually long, narrow feet, an exaggerated characteristic immediately noticeable, of course, to amused undergraduates. One of the first sights Sperry was taken to see by fellow undergraduates at Queens was Streeter's shoes left outside his room overnight for cleaning by the College servant, a customary faculty privilege at the time.[23] Streeter was known as a gentle personality, courteous in his dealings with others and as one who closely linked his scholarship with broad human concerns of the day. He met an untimely and tragic end on September 10, 1937, when an airplane in which he was flying crashed into a mountain outside Basel, Switzerland. He had been returning from a meeting of the Oxford Group, a popular movement founded by the American Lutheran, Frank N. D. Buchman.

Streeter had been ordained in 1899 "despite the fact that his faith had always something of the character of a quest." The author of his biographical sketch points out that "he was more than once attacked as a modernist," especially after his contribution to *Foundations* in 1912. The criticism against him was never forced, because Streeter was generally regarded highly for "the obvious sincerity of his religion and its practical applicability to human problems."[24]

As one of the most distinguished New Testament scholars of his day, Streeter made his reputation with his essay, "On the Original Order of Q," in the *Oxford Studies in the Synoptic Problem* (1911), edited by his older colleague, William Sanday. Streeter's pioneering role in exploring the continuities and idiosyncracies of the synoptic sources was pivotal in the development of modern scholarly methods. The resolution of the problem is still based solidly upon the internal data of the Gospels themselves, although archeological, cultural, anthropological and outside literary evidences are now brought in sooner for corroboration, but only if the veracity of these sources can be firmly established as authentic. Streeter, and those near him like Sperry, were in the front rank of a very consequential movement in Biblical studies.

The functional value of these Oxford contributions to Biblical scholarship lies in the fact that they generally served to compensate an intellectual community for its other deficiencies. Theology in England at the turn of the century was in a state of disrepair. Although there were numerous books being produced by theologians, these efforts were diffuse and suffered for their mere timeliness, being little more than popular nostra prescribed to meet temporary needs. Theology was on the defensive, lacking discipline, and absent systematic or long-term insight. Compared to the growing abundance of testimony about religious experience, theology was often nothing but an ad hoc enterprise. One student of the period in question notes that "the intellectual presentation of the Christian faith was not keeping pace with its practical and emotional expression."[25]

The reason for this over-caution on the part of theologians, as the nineteenth century drew to a close, may have been the fear of possible condemnation by ecclesiastical authorities, especially if they were members of the churches. Tyrrell, for example, paid dearly and was technically excommunicated. They may have feared too adverse public reactions if they became very daring in their views. Other, more complex causes, however, seem best to explain the painfully reticent or, worse, vacant theological offerings in 1900. L. E. Elliott-Binns has emphasized that in such an age of specialization "theologians were conscious of the inadequacy of their knowledge."[26]

Salvaging the intellectual reputation of theological writers was a task defaulted in no small measure to the highly skilled critics of the New Testament, such as Sanday and Streeter. The *foundations* of repair after 1900 were retrenched by those adequately equipped to apply scientific, and hence legitimate, methodology to traditional authorities of faith, perhaps to doctrine at first, but ultimately to Scripture. By 1910, whether it was intentional or not, English culture was rapidly being transformed. England had been a society with the distinctive ability to hold antitheses together, to love the middle way, to embrace the delicate nuance, to strike the proper balance between the extremes. The tensions at the final stages of the Victorian era and during the reign of Edward made reconciliation strenuous and at times virtually impossible. This cultural turbulence was symbolized graphically by the difficulty brewing in theology.

The dominant mood, according to Thomas Langford in his discussion of English theology in the early twentieth century, was a contrary spirit challenging the validity of institutional legacies thought to be dubious because among other factors, "economic considerations were more and more rooted in other than theological or biblical principles." Ideas in art and politics were in flux and reflux. Philosophy became assertive, rejecting its subordinate status to theology. The rise of science and technology were forces contending with faith and sanctity. Secularization was getting the upper hand on society and religion while Christian forms of thought seemed to be weightless. Christian "rituals were evacuated of their meaning—attractive vehicles that carried nothing."[27]

❦

British Theological Modernism

The "self-styled modern" generation that B. H. Streeter and his young colleagues were trying to justify, regarded themselves as post-Victorian, meaning "people of about thirty years of age," which fits Sperry precisely in 1912. Streeter himself was closer to forty than thirty when *Foundations* made its debut. It was a generation "not born, as their parents were, into the atmosphere of pre-critical and pre-Darwinian religion." The distinction between the two generations was noted as "a change from reliance upon, to criticism of, assumptions." The Victorians are attacked in *Foundations*, but not savaged in the manner of Lytton Strachey's later diatribe of irreverence, *Eminent Victorians* (1918). The Victorian optimism "drawn from a capital of uncriticized assumptions," to the authors of *Foundations* (in the words of N. S. Talbot of Balliol) "lay behind their almost pathetic belief in education as the way of all salvation."[28] From that central, liberal implication "progress" was "the bottom layer" of the Victorian mind. The writers of *Foundations* were not so buoyed by a well intended confidence "in goodness as inherent in the natural order of things" or in "the benevolence of nature to the individual." The Oxford authors inclined favorably to one or two conspicuous exceptions in the Victorian climate of opinion. John Stuart Mill was acceptable because of his scorn for those who "take refuge in optimistic Deism."

Also, it is important to note that Thomas Carlyle was palatable because of his negations against prevailing optimism achieved in "The Everlasting No" (*Sartor Resartus*, chapter VII). Carlyle's revolt and preliminary transition from No to Yea was founded upon a young man's nihilism that "the Universe was all void of Life, of Purpose, of Volition, even of Hostility: it was one huge, dead, immeasurable Steam-engine, rolling on, in its dead indifference, to grind one limb from limb. O, the vast, gloomy, solitary Golgotha, and Mill of death!"[29] Carlyle may not have been ultra-fashionable in Oxford around 1907, but he was not apparently discarded with anything like the disdain with which many authors of his generation were treated. Whether or not Streeter cared for Carlyle cannot be ascertained, but that he did not, as editor, challenge favorable references to him in *Foundations* perhaps establishes, by his silence, at least mild approbation.

Meanwhile, the seven pillars of Oxford theological modernity expressed deep concern that a false (Victorian) optimism still survived among a select few who had "disencumbered" themselves of any other convictions. The authors lamented the pedestrian temptation to see too much in everything, a sanguine expectation that something will likely turn up. This hopefulness did not seem warranted by the general order of things. Two things emerge immediately in connecting Sperry with Oxford intellectual continuities between 1900 and 1910.

First and most obvious about these influences is the ongoing acceptability for that "modern" generation of Thomas Carlyle. Sperry had read Carlyle at Olivet College, an experience which he has already described as a turning point. Being predisposed to Carlyle could not have hindered his chances of fitting in with the young, bright minds of Oxford that Streeter tried to unite in *Foundations*. Sperry returned to Carlyle throughout his career as a Rhodes Scholar, at one time preferring Carlyle to the avant-garde George Bernard Shaw whom he had greatly admired at first sight as a wise writer. He complains about Shaw that he is "the apotheosis of cynicism." Sperry later revised his opinion of Shaw and became enormously dependent on Shaw to give weight to his first major work, *The Disciplines of Liberty* (1921). For Sperry, as presumably for his like-minded Oxford associates such as William Temple who, according to his biographer (F. A. Iremonger), was still reading Newman, Kingsley, Ruskin, Browning and Carlyle, the author of *Sartor Resartus* was never out of fashion or anachronistic. In giving his sister some protective, brotherly advice, after their father's death and perhaps while Pauline was struggling with social pressures at Smith College, Sperry recommends for practicality that

> If you haven't read *Sartor Resartus* lately grab it and read especially the chapter on the "World Out of Clothes," especially the last paragraph. Forget what Mrs. Berry [a house mother?] has said and try to imagine what Carlyle would say to you if he found you frittering away your life on Clothes. If I thought you were ever slovenly about dress I wouldn't say this, but you will always be quietly and well dressed.[30]

Not only is Carlyle recommended out of a broad literary familiarity, but he is the vehicle of some of Sperry's deepest thoughts and most personal experiences. Spending Christmas recess in Dublin with his Oxford roommate, Charles A. Bennett (eventually becoming Sperry's brother-in-law and a philosophy professor at Yale), Sperry at the end of 1906 ponders the death of his father who had died at York Beach, Maine the last day of August. He writes to his family that despite the jovial Bennett hospitality he is, nonetheless, prone to "a certain greyness, begotten of too much [sic] books." The true source of melancholy, however, lies beyond overwork as he admits the delayed effects of grief:

> The changes of the summer may have fostered a frame of mind, which was already beginning—for father I have nothing but the same spirit of thankfulness that he is gone free from all his limitations—but on the other hand I know what Carlyle meant when he said he went into a room and found "Sydney Smith and other buffoons prating and jargoning, while death and Eternity sat staring me in the face." I should think less of myself if I didn't go through this sort of thing—it is the portion of every man who tries to solve "the Riddle of the Universe" and finds he knows no more than his fathers.[31]

Sperry relates that while he is a guest in the home of his roommate's family he discovers that "Muriel Bennett has a set of Carlyle's. . . She got at an auction 18 mos. ago. She had never looked into them and I took down *Sartor Resartus* the other night and was amazed to see Carlyle's own signature in ink under the picture at the beginning. She never knew it." Elsewhere in his account of himself to his family, there is even a third mention of Carlyle by way of instructing Pauline that "if she wants to get much nearer the truth—as it seems to me—to read *Sartor Resartus*—especially the chapters of 'The Everlasting No'." Sperry in his enthusiasm claims "Carlyle was a mystic."[32] Except for describing the exchange of Christmas gifts in the Bennett home, Sperry never mentions some other and significant thought preoccupying his mind besides Carlyle and the infinitude of the Cosmos. Whatever feelings he had then toward Muriel Bennett, within two years of that memorable Christmas he had acted upon them, for they were married on December 15, 1908. Perhaps Carlyle was a kind of philosophic marriage broker, or at the very least it can be said a mutual love of books contributed to their "first, fine careless rapture" for each other.[33]

The second point worth noting in the sifting of intellectual seeds and grains that nurtured Sperry during this formative period can be traced directly to the words of *Foundations*. Granted, this work appeared five years after Sperry's departure from Oxford, but given the close nature of the tutorial system, it is indisputably clear that Sperry had access to Streeter's thinking, even those "modernist" ideas in gestation. The regular diet of colloquies through the tutorial method provokes thought and the exchange of ideas in a way that only exceptional lectures can. Sperry was at Oxford when the tutorial system was "at its best." He says, "Streeter was not overworked with tutees and gave me unlimited and generous time." Sperry's debt to Streeter remained an unpayable "major obligation" and over the years they "were in close and constant touch with each other."[34] It is inconceivable, then, that Sperry would not have followed with precision and devotion the pattern and aim of Streeter's mind. A good illustration of the example Streeter set for Sperry is the procedure of discourse Sperry utilized in his first scholarly publication.

While Sperry was the Associate Minister of the First Congregational Church in Fall River, Massachusetts, he contributed a provocative article in 1912 to the *Harvard Thelogical Review* that bears the unmistakable, though also unspoken authority of both Streeter and Tyrrell. The essay deals with

"The Eschatology of the Synoptic Gospels: Its Fidelity to Religious Experience" and is in keeping with the spirit of what is prescribed by *Foundations*. Moreover, the fact that Sperry chose to emphasize experience over explanation relates him immediately to Tyrrell. Although there are no references to Tyrrell in Sperry's article, there are clearly grounds for finding similarities as Tyrrell himself carefully distinguished revelation from theology and considered religious experience as other than a "statement," logically analyzed into knowledge, feeling and will. Given the proclivities of science to make all phenomena explorable and eventually sensible, Tyrrell drew a line through certain "revelation" as beyond the scope of reason. He constantly insisted that both revelational experience and theology had their respective rights and proper boundaries. And further, they were not mutually exclusive, but correlated language and mystery like the parts of a Russian doll comprising the "total experience."[35]

Because Sperry is investigating another aspect of the synoptic problem, his intellectual dependence on Streeter is obviously filial. The problem, simply stated and thoroughly probed by Sperry, is how can the apocalyptic sayings of Jesus have any meaning in a "scientific" world? This question shows that he was listening to the Weiss/Schweitzer problem, too. Sperry cautions students of the New Testament about the perils of a mere scissors and paste reading of the gospel. It is too easy to deny "the authenticity of the apocalyptic matter accredited to [Jesus]," and to dismiss "it as a later Jewish accretion upon the substratum of the original gospel." Sperry points out that "an earlier objective-minded orthodoxy found a justification for and a fulfillment of Jesus' words about the catastrophic consummation of the age in the happenings of Pentecost." He adds a mild rebuke that this solution of the problem "does credit to our predecessors' ingenuity rather than to their candor." Later, and in contrast, subjective-minded believers "spiritualized" the whole matter so that "the Ritschlians merely strike hands with the Alexandrians in the familiar preference for faith-values."[36] Sperry finds any arbitrary solution such as these unsatisfactory and warns that expediency in disposing of the problem leaves the matter open to serious critical objections. He calmly asserts that we have no more warrant for avoiding the twenty-fourth chapter of Matthew than for rejecting the Sermon on the Mount.

It is regrettable, says Sperry, that Jesus "was compelled to have recourse to modes of thought which from the vantage-ground of later centuries seem

scientifically inaccurate and baldly unspiritual; but what are the alternatives?" Sperry realizes exactly what Schweitzer also concluded "that he
prophesied his immediate return upon clouds of glory may be a very real
stumbling-block to his disciples of the twentieth century." Sperry reverses
the logic to prove the point, but also to expose a dilemma infinitely more
serious because "had he [Jesus] been a great anachronism and foretold his
part in the realization of the increasing purpose, in terms of 'the ascent of
man,' he would be a hopeless riddle." The bothersome catastrophic language of the first century presents very awkward cognates to users of sober,
present-day terminology preferably describing spiritual progress. It cannot
be done without impugning the long-term results of Christian faith. Jesus
is not a plastic prophet recasting his words to fit our modern idiom. "Even
the most jealous conservatism is now repudiating that conception of the
incarnation which would make of Jesus a thesaurus of all wisdom."[37]

The specter of Sperry's concern is over "the general indifference and
antipathy to the apocalyptic matter in the gospels" which "seems to arise,
not from a repudiation of that mental relativity which led to a use of the old
imagery of Daniel, but rather from a profound distrust of the catastrophic
mood which colors all Jewish eschatology." The modern mind, until the
world wars were consciously assimilated and the nuclear age was born,
could not entertain in its wildest imagination anything like cataclysm,
"dis-creation" or the eschaton. Put this way, the modern mind could
imagine nothing other than progress. Sperry suggests that there is wisdom
to be drawn from the unpalatable eschatology of the gospels which is to
acknowledge—contrary to science and popular culture—the discontinuity
of progress (this before recent notions of entropy):

> We can forgive the apocalyptist his symbolism, but we cannot accept as
> religiously valid for the present day his theory of chaotic and discon-
> tinuous progress. The sayings of Jesus about the end of the age are
> dominated by two ideas, suddenness and unforeseeability.[38]

What Sperry ascertains convincingly is the corrected premise and new
willingness "to ignore the conception of continuity which has hitherto
seemed a necessity for science," and to validate instead spiritual experience
itself as it is presented in life. Sperry offers the powerful example of
religious conversion, documented in the Gifford Lectures by William James
and published as the *Varieties*, as "a felt indubitable certainty of Experience"
(to quote Carlyle), which even "the decent mechanical theology of the times

cannot boast."[39] In terms of religious experience and expression the sudden (or apocalyptic) is as legitimate as the gradual (or the evolutionary, that is scientific explanation). The problem is not how the experience is explained, but how it is met when it comes. Experience precedes theology. If one worships the Principle of Continuity to the exclusion of all catastrophism, the unforeseen opportunities of the future and its as sudden trials will find him inevitably sleeping.

It is not required of the twentieth-century Christian to be clever and dovetail the archaic imagery of Daniel into contemporary conditions. What matters, concludes Sperry, is whether the oft heard refrain, "Watch, for ye know not," has, in an era demanding the certainties of science, a divine immediacy. The age which had been faithful to parables of growth as demonstrating a kind of proto-Darwinian philosophy, need not simultaneously dispose of the profound religious experience asserted in the dramatic language expressing Jesus's conception of the future. As science and philosophy adjust to the asymptomatic inconsistencies of nature, so too, Christianity has had to abandon certain of its laws of continuity. The prior scientific ardor for demonstrating a uniformity of process and of minute continuous change need to be challenged and balanced by an equally strong possibility of the catastrophic element in experience (wars, pestilence and death). Sperry observes that when the biologists and philosophers begin to evoke principles of limited randomness in the cosmos, they are already at one with the complete experience represented by the eschatology of the Synoptic Gospels.

Several things about Sperry's eloquent essay are remarkable *vis-à-vis* the definition and controlling check points of a modernist offered by William R. Hutchison in *The Modernist Impulse* (1976). Hutchison's prospectus for modernism is three-fold: immanentism, cultural accommodation and religious progressivism. Ostensibly, Sperry is every inch a modernist and Hutchison depends upon him as such to hold the several beads of his argument on a common strand. Hutchison's group portrait of the modernists while adequate in general terms, perhaps does not account fully for certain shadows of thought that may actually project in such a way as to keep persons like Sperry inadvertently out of the picture. This does not mean that Hutchison's delineation lacks breadth or requires expansion. It may mean, however, that one's present investigation of vanguard Protestants, because of Sperry, is now forced to deeper, subtler levels of modernism than space in Hutchison's important work permits.

Sperry does not exactly fit Hutchison's profile. The fact that Sperry is exploring seriously eschatology and religious experience in 1912 hints at something like an implicit transcendent theology or at least not full endorsement of a comfortably posed immanent one. Religious experience was certainly part of the liberal emphasis and concentrating on it is not excluded by Hutchison's definition. The methodology at this juncture is not in question, for Sperry was thoroughly modern in his approach to the problem. But where that exploration of religious experience leads seems to point out some discrepancies not covered by Hutchison's general hypothesis.

Secondly, Sperry is hardly a cultural accommodationist because his article in the *Harvard Theological Review* initiates a frontal assault on the prevailing scientific and historical assumptions of development and progress. There is a counter-cultural tone in his argument. Science does not hold all the answers. And religion is not an extension of culture, but a separate entity—in the world, but not of the world.

Thirdly, while Sperry does not dispute the realizable Kingdom of God, he realizes the prospect may not be a gentle ascent to the mount overlooking the promised land. Sperry writes, "We accept the fact of the increasing realization of the Kingdom and the continued operation of the person of Christ in the sphere of faith as proved, while we recognize in the form of the apocalyptic matter of the gospels 'that relativity which attaches to all that is human'(Sanday)."[40] Most modernists, according to Sperry, have tended to reject the catastrophic, the sudden and the unforeseen. And this flawed assumption, especially needs to be re-examined. Sperry recalls the many cases documented in James' *Varieties* whereby the "progressive" agencies of state, philanthropy or science had practically abandoned "disturbed" men and women "to the logically suicidal ravages of their own transgressions" only to learn later that religious experience "brought them the sudden and the unforeseen [which] achieved their salvation."[41] Apocalypticism recognized the immediate effects of crises and revolutions—truly modern phemonena—which pre-war optimism grossly neglected in its sugared social gospel.

What is so striking about *Foundations* and the simultaneous appearance of Sperry's essay on eschatology seems to be an assessment of "the Modern

Situation" that is predicated on a minimum of romantic idealism. It is a pre-war realism perhaps unknown except in some of Joseph Conrad's novels such as *Nostromo* (1904) and *The Secret Agent* (1907). It is the kind of modern realism expected in what is known as liberal, post-war disillusionment. Instead, one finds something of that mood in advance of the Somme and Gallipoli and Versailles. In spite of outward peace and the Edwardean spirit of indomitable self-complacency, the seeds of the coming tragic years were gradually sprouting. The period of boundless romantic confidence was beginning to show signs of wear, as if the weariness of "the world before the flood" had come upon it. The perceived lost momentum of optimism impressed the writers of *Foundations* palpably because "the assumptions of Mid-Victorian liberalism have been going bankrupt. . . The skies have darkened and men's minds have become more sombre."[42]

A creeping pessimism in the late Victorian era is quietly demonstrated in the recesses of literary sources. Matthew Arnold is one outstanding example:

> The glow of central fire is done
> Which with its fusing flame
> Knit all your parts, and kept you one.

These lines vaguely anticipate Yeats's post-war "eschatology" when "Things fall apart; the center cannot hold" (1921). The opening passages of *Foundations*, while an extension of some minority opinions at the close of the nineteenth century, does not seem at all typical of contemporary Protestant theologians. If the theology were to be carried forward to new results, then certain modern realities had to be squarely faced, but not by directing excessive energy to the refutation of outside criticism. Rather than older, abstract solutions and postulates of romantic idealism, the problems had to be addressed by the presupposition that theology is first an interpretation of religious experience. Moral absolutism was gone, materialism and nihilism were new powers with which to reckon. An empirical basis for theology was called for because of "the mere scale and range of the world in size and time has prompted a philosophy of relativity wherein nothing is absolutely true or right at any passing moment."[43]

The emphases made in *Foundations* seem remarkable in that they came before the Great War and from the "lost generation" that included such promising, premier scholars. W. H. Moberly of Lincoln College, Oxford asks rhetorically, "Does the optimism, which we proclaim, in fact make the issue of goodness and evil unreal? Does the union of man with God, which is the centre of our philosophy, in fact make human selfhood unreal? The appeal here," he says, "is to actual experience." Moberly explains what is meant by "actual experience" which can be, all negative assumptions aside, authentically optimistic in the modern world. He cautions that "Christian optimism, with its 'heaven' in the future, is too naive, too much like a fairy story. The true optimism is of sterner stuff, and is from a human point of view more austere." The example of Shakespearean tragedies comes to mind because no happy ending is ever promised, but there is, nonetheless, the residual feeling that "nothing is here for tears."[44]

Non-German Channels of Influence

Whether or not *Foundations* represents any early, portentous, significant or unusual shift in theology is beside the point in discussing the particular outlook of Sperry which the work engendered. What matters, it seems, is that in all likelihood Sperry returned to America with a critical realism that was not generally shared among his American contemporaries, some of whom were former graduate students in Germany. It is hard to imagine William Adams Brown, Shailer Mathews, the early Reinhold Niebuhr, Harry Emerson Fosdick or Henry Nelson Wieman thinking along the lines of *Foundations* before 1914. What is, moreover, deserving of deep interest here is the possibility that Sperry was better prepared for the human realities of the 1920s and 1930s than other American liberals because he anticipated the necessity of theological corrections (like those of neo-orthodoxy with regard to human nature) sooner than those who were connected to continental (as opposed to British) sources. It is no small point that of the eight American religious liberals studied categorically by Kenneth Cauthen not one prepared graduate work at a British university. Looked at another way, of the six who studied abroad, all six were in Germany for varied lengths of time.[45]

Sydney Ahlstrom raises a valid question about what has influenced American thought by asking, "Do not Americans show a propensity for the thinking that has characterized the German intellectual community?" This propensity toward continental influences "seems to be something more basic than attraction to mere cleanliness, efficiency, good plumbing and fine beer." Ahlstrom is convinced that "there is an underlying element of temperament that has made the German-American intellectual relationship so close." He boldly declares that "an American without that intellectual affinity is difficult to imagine."[46] Ahlstrom is correct in venturing to say that no explanation of American theology would be adequate without accounting for the American preference for German sources of thought. But here we must take into account the valid exception and note it for how it stands apart in the crisis decades between the world wars. That the strength, power and one-sidedness of the German-American relationship is irrefutable should not automatically preclude the added value of lesser known intellectual consignments in American thought.

There is an important, though subtle difference to be drawn between British and German intellectual sources which ostensibly diverge little, if at all. Without putting too fine a point on their distinctive presuppositions, but because British and German philosophical conclusions often bare mutual resemblance, it is necessary to note what Hans-Georg Gadamer has called "the hidden constants."

An indication of "the hidden constants" behind the British approach to discourse comes from the Harvard philosopher Charles S. Peirce who in 1871 gave a long review of George Berkeley's empiricism. Peirce expressed the widely accepted view that British philosophy through the nineteenth century had its own peculiar national tendencies: "From very early times, it has been the chief intellectual characteristic of the English to wish to effect every thing by the plainest and directest means, without unnecessary contrivance." Peirce pointed out the strong preference "for the simplest theories, and a resistance to any complication of the theory."[47]

Over against this description is a picture in contrast of German philosophy rendered by Lewis White Beck who writes about the peculiar nature of that intellectual tradition. "The form is generally didactic, systematic, encyclopedic, prolix, humorless." In the nineteenth century German university the expectation was that a professor would produce his own multivolume system and start his own school. Beck suggests that loyalty to a particular school of philosophy among German academics was a feeling equal to the intensity an English university graduate might feel for Cambridge, but hardly for Cambridge Platonism.[48]

Hans-Georg Gadamer in his influencial work, *Truth and Method*, traces the difference between British and German intellectual traditions to the idea of "common sense" in a national culture, and from that point, he assumes, all other differences of temperament and analysis derive. Gadamer makes clear that "common sense" as a concept with a moral element has remained in place since eighteenth-century Scottish philosophy and is distinguishable from the German concept *der gesunde Menschenverstand* ("sound understanding"). "Whereas in England and the Romance countries the idea of *sensus communis* is not even today just a critical slogan, but is a general civil quality," in Germany, he writes, this concept "took a direction greatly divergent from the original Roman meaning of *sensus communis*, and continued a scholastic tradition."[49]

By 1925 it was estimated that over the course of a hundred years ten thousand American students had attended German universities.[50] Until the gift of Cecil Rhodes was made there was nothing in Britain that resembled anywhere the American student migration to the continent. Even after the opportunities opened for Americans to study at British universities, the statistics about that expansion could hardly be compared to the other, long-standing development in Germany that simply overmatched the competition to attract American students. Ahlstrom's quantitative judgment cannot be disputed. After all, "if, contrary to the fact, one could imagine all America's intellectual ties as having been exclusively English down to World War I, then the events of the 'Thirties' would be very hard to imagine." In any event, says Ahlstrom, "such was not the case."[51]

Ahlstrom and other historians, however, in paying close attention to the obvious quantitative evidence in the question of outside influence on American thought have overlooked another, if minor, part of the story. They have passed over the qualitative difference of other, non-German theological furnishings, which cannot be measured by the numbers alone, even if those incontestable figures dominate the scene. Ahlstrom's categories of influence are of two main divisions—the persuasive and the provocative, which, as he says, "often interface in a complex way."[52]

Willard L. Sperry was not a figure in the twenties and thirties who was *provocative* in the way Reinhold Niebuhr or Harry Emerson Fosdick commanded attention and provoked controversy. Sperry, perhaps, lacked for the polemical opportunities that Niebuhr and Fosdick found early in their careers. Lacking the reputation of a provocateur does not, however, mean passivity or truncated influence. In fact, Sperry's quiet British style of thought in American religion was converging with continental forces at a critical juncture. Walter Marshall Horton, a highly acclaimed spokesman for a moderate neo-orthodox position, concluded in the mid-thirties that "very grave issues hang upon our decision whether to take the turn indicated by the Barthian sign-post, or to follow the road on which contemporary English theology is travelling."[53]

It has been self-evident for a long time which road American Protestant liberals followed. Historians have gotten much mileage out of the fact that the Niebuhrian steam roller paved the road originally mapped by Barthian thinkers. Niebuhr, of course, routed his own scenic detour, but arrived roughly where continental thinkers suggested. Meanwhile, it is often wholly forgotten that up until 1940 contemporary English theology in William Temple and L. P. Jacks, to mention just two examples, proposed going by another way. The leading American spokesman for these alternate positions, and also the American most personally connected to Jacks and to Temple, was Willard Sperry. And it is the quality of Sperry's persuasiveness, perhaps at times too subtle and thereby, too English, that becomes the main burden of any treatment at hand of his life and work. No other American Protestant liberal of the first order, save Sperry, was intimately associated with the professed English options which Horton said still existed fifteen years after the First World War and which commanded in some measure an American audience. Young American theologians, such as James Luther Adams, who had even been Sperry's student at Harvard, were still going to Germany in the thirties for advanced study.

The qualities of Sperry's "Englishness" date naturally to his student days at Oxford. His prophetic message in American religious thought is clearly more persuasive than provocative. The English intellectual background of the twentieth century, meanwhile, must be taken seriously as being neither completely persuasive nor provocative. Failure at a single, popular level at being persuasive, however, does not necessarily mean that such acts of persuasion have been inhibited from quietly and patiently opening new ways of thought. William R. Hutchison observes that lesser known theologians from atypical backgrounds should be seen as sometimes getting a decisive advantage over the popular luminaries. He comments that "Sperry might have made some personal capital out of the fact that he himself, well before Niebuhr had been heard of, had expatiated upon the consciousness of sin and suffering" as the original tenor of Christian experience. Instead, Hutchison finds it remarkable that with no evidence of a jaundiced eye Sperry rejoiced "with a certain fearful joy" that he was seeing his position articulateed at last.[54]

The combination of Sperry's modified Calvinist horizon and straightforward Oxford launching pointed him squarely in a liberal direction, but one that uniquely conveyed English *"foundations"* to an American audience. Sperry became very much like a money-changer at a major crossroads, translating the ideas of one place into the equivalents of another, or breaking down the higher notes of the university into the smaller denominations of the commonplace. He traded almost exclusively in the intellectual currency of figurative dollars and pounds sterling while many more others of his generation traded the coin of pure silver and German marks.

An Unexpected Source: George Tyrrell

The diversity of experience at Oxford brought Sperry into regular contact with the continuity of the catholic Christian mind, a frame of reference far richer than any provided solely by American Congregationalism. Ironically, the sympathies acquired for the Church of England and Roman Catholic Modernism greatly overshadowed any previous strong feelings Sperry may have had for English Nonconformists. Next in significance, after Streeter's enormous influence upon him, Sperry followed with protracted interest the opinions of Father George Tyrrell. Tyrrell's point of view gained hold of Sperry progressively and perhaps filled a void left by Streeter who, ten years after the Great War, recanted some of his earlier, modernist sentiments. Streeter was led away in the twenties from a position of absolute idealism (pre-war liberalism) by the "new" psychology. This, in turn, placed Streeter in the otherwise unlikely camp of a "new" evangelicalism.[55] As a result, Streeter and his wife became active in Buchman's Oxford Group Movement—much to Sperry's sorrow and dismay. The Buchman group was theologically liberal, or at least vaguely antinomian, but it just was not politically liberal. By the late twenties and until the mid-forties, with Streeter drifting away from an earlier liberalism and then dying tragically in a plane crash, Sperry formed and maintained close contacts with another English theologian of well publicized liberal views, the Unitarian, L. P. Jacks. Thus, through Jacks Sperry was, at last, brought into direct contact with the English tradition of Non-Conformity. Because

Jacks entered Sperry's orbit after the American had already left Oxford, the necessary discussion of their relationship must be deferred.

Meanwhile, as the twentieth century opened George Tyrrell (1861-1909) had clearly become the leading spokesman and focus of the Modernist movement which more or less died out after his time, although later liberal impulses in Roman Catholicism can be traced to the Modernist challenge. Tyrrell ran afoul of the Vatican, drawing papal condemnation (Encyclical *Pascendi dominici gregis*, September 8, 1907) and then finally, a month after the *Pascendi* was issued, he was excommunicated for "the synthesis of all heresies," which had been denounced as Modernism. The Modernist tragedy was anticipated in large measure by Matthew Arnold's own intellectual disposition as a person left "Wandering between two worlds, one dead,/The other powerless to be born." Tyrrell and his fellow Modernists felt that in being forced to compromise on intellectual inquiry and honesty, they were left "between two worlds"—the old world of inflexible (read "infallible") orthodoxy and the new world of incipient secularism.[56]

Tyrrell had been a convert to Roman Catholicism; so, there is, naturally, enough of John Henry Newman's pattern of mind found in Tyrrell to make some of the inevitable comparisons seem favorable. Tyrrell, however, while a man of brilliant endowment was very unlike Newman in that he had less patience in the face of authority. Newman was, perhaps, drawn to authority because he required it in his constitution; Tyrrell was drawn to it because by nature he needed to resist it. Some have explained the tensions in Tyrrell's genius as being a cross between mysticism and an Irish temper. Regarded as the leading apostle of the Roman Catholic Modernist movement, Tyrrell possessed the fixation of a martyr raging with single-minded guile toward a mission. After ten years of intensity and remarkable production bringing into print some important polemical works, Tyrrell, having sacrificed himself to the cause, burned out right at his prime and died two years after Rome deprived him of the sacraments.

Tyrrell defined a Modernist as "a churchman, of any sort, who believes in the possibility of a synthesis between the essential truth of his religion and the essential truth of modernity."[57] Broadly speaking, this characterization would carry Willard Sperry in its sweep so that his own lifelong task was to serve as a mediator, a cultural arbiter between the two worlds of historic religion and modern science. Tyrrell, however, had a far more difficult problem in that role because of the bitter contention between himself and the controlling institution to which he belonged and wished to remain loyal. Tyrrell's gravest mistake may have been that he out-positioned himself politically. He was always an "insider" pushing out against a surrounding fortification. Sperry, on the other hand, was simultaneously an "insider" and an "outsider" veering between two cultures.

The uproar that Tyrrell caused was due to his frustration with the "ossified" theology of Roman Catholicism which had stood in the way of making it possible for that tradition to come into valid relation with the modern world. Failure on Rome's part to respond in an up-dated mode of thought would, in Tyrrell's mind, mean trouble for all churches, not just the Roman Catholic Church. Tyrrell said all Christians must take an interest in the Modernist Controversy and "hope that their respective Churches are not outworn, are not dead but sleeping." Tyrrell's desire to expand his base of support was premised on the belief that "if Rome dies, other churches may order their coffins."[58]

Tyrrell's agenda for the Modernist of any faith—Roman Catholic, Anglican or Nonconformist—is clearly articulated in the Preface to his final work, *Christianity at the Cross-Roads*: "The time has come ... for a criticism of categories—of the very ideas of religion, of revelation, of institutionalism, of sacramentalism, of theology, of authority." Tyrrell argues that "the current expression of these ideas is only provisional, and is inadequate to their true values." And this, Tyrrell maintains, is in keeping with the orderly process to improve Christian "self-consciousness." The element of paradox, always evident in Tyrrell's dialectic thinking, comes to full force in his swan song:

> The Modernist's confidence in Christianity may be misplaced, but it cannot be despatched in a smart article or encyclical. We may be sure that religion, the deepest and most universal exigency of man's nature, will survive. We cannot be sure that any particular expression of the religious idea will survive. Nay, we may be sure that all must perish, that none can ever be perpetual and universal save that which shall at last recognize and conform to the laws of the religious process, as they come to be established by reflection on wider experience.[59]

Tyrrell declares that the ultimate problem was "not Catholicism, but Christ and Christianity." And "should Christianity be unable, or unwilling, to conform to these laws, it must perish, like every other abortive attempt to discover an universal religion as catholic as science."[60] This Modernist view—often confused mistakenly with liberal accommodation to the *Zeit-*

geist— must be carefully delineated from liberal Catholic or even liberal Protestant readiness to indulge science disproportionately to Christianity. Tyrrell was not about to surrender or devalue religion in order to confirm its truth scientifically. On the contrary, and paradoxically, Tyrrell attacks the orthodox static positions, but not from a liberal perspective of present-mindedness. He makes his contention based on internal (scholastic) arguments, taking on all comers with their own weapons like David possessing the sword of Goliath. It is essential to comprehend that Tyrrell was a Modernist, not necessarily a liberal as that term was used then and now.[61] While not as vigorous a critic of liberal Protestantism as he was of his own church, Tyrrell reserved the other sharp edge of his sword for that non-Catholic company with whom he was syndicated in spirit. He contemptuously faults "liberal Protestantism, with its bland faith and hope in the present order, its refusal to face the incurable tragedy of human life."[62]

Tyrrell was not always the iconoclast. His main interest was actually a positive one in trying to reorient the spiritual priorities of his generation. Religious experience he placed prior to theology. Theology, as a consequence, was not so much the queen, but the consort—always in service to the shared fate of genuine religious awareness. This is very much in keeping with Arnold's commitment "to see life steadily and see it whole." Tyrrell's first priority was to ground religion on the firm basis of experience, a form of thought Sperry adopted and applied in his interpretation of eschatology in the Synoptic Gospels. Near the end of Tyrrell's life, he reinforced what he had previously decided about religion:

> We do not need to prove religion to men, but to show them that they are religious. That religion which we "prove" is not the substance, but a particular form and interpretation of religious experience—not the divine, but some particular image, symbol or conception of the divine. What we experience (be our creed or non-creed what it may) is a Power that makes for Righteousness, i.e. that subjects us to an universal, super-individual, super-social end, of which we have no distinct conception, and which we can only figure to ourselves in symbols, images, whether spontaneously or by deliberate effort of thought.[63]

Tyrrell was not a shaky-minded empiricist lacking nerve. He argues for "participatory" epistemology by giving ample room for the fashioning and the finding of truth. For Tyrrell "religion is not a dream, but an enacted, self-expression of the spiritual world—a parable uttered, however haltingly in the language of fact. It is . . . construction that has been forced upon us and verified by our experience." He issues a further note of caution to positivism that no one, particularly a scientist, can merely "think to get to any fact, even the commonest without faith and intuition."[64]

In more ways than one and from an early point in Willard Sperry's career there is much that is patently derived from Tyrrell's philosophy of religious experience. In Tyrrell one finds stress on Christian "conscience" and "conduct," the paradoxical coalition of immanence and transcendence in his theology, the delineation obviating a premature and misspent reconciliation between religion and science, the careful distinction between "the language of prophecy" and "the language of exact thought," and the noble attempt tò express the essence and distinctiveness of Christianity without reducing it to the triviality of mere banner aphorisms. Fundamentally, if ironically, Sperry's ideas converged with Tyrrell's. The irony is that a Protestant continued and promoted Tyrrell's thought down through the years and across an ocean. The themes highlighted in the corpus of Tyrrell's thought bud and bloom subtly in Sperry who happened to be in England at a formative period of life just at the height of the Jesuit's notoriety. What is more, it is Sperry's distinction to be the only, or perhaps one of but a few significant American Protestants, who relied on an English Catholic Modernist (and, from one angle, a heretic). Sperry was consistent throughout his adult life in a profound devotion to Tyrrell's cause. The earliest indication that Sperry was cognizant of and drawn to another unusual and unlikely intellectual source (the first being liberal Anglican biblical scholarship) probably is recorded while he was preparing for Final Examinations at Oxford. Much that he commends to his theologically distraught sister, Pauline, is in keeping with the views of Modernist proponents such as Tyrrell. Taking time out from acutely rigorous study to write in long hand, Sperry casually enumerates his current theological opinions:

> I can't say much to you re your theological difficulties, for I'm in the seething pot myself—but two or three things are close to me a) that [Robert Louis?] Stevenson is not the last word on religion and you are much better back to the gospel of John, b) that Christianity is a mood of life and not the intellectual assent to everything found in the Bible or the Creeds, and that we are to be known by our friends and not by our attitude to the Virgin Birth, c) that in the last analysis we must be content with an honest agnosticism. . ., d) that on the other hand, we are justified in proceeding on the assumption that for all practical purposes certain great facts about God and Christ are true, though they cannot be [?] demonstrated, e) that we are not to disregard all the capacities for mysticism which we possess,

though they may lead into experience which we cannot analyze, f) that the sooner we close our Shaw and open our Carlyle the better. . .[65]

Sperry while still in his early twenties was already on his way to inheriting "the common tradition" of English spiritual writers and literary figures represented tangibly in Tyrrell. On several points, Sperry sounds like Tyrrell slightly distilled, yet there is no sense whatsoever then or later that he is a mocking bird to Tyrrell's sparrow song. Tyrrell says, for instance, "Christianity was, therefore, not a religion, but a spirit, mode or quality of religion, which might be found in various religions, but never apart by itself, as it were 'a subsistent quality'." He continues, "To speak of 'a pure unadulterated Christianity' is really nonsense."[66] That is the same spirit which Sperry himself accords in professing that "Christianity is a mood of life." The emphasis in this shared affirmation is on the primacy of feelings and conduct.

Sperry's postulate of sincerity, that religion must incorporate "an honest agnosticism," again sounds much like Tyrrell. Sperry quotes Tyrrell frequently in sermons preached through the ensuing years as exemplified in "The Testing Ground of Prayer" which cites this passage from the Jesuit's work: "The honesty question always riles me. . . At least, let us confess that there are degrees of honesty as there are of reality. For the rest, it is enough if we try to be honest and purge our dishonesties with all diligence. The best symptom of progress," Tyrrell iterates for Sperry's homiletic purposes, "is a growing sense of one's manifold insincerities."[67]

Sperry mentions to his sister the necessity of objective realities in religion. Again Tyrrell confirms Sperry's summary in elaborating that "the sense of an absolute opposed to his relativity, an infinite to his finitude, a permanent to his evanescence, an actual to his potentiality, a repose to his restlessness is the ground work and canvas on which man's rational life is broidered." Tyrrell rehearses the reality of religion in terms of human experience (as opposed to thought), "That we can feel and suffer from our relativity, finitude and evanescence, means an under-consciousness of an Absolute, Infinite, and Unchanging, that we must for ever try to express in our thought and action as in terms of another order of being."[68]

Sperry's interest in the capacities for mysticism, "the guarded powers of wonder," are, unlike some liberal Protestants, steadfast throughout the subsequent years of his intellectual activity. He gives the topic a thorough review in his Ayer Lectures of 1929: "The mystics never doubt or deny the existence of God in the world around. On the contrary, because they believe in the God without they turn at last to find the God who is within. That is their mature childlikeness."[69] Of Tyrrell's own credentials and capacities for mysticism there is uniform agreement beginning with a classic autobiographical account of his conversion as a youth while attending Mass:

> Of course it was mere emotion and sentiment, and I set no store by it then or now, but oh! the sense of reality! Here was the old business, being carried on by the old firm, in the old ways; here was continuity, that took one back to the catacombs; here there was no need of and therefore no suspicion of, pose or theatrical parade; its aesthetic blemishes were its very beauties in that mood.[70]

The experience of which Tyrrell speaks forms over time "a common language of self utterance" and this is how theology evolves—only after prior and authentic experience.

Sperry's daughter, Henrietta Wilson, recalls as a child hearing of Tyrrell at home and "seeing his books on the shelves."[71] The best corroboration of Tyrrell's influence on Sperry comes from Sperry himself in a footnote written in the pages of *Those of the Way*, a pithy devotional manual published after a Lenten lecture series of that title. Sperry fervently defends Tyrrell's combination of piety with intellect, saying, "I owe more to the writings of Father Tyrrell than to those of any other modern author, in my endeavor to understand what the Christian religion was at the first, what it always has been at heart, what therefore it should be."[72]

Sperry came back to America a decidedly changed individual. While home he would look to England again and again for something Thomas Hardy describes as "either directly seen, or miraged in the peculiar atmosphere." At Oxford the steady memories gathered about a whole life, not just an intellectual one. Sperry had the opportunity to row on the college eight. In characteristic modesty he reported that the physical work on the river was not exactly a retreat from the fine eighteenth-century setting of the Queens library:

> You see rowing has its disadvantages and one of them is that you slide about a seat so hard and so long that you gradually wear a hole in yourself and sitting down is a very painful process, as one might suppose.[73]

Sperry was an accomplished member of the college crew, but his chances for a Blue (i.e., rowing for the University, particularly against Cambridge) were spoiled by a rowing form acquired in boyhood in a skiff. Rowing in Maine produced a choppy motion as opposed to the graceful pull of a true English oarsman. He, nonetheless, rowed a winning boat in the intercollegiate races which, as custom dictated, meant he was presented with his section of the boat and the oarblade. As mementos, a sacred place for them was reserved among family furnishings. "The piece of boat made an ugly sort of cupboard, and the oarblade hung over the fireplace in his study at home."[74]

His success at Oxford was not limited to athletics. He was elected to one of the prestigious clubs at Queens, so that he enjoyed a modicum of social as well as athletic fortune. This particular invitation came "by strength of silent example" in spite of being a teetotaler, one of four nondrinkers out of a hundred and forty men in Queens, an exceptional feat in affability given the collegiate pressures to conform.[75] None of these accomplishments, however, were as impressive as earning First Class Honors in Theology. The significance of an Oxford First was of such magnitude as virtually to guarantee from that moment on all the courtesies and university opportunities closed and unknown to the aggregate of the many near misses. Streeter carefully groomed (and promoted) Sperry for his First believing him to be "the best prepared man he ever sent in for the Theology Schools."[76] In the British system one's eventual academic career usually hinged on the prerequisite of earning a coveted First.

In three ways, then—athletics, clubs and academics—Sperry, coming from a small midwestern American college, made his mark at Oxford, though in truth, the greater mark was the one Oxford left on him. In a fourth and deeper way also, Sperry cemented his English loyalties for good when he met his roommate's sister whom he married in 1908 with Canon Streeter officiating in Dublin. As his time at Oxford drew to a close, Sperry declares his acquired Englishness by recalling Ruskin's description of America as "a fresh and very ugly country." Sperry, displaying half-in-earnest sophistry in defense of his newly adopted homeland of the spirit, decrees "England as a newer country than America" because the great reforms of the nineteenth-century "changed her whole way of looking at things." The American Civil War, says the American Oxonian, "didn't seriously change the American attitude—the American idea—the American heritage."[77]

The double feelings embracing English chauvinism and American deprecation placed him between two worlds of conflicting loyalties—the one, into which he was born, was partly unacceptable to him, the other, lacking birthright covenant, in due measure was unaccepting of him. He was always a visitor never a dweller at Oxford, never, as he had hoped, the integral connection of another world in the Senior Common Room. After the Second World War he saw Queens slipping away from his comprehension, "ingrowing and academic in the pejorative sense."[78] This was the part of Oxford that for Sperry could never be "directly seen," but appeared only "miraged in the peculiar atmosphere." As he himself realized when he was "turned down on the election for boats captain. . . it wouldn't do to have an American running boats."[79]

Oxford was the great testing ground in Sperry's life. From there he first tried on the ideas that would serve and govern his life's work, confirming the dominant purpose of the University to connect truth and virtue. Three phases of metamorphosis seem apparent in Sperry's constructive Oxford period—developing his intellect, testing his energy and claiming him for a higher, guiding purpose. It all began to point toward the parish ministry back home, after a year of re-entry preparation at Yale. First, Sperry came to maturity by thinking deeply and critically:

> I'm quite sure most of us are too dogmatic and will talk too easily about things in the last resort we know nothing about. It is a narrow path we travel intellectually at any rate I can't understand the man who goes plodding along as [assuredly?] as if he had all Broadway to himself— though I envy him. I shall be a very erratic and unusual sort of minister, either a howling success or an immense failure.[80]

After cultivating his critical abilities, Oxford showed Sperry what his limitations might be, particularly where one necessarily draws the line in his persistence. Enduring as well as merely performing is the second measure of an education's abiding effect. Sperry became quite weary of books, exposition and drudgery, a curable psychological peril of graduate studies. Coincidentally, his middle sister, Pauline, also found the ends of her study impractical and interminable. The expanse covered in an academic course often seemed to them both far too distant and un-reasonable. Drawing from the discipline of rowing, Sperry tells his sister, "the better fitted we are in scholastic ways, the larger service we can render in the end." Sperry acknowledges that his advice is as much self-encouraging as it is intended to cheer his studious sister. In spite of the strenuousness, he confides, "I am too young to settle down to a life work and so are you. We must be content to go on getting ready. . ."[81] He had, after all, already had a strong dose of New England earnestness and mission.

Finally, having attained a sense of self-knowledge through independent thinking in relation to primary intellectual sources and increased reserves of concentration, Sperry foresaw and claimed his higher resolve through life itself. Six months after his father's death, his life's work was submitting to the predisposition his father shaped unawares—to help people find meaning in life and obtain strength for living. He reveals to his mother, "I find I'm more and more ready to see life whole, to reckon some with death itself. I am no better than my fathers that I should know why it all is, or ask more than my three score years and ten.... I think I can begin to understand what your loneliness must be."

When Sperry embarked for study at Oxford, his father invoked parting words from Ezekiel (2:1) that cohered in the strongest way possible, "Son of Man stand upon thy feet." These anchor-like impressions from home, ultimately touching him in a way Oxford could not, "meant everything" to him "in beginning life anew,"[82] certain of "the central stream of what we feel indeed."

CHAPTER 3

Developing a Theology
of Second Thought

". . . traditional belief in New England retained its continuity and priestly unction; and religious teachers and philosophers could slip away from Calvinism and even from Christianity without any loss of elevation or austerity. They found it so pleasant and easy to elude the past that they really had no quarrel with it."

—George Santayana[1]

Yale and Ministry

IF THE OPPORTUNITY of going to Oxford had been entered with many initial misgivings, then Willard Sperry's success after three years there proved that an undergraduate education in a small midwestern American college did not disqualify him for work in a great and ancient European university. Rather, Sperry's self-fulfilling adjustment to an overseas culture was carried further than the contentment of being a comfortable tourist. His loyalties now stood four-square against a deeper background of England, not merely New England. He had acquired a homeland of the mind and with it an enthusiasm that was bound to be problematical in returning to America because the two cultures, though intimately connected, were, nonetheless, at that time very different. Sperry's difficulty was more serious than that of an American literary expatriate who had perhaps angrily renounced the small town new world for the authority and stability of the old one. He was not turning his back on America, but turning his face toward America and in entering that narrow passage between two identities he was determined to bring England with him rather than leave it forever.

Reentering American society, having been convinced, if not converted, by the ordered dignity of English ways, was not necessarily an educational advantage leading to an instant theological career. Typically, Germany, not Britain, was the acceptable point of departure for all but Episcopalians into

American Protestant life and thought. Whatever anxieties Sperry felt in the first place about Oxford were set to rest in terms of that particular experience by earning the First in Theology and by marriage to a stunning and brilliant young woman whose own church affiliations were with Anglo-Catholicism. These earlier misgivings that once centered on Oxford, however, were transferred geographically, and ironically, they deepened as Sperry considered his return to America, in many ways an unwelcomed stranger in his own country. It is in this context that Sperry's professional pursuits and theological passage from England, potentially in drift, were protected by the firm mooring which a year at Yale Divinity School (like his father) would supply. This prudent decision was intended to give him some local point of entry into the American ministry.

Academically, the year proved useful and earned Sperry a "modest M.A." There he worked in philosophy under Professor Charles Montague Bakewell and prepared a thesis on Aristotle's criticism of Plato's doctrine of ideas. Meanwhile, he continued his studies in church history "on down after Chalcedon in the classroom of Williston Walker." About the renowned church historian, Sperry, looking back upon many years declared that "he was by all odds the best lecturer whom I have heard in any college or university."[2]

Moreover, besides the inspiration of Walker, Sperry "got also a hint of saintliness from the lectures of Frank [Chamberlain] Porter" who had taught Biblical theology. Others have noted that same quality of Porter's teaching which was a power that "lay in the richness of his thought, the transparency of his spirit, the gentle self-effacement of his character."[3] Sperry found Porter appealing for other reasons, too. Coming out of the German university experience, Porter's frame of theological inquiry had a different shape than the one Sperry would eventually form and describe for himself. But one can trace in the Porter of substance, not just in the man's charming personality, the converging theological questions which the mature Sperry took up after him. Porter, for instance, was critical of both Liberal and Ritschlian theology. His commentary and quest focused on the problem of faith and history, because in his view, "Liberalism substituted for Christ the Christ idea, whereas Ritschlianism was tied to the Christ of actual history."[4] Since both could not be right, Porter wondered if Liberalism were Christian and if Ritschlianism were reasonable. Sperry posed the same query to his own Modernist position and to the competing Barthianism.

What is even more suggestive of the unconscious intellectual associations between Sperry and his Yale professor were the debts Porter's thinking owed to Coleridge, Wordsworth and Horace Bushnell. Wordsworth, in particular, became a key figure in Sperry's understanding of religious experience and its meaning. Porter, likewise, found in Wordsworth his whole principle of Biblical interpretation as a parallel to the purpose of poetry which is "truth, not individual and local but general and operative, not standing upon external testimony but carried alive in the heart by passion—truth which is its own testimony."[5]

Porter developed several hermeneutical canons which paid special attention to "the power of the mind to clothe its deepest feelings" into a language of faith and emotion that transformed things seen into symbols.[6] These issues have parallel expression in Carlyle, so it is not surprising to find Sperry making similar use of this hermeneutic method. Interestingly, Carlyle, Porter, and Sperry are united in a lifelong preoccupation with the problem of the language and expression of faith and emotion and its significance in deeper thought. For Sperry symbols, language or "clothes" mediated between objective and subjective truth:

> Religion may have to get along without the full [naked] measure of objective truth, because our knowledge of the universe is forever short of the total fact and often in error as to detail, but it cannot dispense with the other kind of truth, namely that agreement between our convictions as to reality and the words and deeds [and "clothing"] used to express those convictions, which we call sincerity.[7]

After Sperry's unofficial probationary year at Yale, and now having brought his Irish wife, Muriel Bennett, to New England, he was ready to embark upon his father's calling. The provisional time spent at Yale, however, did not preempt a series of false starts which Sperry had anticipated and had hoped to avoid. He had become comfortable with the idea of being ordained in the Episcopal Church because the "manners" of his "hereditary American Congregationalism seemed...rather sloppy and untidy" beside the proprieties of Anglicanism to which he had grown accustomed in Oxford. While his father had been a Congregational minister, he reasoned that his loyalties could be easily transferred because on his mother's side of the family there were a number of Episcopal rectors. For these reasons Sperry supposed that he might be more at home in the Episcopal ministry. Through a rector of a New Haven parish, Sperry arranged an interview with the Dean of the Episcopal

Theological School in Cambridge. When asked for his position on the Virgin Birth, the bodily resurrection of Jesus and like doctrinal points, Sperry gave his "general opinions—rather than convictions" as they had been formed under Streeter's tutelage. The Dean advised that Sperry not apply for Episcopal ordination and many years later Sperry recalled, "I think he felt, not without warrant, that he did not know what he might be letting the Episcopal Church in for, in the case of an unknown Congregational maverick tainted with modernist heresies from England."[8] And yet, while the matter was settled with finality, Sperry came to feel over all the intervening years that "culturally" he was an unrecognized Anglican.

Meanwhile, having been rebuffed by the Episcopalians, he applied to the New Haven Association of Congregational Ministers for a license to preach. As is still the case in such matters, he had to appear before a committee and make a brief statement of faith which was also a matter of conscience. Having presented an earnest statement of his beliefs, young Sperry ended with the imprimatur of weighty historic words, "Here I stand, God help me, I can do no other." The entire exercise cost him much agony and the outcome forever soured him on denominational hierarchy as he explains what ensued in an autobiographical essay:

> That quotation was greeted with a howl of laughter from the assembled company of ecclesiastical thugs. If they had taken a snake whip and struck me across the face, they could not have hurt me more. The pain of that cruel laughter still lingers in my mind and heart as a wound which has never healed... it was my taste of the brutality of organized ecclesiasticism. True, at this distance I can see the discrepancy between the Diet of Worms and my appearance before the New Haven Association. But the heartless reaction of that gang of theological ruffians gives a clue as to why some sensitive and conscientious young men do not enter the ministry today.[9]

Momentarily distressed as to his fitness for ordination into any Christian ministry, Sperry appealed to a local minister for advice. He visited a prominent Congregationalist figure, Newman Smyth (1843-1925), who was, in his generation, one of the leading and controversial Andover liberals. Smyth was invited to succeed the theologian Edwards Park in 1881 which sparked a faculty furor. Smyth, instead, stayed in the parish ministry for the entirety of his career, though for twenty years he was a Fellow at Yale while serving as Minister of the First Congregational Church of New Haven, making him more than an honorary academic, but also a scholar and an author in the genteel tradition.

During his distinguished ministry Smyth devoted much of his energy to ecumenism and boldly declared in 1908, the year of his retirement and near the time Sperry came to be counseled, that the "Protestant era" was ending. His book *Passing Protestantism* (1908) was a pioneer work in the ecumenical movement. His ecumenical vision has been regarded as liberal rather than reactionary, probably because of his ready acceptance of a "mediating modernism" largely contingent, he felt, on the outcome of the experiments of Roman Catholic Modernism. A shared interest in Tyrrell's success or failure, however, was not what had precipitated the first and perhaps only meeting between Smyth and Sperry.[10]

In the study of Dr. Smyth, Sperry explained that his intial concern for religion had grown out of his brooding over the death of a friend and then later the untimely loss of his father. The mystery of human life and the meaning of eternal life were the major concerns of his mind, and not the incidental and peripheral issues of such questions as the Virgin Birth. Reassured by Smyth that to stand fast on the one or two convictions he already held, while wanting other articles of faith and doctrine, was a sure foundation from which the work in the ministry could extend. With this affirmation Sperry went on to enter the ministry of the Congregational Church into which he had been born.

In the autumn of 1908, he was called to the mill town of Fall River, Massachusetts, to be associate minister of the First Congregational Church. The minister was William Wisner Adams, then in his late seventies, but an energetic, disciplined and erudite man, from whom Sperry learned much about preaching and practical church matters. These first few years in the ministry under the guidance of Adams were of such positive consequence that Sperry referred to the experience constantly from the later vantage point of Harvard. Adams was an excellent model. The senior minister stayed well informed through the latest theological publications of the day, which at that time were focused mainly on biblical criticism. "Much of it went beyond his own position, and the margins of his books were cluttered with his single devastating comment, 'Bah!' However, he knew what was going on. From his watchtower on the walls of his church he looked out over the confused theological scene, and reported back to his parish that, although there were many foes in the field, the faith was still intact."[11]

Through his mentor, Adams, Sperry gained insight at an important theological intersection where the nature of religion crosses the business of ethics, which to Sperry's benefit was "little short of a kind of conversion in maturity." In preparing for the ministry Sperry had had a youthful infatuation with Tolstoi's ethical idealism, a rigid and uncompromising set of Christian principles distilled from Tolstoi's religious writings such as *My Confession* and *The Gospels in Brief*. This influence of absolute imperatives would become manifest in Sperry's later pacifist position expressed publicly through the war years, 1914-1918.

Sperry, however, was not Tolstoian in any strict or practical sense of what that connotes, but he was nevertheless attracted to some of Tolstoi's philosophical musings and admits that as a theological student he "was under his spell." Tolstoi, apparently, was still in vogue from the 1890s through Sperry's day at the turn of the century, having influenced social reformers such as Jane Addams, the founder of Chicago's Hull House.[12]

Sperry's self-described "Tolstoian period" was a liberal variant of pre-1914 "antimodernism" which had been injected into American culture by vague pastoral doctrines of the "Simple Life." When Sperry later refers to his "Tolstoian period" while in his twenties, it is symbolic of an immature readiness to renounce the world— its politics, its economics and its divisions. Some of this idealism (and anarchism) never ceased influencing Sperry's middle sister, Pauline, whose stand against taking a loyalty oath as a university professor in Berkeley became a celebrated case in the McCarthy witch-hunting days. Sperry, meanwhile, outgrew these tendencies as he faced in the ministry the realities and complexities which made Tolstoi's ideals impractical in the "real" world. In a letter from 1938 to John R. Mott, Chairman of the International Missionary Council and called "American Protestantism's greatest statesman," Sperry clarified the process through which he had once passed in his early theological development:

> So far as the Christian "good news" is concerned, I have long ago given up the attempt to find in the Gospels or in the New Testament literature verbal rules to determine our conduct in the 20th century. I went through that phase in the days of Charles M. Sheldon [a Congregational minister and author of the popular *In His Steps*, a novel exploring the hypothesis of a modern church taking seriously and literally the precepts of the Sermon on the Mount] and during my Tolstoian period as a theological student. I did not find that it worked on those premises. We must have the courage of Christian originality while not claiming novelty. The Christian life is a first-hand adventure and not an imitation.[13]

Tolstoi understood Christianity as a religion with a firm metaphysics and ethics, the latter a consequence of the former. What was clearest in the Gospels to him was the ethical vision because this is what the life and teaching of Jesus Christ most forcefully proposed. While in accord with much of the social gospel, this ran counter to the rediscovered importance of Jesus as an apocalyptist. Tolstoi's premise led to a theology of perfection, an answer to the question, "What must I do?"[14]

Tolstoi reduced the teaching of Jesus to five principles, one of which was "Thou shalt not foreswear thyself"—i.e., pledge away your future. Sperry did not, for instance, find this objectionable in Tolstoi. He explained in a short discourse on pacifism addressed to his daughter that

> The idea has difficulties. On that basis how do we sign on for anything, a profession, marriage, etc. The difference being, however, that we make these decisions as the actual occasion for them comes along. I think Tolstoi was arguing against deciding in advance—before the event—what you would do. The trouble is that when the actual thing comes it isn't at all what you imagined it would be. There is something to be said for being a free unpledged agent.[15]

Sperry was Tolstoian only to the extent of rejecting premeditated and arbitrary convictions. His Tolstoian self-reference is often a kind of code word for his experimentation in pacifism and nothing more. Beyond that, Sperry did not subscribe to anything else in the complex Tolstoian package of idealism such as celibacy and ceasing to believe in private property. Sperry would part company with Tolstoi even on the practice of pacifism, leaving only these general, but favorable comments to his daughter:

> He was a question mark set against all the conventions of Western society. He made it challenge its axioms. But he really didn't have an answer to any one of the questions he asked with such dramatic force. ... the man did make you question your own conventions and therein lay his value to his time, and perhaps to all times. There is also, a nice tale of his holding up all his rich friends for money to give to the poor of Moscow, and after he had collected a large sum, hunting for worthy recipients. But not being able to find one person who was morally fit to be helped he gave the money all back to his friends. He had that kind of devastating consistency.[16]

While a ministerial neophyte and not yet aware of alternatives and challenges to the validity of the Christian ethic, which Nietzsche, in particular, represented, Sperry admitted in retrospect that "the subsequent discovery that there were serious persons in our world who questioned the validity of that ethic was the one bad theological shock that I have ever experienced." Sperry remembers that the manner in which the poisoned arrow of "Anti-Christ" got between the joints of the armor of his "theological overconfidence" was in reading a book called *The Religion of All Good Men*. It was written in 1906 by H. W. Garrod, the English spokesman for Nietzsche.

Nietzsche criticized the Christian faith both as a spurious option to Jesus's real way of life and as being opposed to reason. These two criticisms are essential for understanding Nietzsche's attitude toward reason, which he valued most highly. In general, his most original criticism of Christianity was his attempt to demonstrate how from the start resentment (toward unbelievers and "the world") has been the heart of the so-called religion of love.

That Sperry was jolted by Nietzsche's harsh assessment of Christianity is a point of ever increasing importance because that experience not only represents a personal watershed, but is also symptomatic of a broader complacency in liberal Christianity that existed at the turn of the century and continued through the Great War. In light of Nietzsche Sperry discovered liberal Christianity had grown soft and had failed to question its own motives in readily accepting a doctrine of divine immanence, a realizable Kingdom and adapting to every modern urge. In accordance with Nietzsche's general challenge, perhaps "love" was not the incentive behind liberalism's premises, but "resentment" which required something besides the final word of liberalism's own schemes of salvation. The theological shock Sperry received in his introduction to Nietzsche was a glimpse of what correctives he had to consider during and after the world war. In this sense he had an advantage over contemporaries such as Fosdick and Niebuhr who did not realize the problem of liberal Christianity's lack of introspection until much later. However unprepared Sperry might have been to have his ("Tolstoian") ideals questioned at a time of Protestantism's cultural supremacy, his reaction was in some real measure indicative of how proportionately presumptive liberalism had become and what further disturbances and beguiling dangers were in store for it.

Meanwhile, the chief preoccupation Sperry had early in his ministry was the practicability of the Christian ethic, assuming it was the last word on all matters of conscience and of religion. It was the problem of the usefulness of Christianity which Sperry tracked and followed toward "a semi-mystical devotion to the person of Christ."[17]

A turning point in Sperry's understanding of the nature of religion arrived when old Dr. Adams preached to his people an annual sermon on the recent developments in astronomy. The following Monday morning the young associate ventured to ask the senior pastor what use his sermon served to a congregation absorbed in the making and selling of cotton fabrics, situated next to the conditions of people who were poor and underpaid. Adams, exercising the privilege of age, replied with detachment, "My dear boy, it's no use at all, but it greatly enlarges my idea of God." For Sperry the words came almost as a blinding light, and what he articulated about this realization approximates the late phase of H. Richard Niebuhr's "radical monotheism":

> In so far as I had ever thought of God, it was only as a hazy Veiled Being in the background of Christ. But from that day to this the idea of God, rather than the ethic of Jesus, has been the center of my religious thinking. Nothing seems more important than "greatly enlarged ideas of God." I have not given up my initial concern for the ethic of the Gospels, but that ethic is now set in the framework of my thought of God, and does not stand or fall as an independent system. Hence, I have never been able to share what was, some years ago, the attempt to isolate and salvage the ethic of Christianity, while letting its theology go.[18]

Sperry profited enormously from the example of Adams in other ways than exposure to a vigorous mind, undaunted by growing old. Adams was not only scholarly, but he was a gifted pastor. As evident from a plea Sperry made to his sister, Pauline, Adams had instilled him with high intellectual standards for the pulpit: "Don't ever be one of the people who ask their minister to bring religion down to them, to popularize it, will you? It's suicide for the church and nothing else."[19] But Adams also taught him to stay close to the people of his parish individually and in their homes. From the older minister, the younger one learned the art of pastoral calling and of its hidden rewards that sometimes will rejuvenate the caller:

> I am trembling on the dizzy verge of twenty nine, and was feeling quite grey headed, until I dropped in on a parishioner this afternoon and found Dr. Adams [already] there, aetas 80, beating the knees of the parishioner, aetas 87, like a couple of young bloods: I feel younger since then. There are some people. . .[like Adams] who will never grow old, they will pass instantly from their first into their second childhood. It's not quite clear to

me whether such a transition is to be desired or not, but age is a relative matter.[20]

Fall River, a kind of social Siberia compared to Oxford and New Haven, grew on Willard Sperry and grew to be important in keeping his higher theological contemplation checked by the pedestrian and daily needs of religion. The Sperrys had ready access to the cultural advantages of Boston, and though neither Willard nor Muriel were well disposed to the provincial life of a small textile manufacturing city, they would never have survived those years there if they had shown habits of snobbery, which is not to say that Fall River did not at times amuse and frustrate them:

> Why I even think Fall River is preferable [to Boston], we have a few human crudities left yet, we have not refined ourselves away to the vanishing point. We sometimes call over twenty minutes, and occasionally leave two cards on a widow, and now and then we put our feet on the mantlepiece, in short I may say that the task of creation is still unfinished here, therefore, there is some use in being alive.[21]

There were other times, however, when Sperry struggled to put the best face on provincialism. Undertaking a long-term adult class in the Bible, Sperry attempted to induct members of his church in the methods and findings of modern, higher criticism. At the beginning of this endeavor, a kind of group Pygmalion project, Sperry confided to his sympathetic middle sister, "Well, I might as well have been Servetus." In this vein, he continues,

> So far as Fall River is concerned all the travail and agony and bloody sweat of scholarship for the past hundred years, might never have been. To these people here every "higher critic" is a concrete illustration of a personal Devil. Sanday has horns, Driver has a forked tail, Streeter shows the cloven hoof, Williston Walker carouses with night hags, and as for Benny Bacon, he eats little children i' the dark o' the moon!! It's so hard to feel for all the man (sic) who have given their best powers to a kind of relentless search for Truth that they shall be looked upon as deliberate enemies of all that is good and true. . . I feel how futile it is to dash one's brains out against a parish that was hermetically sealed up against new ideas about 1829. . .[22]

Sperry's first personal test of composite liberal learning not only pitted him against entrenched parochialism, but led to a deeper introspection about the value of modern theological ideas and progressive approaches. He considers early in his ministry the isolation of intellectual activity within the church, writing that

Confessedly it would be easier not to think, orthodoxy is the most comfortable modus vivendi, but what if one can't be orthodox, what if the mind God gave one and the training the world has given one won't let him settle back on the bosom of Calvin or Augustine or any other worthy, what if one is cast out naked into the dark and told to hunt for himself, what then?[23]

At this juncture, just before 1914, Sperry is deliberately exploring his own internal limitations toward the traditional liberal emphasis on human reason, while also measuring the boundaries of traditional church doctrine that one may try to extend without crossing over into the land of heretics. The tension between these opposing forces remained mostly private while in Fall River, until the First World War when his pricked conscience provoked within him a public voice on a controversial issue—Tolstoi's doctrine of nonresistance. Meanwhile, the day finally came when Sperry later looked back upon his venture in teaching a high level Bible class as a successful experiment in pedagogy. He led them over a succession of years through the Hebrew prophets and the historical books of the Old Testament on down to St. Paul's Epistles and thus finally to the Gospels—and not merely to the narrative story, moral teachings and the parables, but to the apocalyptic interpretation of the Gospels as found in Schweitzer's *Quest of the Historical Jesus*. About his class, he remembered that "they were loyal to the end." After initial fits, starts and frustration, Sperry changed his mind about general church obstancy to advanced learning in the Bible. "This experience persuaded me," he writes, "that given time and opportunity to do so, it is not impossible to interest the laity in such matters. But it cannot be done in any single thirty minute sermon."[24]

Sperry's pastoral role model, Dr. Adams, died while Sperry was in the parish, and so Sperry succeeded him as minister. Adams's pastorate fell just short of a full half century, yet Sperry appreciated his predecessor's life and achievements mostly for their rare quality of spirit, not solely for their recorded length of years and service, saying in his funeral sermon, "He was gloriously indifferent to the outward responses to his work, but [was] scrupulously critical of its inward spirit and purpose." Further, Sperry admired Adams because he

> . . . conceived of his ministry as a glorification of God, a revealing character of God. He lived in a day when a hundred other ideals are cherished by the Christian ministry. Men wish to be known as pulpit orators, to build up large and successful parishes, to increase the budget each year, to have crowded congregations morning and evening, to write books that shall be

> widely read, to be prominent in the denomination. All these ideals Dr.
> Adams put resolutely behind him. . . . [D]enominational politics he ab-
> horred, definitely preferring to remain in comparative retirement that he
> might give himself more unreservedly to his own work. . . [H]e had no
> respect for ecclesiastical machinery. . . . He wished people to come here to
> worship God, not to hear him. [25]

Sperry's eulogy of Adams hints with more than subtlety at the kind of
learned, independent ministry Sperry himself embraced and encouraged
from that time through his own increasing parish demands and subsequent
university responsibilities. Sperry's preferences became practically identical to his clergy "tutor," of whom he recalled that

> he playfully pleaded guilty to preaching over the heads of his people. For
> forty-eight years he even took a certain pride in this charge, because it
> bespoke the common assurance of his people, that he had refused to sell
> his ministry for the kingdoms of this world. . . . He is said to have lived in
> his study, with his books, away from actual life. But it was the real world
> in which he lived, and your world and mine of shuttles and looms and
> ledgers is the dream world. [26]

Sperry continued to serve in Fall River for two years after Adams's
death before he was called to be minister of the Central Congregational
Church in Boston's Back Bay. His first impressions of Boston are of "its
complacency." "It is such a finished and finite place. Bounded on the North
by Emerson's Essays, on the South by Boylston Street, on the East by 1620
and on the West by the Obituary Column in the *Transcript*." [27] Sperry's first
view of his new environs was remarkably similar to George Santayana's
final consideration of the city, before leaving New England in 1912. The
Harvard philosopher believed that "Boston and Cambridge in those days
[before the turn of the century] resembled in some ways the London of
Dickens: the same dismal wealth, the same speachifying, the same anxious
respectability, the same sordid back streets. . . the same odd figures and loud
humor, and, to add a touch of horror, the monstrous suspicion that some of
the inhabitants might be secretly wicked." [28]

The work in Central Congregational Church, one of the "problem"
parishes, was not necessarily that of a preaching post, but it was also not
an experimental station of conscience for the social gospel. While it was
made up mainly of professional people, Sperry nonetheless dealt with
serious church financial pressures and local community and pastoral needs
in due course. Often the indigent needs were urgent and did not pertain to

the regular membership. The church's location was not far from the train station which meant the occasional troubled person drifted into town stopping at the nearest church for assistance. Sperry's accessibility is noteworthy in a time of a more formal etiquette that conveniently sheltered clergy from unplanned interruptions. In one instance he spent an inordinate amount of time counseling a stranger who contemplated suicide.

Most clergy of the time were not yet well equipped in the tools, knowledge and method of psychology, relying on "seat of the pants" strategies or on a traditional "cure of souls" for even the deeper problems of life. In Sperry's case evidence is offered that he was something exceptional in this regard, demonstrating what today is known as directive technique in pastoral counseling (as opposed to the popular Rogerian counseling of the 1960s). In characteristic modesty, Sperry tells a fellow minister what he did with the man so profoundly troubled:

> I got the story out of him on the sound theory that he would be in much healthier condition if he objectified his trouble. This I take it is good psychology and good religion. I made him tell me everything . . . I then urged him to pray for himself then and there, which he did. It was very hard for him to do it but after he had done so and I had shared [my thoughts] with him he seemed to feel vastly relieved. When he left me he assured me that he was now on top of his trouble and would take the first train back home in the morning. I offered to care for him that night and to see him off in the morning, but he said there was no need.[29]

❦

First Stage Pulpit Theology: Pacifism

Six months after his arrival in Boston the First World War broke out in Europe and if there was any single great experience of his life after Oxford, it was trying to reconcile his private thoughts with his public role at this crossroads of global history in August 1914. If Oxford shaped him theologically, the First World War and its aftermath reshaped that theology. And because his was not a systematic theology, as Oxford was not a systematic course, he was more likely than other major American Protestant liberals (who happened in the main to be by-products of German systematic theology) to change his mind sooner. Sperry's was a programmatic theology, and his pulpit work during the war years emphasized thinking that did not have to adhere to the consistencies of a systematic exposition of doctrine. What began to set him apart from his generation was the issue of nonresistance, a decidedly minority position in the face of a popular international cause, a cause not unlike the social gospel, trying to save the world for Western ideas.

The public function and verbal performance of clergy in times of national crisis, has usually been heard as an amplification of a call to arms. Throughout its general history spanning three centuries, the American pulpit has been mostly nationalistic in the face of United States involvement in foreign war; sometimes the American pulpit was even bellicose, able "to metamorphose any national conflict into a struggle between God and the Devil, and to apply the sulphanous trappings of orthodox theology to their denunciations of the current foe."[30] Once the war was on in Europe and before the United States entered it, most of the Protestant preaching pertaining to the theme of war showed no impulse toward the Tolstoian spark of pacifism. In fact, and ironically, the war was heartily endorsed, and scriptural reasons furnished, by such disparate wings of American theology as premillenarians Isaac Haldeman and Frank M. Goodchild on the one hand and modernist interpreters such as Shailer Mathews and Harry Emerson Fosdick on the other.[31]

Fear and propaganda tactics were periodic, perhaps regular in the American pulpit. German atrocities were regularly paraded before congregations and the Kaiser was hanged symbolically, if not in effigy, off the rail of many of the most dignified pulpits. The renowned Congregationalist minister of Brooklyn, S. Parkes Cadman spoke out against students refusing to engage in military drill and exercise, calling them "parasites and suckers. . . rubbish." The literary and sentimental preacher, Henry Van Dyke, declared that he would "hang everyone. . . who lifts his voice against America entering the war."[32]

"Once we were safely in the war," recalls Granville Hicks, "all these gentlemen of God settled down to the gaudy business of egging on their parishioners. The flags inside and out of every sacred edifice proclaimed that the church had become an official recruiting station. . . teaching the laity to hate the Huns with true Christian fervor. Every denomination that held a convention during 1917 hastened to endorse the war."[33]

This contentious interpretation of Granville Hicks, which Ray H. Abrams popularized in his 1933 book, exaggerates the bellicosity of Protestant leaders. There were indeed extreme positions articulated. John E. Piper recently offers, however, the judicious view that "most denominations and agencies shared neither the pacifist nor the militant opinion." Rather, a large middle ground was held to defend traditional Christian imperatives such as service to those in need and loving one's neighbor. Pacifist crusades in the 1920s were predictable reactions within the establishment clergy ranks to some of the heated pulpit rhetoric of the war.[34]

The Christian ministry, perhaps for its faltering social prestige and professional status, became publicly active or even muscular, trying to prove that it was not in its character to walk away from a fight. Nor was it natural for it to remain an uncommitted spectator removed from the raging of great events.[35] Harry Emerson Fosdick during the war, unlike Willard L. Sperry, saw no tension between true patriotism and New Testament Christianity. Fosdick's just war theory argued from the pulpit that

> We never were so excited about anything in our whole lives as we have been about this war, we never felt the deeps within us, the passion for sacrifice, as during this war. . . Combativeness is an essential element in Christlike character. . . . There are some things in this world that are intolerable, and the man who will not say so, and fight, cannot save his soul. Sin is to be crushed by militant righteousness.[36]

Fosdick, while preaching at Stanford University, pointed out the incongruity of Christianity and war. But for Fosdick at this time, war was necessary surgery, the cutting out of evil which had no basis; it was a creative and positive act.[37]

Meanwhile, the issue of war's religious propriety remained in doubt for Sperry whose preaching regularly explored the doctrine of Christian pacifism without ever fully committing himself to it like the Mennonites or the Friends. More than staking out a position he was also testing the outer limits of his church's principles of the free pulpit, especially in a local climate of opinion that convened mass meetings at Tremont Temple to adopt resolutions indignantly repudiating "the utterances and actions of certain so-called pacifists."[38] It was one thing to pose and examine the dilemma of war and the Christian ethic in an academic journal, as John M. Mecklin did. But it was an entirely different thing when it required that added measure of courage to think out loud in a pulpit about one's uncertainty as to the nature of ultimate religious loyalties. A scholar may rightfully conclude, as John M. Mecklin did, that "the only thing that the present immediate struggle can decide finally for us is the purely material and physical question as to which of the two groups of contestants is able to utilize most skillfully and effectively the material forces at their command for killing men."[39] But a congregation, often able to hold surprisingly high thresholds for ambiguity, will not long let matters of war be discussed in church only in metaphorical terms, no matter how graphic, but eventually must demand that theological and biblical idioms be spoken. These conditions made Sperry's task all the more urgent and pressured.

His Thanksgiving sermon for 1914 preached in a union service made up of several Back Bay congregations did not merely rehearse the early history of Massachusetts; he also talked about the issues of the day in a prophetic vein, calling people out of "comfortable complacency" to be gathered on a day which "we remind one another" not "how safe it is to be an American," but "how risky it is." He said that since August of that year "America is no more exempt than the old countries... from a collision of ideas" which is much more than a geopolitical collision between conflicting nations. Sperry says here that Tolstoi's twenty-year-old prophesy of what total war will be like comes "like the heavy, monotonous insistent fall of a trip hammer." Tolstoi foresaw the conditions whereby people "will go to freeze, to starve, to be sick, to die from disease, and finally they will arrive at the place where they will be killed by the thousand, and they will kill by the thousand themselves, not knowing why..."

Sperry initially viewed the situation of war in Europe from the perspective of an ethical absolutist, perhaps arguing as a liberal postmillennial apocalyptist, a crusader convinced of his ultimate righteousness, because in his view, it was not in the end a political problem. Further, he did not suggest political isolation as a solution to a moral dilemma. "We cannot be neutral upon the conflict of moral ideals which now outwardly and visibly rages." Sperry warns that if sides must be taken that it not be a choice of one state against another, but to bind corporate idealism to the gospel of Jesus. "Christ and Anti-Christ stand face to face, and there is no such thing as a possible and honorable neutrality."[40] Sperry returned to the analogy of the New England Puritan settlement to complete his thought to the extent that the foreground of Thanksgiving was set to a background of risk, making the moral venture of faith imperative and political loyalties secondary.

Sperry continued this controversial theme into the following January with two long sermons delineating the theory and precedent of his pacifism. Toward the end of 1915 he led a Bible class in the study of the

Sermon on the Mount to augment, and perhaps to repair the damages of his preaching activity. In none of these materials does Sperry delve into specific issues of American foreign policy. He also seems to avoid sensational descriptions of war's cruelty, instead keeping his discussions on the higher abstract level of theory and history.

Sperry's sermon entitled "Non-Resistance" derives from the Matthean (5:39) text, "Resist not him that is evil," and he calls to mind the example of William Lloyd Garrison "who was before his time" in the practice of non-violent protest. Sperry claims that "practically all Tolstoi's religious writings resolve themselves into figures upon this one theme, you must not resist evil with evil, you must overcome evil with good." And that was initially Garrison's by-word in founding (1838) the short-lived "Society of Non-Resistance." From that premise and point of continuity, Sperry entertains the question, "What is going to stop the war?" He mentions the possibilities of economic insolvency, military exhaustion and a general spontaneous uprising of the common people. What Sperry finds so disturbing is that no one mentions religion and that H. G. Wells is probably right in saying that "Christianity is silent."[41]

Sperry is adamant that Christian faith requires a definitive response to war because "Protestantism either admits a 'half-way covenant', or, as in latter times, 'spiritualizes' the letter of the gospel. Everywhere there is this ethical 'bi-metallism', by which the original currency of the Kingdom has been debased . . . This modified Christianity is the Christianity which is now declared bankrupt."[42]

Sperry carefully reasoned that nonresistance was indeed a historic Christian axiom, a central article in the counsels of perfection. He explains that "non-resistance differs from forgiveness only in its direction. For while forgiveness is an act of retrospect, non-resistance is an act of anticipation." The analogy led to the further assumption that if nonresistance is unjustifiable and impracticable, so too is forgiveness, because they are one and the same thing. On this point Sperry emphasized that there was a vacuum in the world which this kind of thinking could fill if the preachers themselves would only adapt this "peculiar Christian policy." He was right in assuming that unless clergy preached this message, that no statesman, no socialist, nor any economist could be expected to appear as advocates of this radical peace program. But he was naive in believing that the ethical imperative of Christianity could sell itself merely by the persuasive air-tightness of its own internal logic. Sperry was a little dreamy-eyed in believing that with enough faith in preaching the doctrine of non-resistance "we shall find a world ready to listen."[43]

The very next sermon which he preached, "Christ Our Peace," was even less ambiguous in calling for a higher moral commitment than just taking sides in war. Sperry drives head-on into the issue of American patriotism, beginning with the assumption that "from the standpoint of a universal ethic patriotism is a standing contradiction."[44] Calling into question the impulses of nationalism and patriotism, he posits that as an institution it cannot stand because in the end it is a house divided against itself. Meanwhile, every person "in Christendom is a member of some nation, but he is also a member of some international society, a brotherhood of labor or scholarship or religion. And it has become increasingly difficult for the modern man to decide which of these communities constitutes for him the true society wherein he realizes himself most genuinely."[45] Here Sperry is advocating a prior world citizenship above one's nascent loyalty to a country, while recognizing that the price of that broader emphasis is an inner chaos, "a chaos that sometimes becomes conflict."

Sperry notes in this pulpit exposition that movements other than Christianity have pressed the claims of the gospel which speak of knocking down national barriers in order to unite people, which is the goal of the gospel. He praises socialism, feminism and the international community of scholars for asserting a Christian ideal which the Church itself thus far had failed to make known with any vigor. Sperry dismisses the argument of those who insisted that culturally church and state are inseparable, and consequently, the Church could not be an independent voice undermining the State. It is, in Sperry's view at that time, a specious assumption that the two are inseparable. Rather, Sperry goaded his congregation with what for them would be the distasteful example of Roman Catholicism, reminding them "that when Protestantism divided Christianity in Europe along national lines, Romanism refused its blessing to any arms, and prayed for peace in all nations; it remained truly catholic, and therefore genuinely Christian."[46] This according to Sperry "must be written down to the lasting glory of Roman Catholicism."

Sperry later in the sermon invokes the Protestant heritage too as reenforcement of an ideal that must finally transcend national loyalties. In this instance he calls to mind the warrior example of Oliver Cromwell, finding an ironic twist in how patriotism is to be supplanted by the gospel. Sperry writes,

> It is said of Cromwell's cavalry that when it went into action the men rode in a solid block, boot to boot, the heads of the horses behind at the tails of the horses ahead, and when this mass had crossed a field, it was as though the fist of God has swept the place... Sometimes one needs to get this iconoclastic mood to understand our religion. Christianity, so far as life's lesser loyalties are concerned, is veritably the fist of God. It crosses our world and crushes down all the petty artificial barriers that we set up between ourselves; it leaves nor classes, nor sexes, nor races, nor states, but only human souls. It leaves personality, naked and unashamed, and alone deserving the name of the child of God.[47]

Sperry uses the terms of "muscular" Christianity, in effect, to pull a metaphorical punch for the purpose of showing that the fist of God can also land on the chin of the patriotic Christian militant "marching on to war" as easily as on any one else. Finally, he gets to the heart of the matter in asking, "Who is the patriot in America to-day?" And while his inquiry is posed in 1915, and might have been treasonous in 1918, it is still a loaded question for any public voice to address openly and in the midst of conflicting public loyalties. Sperry denounces "the trader who is looking for advantage from the war. . . the soldier who preaches a bigger army. . . the statesman who sits at the receipt of custom jealously guarding his revenues." He goes on to state that "surely the patriot is the man who is pledged to making his citizenship the expression of his religion... It is not Caesar who claims us but Jesus." And this reasonable conviction, a peroration, is then taken one step further with added specificity and potential controversy: "The only patriots who can serve America now are those who are Christians first and Americans second." [48]

If anything Sperry articulated in early 1915 was the equivalent of waving the bloody shirt these sermons clearly represent not only an exceptional message from the mainline pulpit, but also an unacceptable interpretation of events in the popular view. If there was any "socially correct" bandwagon to join, it was not the one Sperry followed. The Protestant preachers were not uniformly propagandists for the Allied war effort, but even moderate voices such as Harry Emerson Fosdick, Shailer Mathews, George A. Gordon, Yale's Benjamin Bacon, the Universalist Frank Oliver Hall and the Harvard Unitarian, Francis Greenwood Peabody were offering reasoned, sometimes caustic expositions about the errors of pacifism.

Among his peers Sperry was decidedly in the minority, gambling instead on his own sense of righteous indignation.

What he stated publicly were feelings held in private conscience that never seemed to deviate into any discrepancy between what he said and what he thought. Writing to his mother he expressed the opinion that "war doesn't settle anything or get us anywhere. I should feel it was just an unutterable calamity, a kind of terrible wrong. *I couldn't find God in it at all* [emphasis added]. Indeed I shouldn't want to. I should feel that the world had put him out of court, and therefore could not expect to keep him in court."[49]

As to the reaction elicited by Sperry's public declarations it was surprisingly minimal, while elsewhere pacifist pronouncements moved congregations to drastic remedies, usually ridding themselves of the preacher. John Haynes Holmes of New York's Community Church preached pacificism consistently and his congregation eventually walked out on him.[50] The Quaker scholar (and later Sperry's colleague on the Harvard faculty), Henry J. Cadbury, who was teaching at Haverford College at the time wrote a letter to the *Philadelphia Public Ledger* (October 12, 1918), using Haverford stationery, "against the orgy of hate" and the spirit of "revenge. . . which is the greatest obstacle to a clean peace." Within days of Cadbury's published letter, he was forced to resign in spite of saying to the faculty (ironically, of a Quaker college) that his attitude was one of "confessed indiscretion and sincere penitence." For this expression of conscience Cadbury became known, though unintentionally, as one of the celebrated martyrs to academic freedom.[51]

Sperry, more than likely, prepared himself for the fate of public persecution, but there is no evidence that he suffered at all for his views. To the contrary, he may have been very frustrated that his public commentary did so little to stir much controversy. With regard to a series of Vesper sermons on the topic of war he drew larger than usual audiences, but confessd, "I am plumping into the mud with both feet and making a splash even if I am not getting anywhere. But I do feel very strongly that it is a time when Christian people ought to be thinking in the terms of absolute ideals as well as of immediate expedient." He reasoned that while "the counsels of perfection" may be unobtainable, for all of your good intentions set against the impracticality, those high standards which are, nonetheless, before your mind can "lend a certain bias to your conduct, that otherwise would be missing."[52]

Further, it is almost startling that among the many pacifists discussed in the influential Abrams study, *Preachers Present Arms,* Sperry is never mentioned, and this in a work that contains the views of otherwise obscure ministers. This is all the more surprising because the Abrams book is so single-mindedly slanted toward pacifism. What Abrams ignored was the work and thought of those who reluctantly accepted the war while agonizing over their roles as church leaders. By 1933, the date of the book's publication, one would suppose that given Sperry's position at Harvard and stature in the Protestant community, he might have been regarded as a fairly prominent pacifist during World War I. That he is overlooked entirely is either a gross deficiency in scholarship or must be accounted for in some other way.

The peak of controversy having to do with patriotism and pacifism would have come, naturally, when American dough-boys were first shipped abroad. Sperry's views were expressed well in advance of direct American involvement by at least three years and in some respect whatever energy he had for the cause was spent prematurely. By the time American soldiers were sent to France he found himself "unable to part company with youth going off to battle and tried to do what [he] could for them." This is not to say that he was no longer aware of "the tensions of a permanently uneasy conscience over the whole problem of militarism and pacifism," but that he had internalized the issue where other pacifists were only then exploring and articulating their positions with the public. And in public he modified his views to focus on the kinds of pastoral needs soldiers and their families required, while never endorsing the war.[53]

The lines had fallen unto him in disturbing places. Liberal, ethical emphases were antithetical to the conditions of a world turned upside down by war. Sperry was torn by being placed in that middle ground between one's ideals and his subsequent guilt feelings at his incapacity to do more, let alone to do right. "I am in danger of ceasing to be a Christian," he tells his sister. "Pacifism needs more guts than it has. It is sentimental. You have the idea, anarchy! [Pauline throughout her life flirted with radical political theory] The only trouble is we shall each have to get an island. The world isn't any more ready for this absolute naked idealism of the socialist or anarchist than for the Christian." Sperry continues his observation, adding the hasty disclaimer, "But don't tell mother I said so," that the only two places one can be consistent on this earth is "a hermit's cell and the grave, and both these places are peculiarly ineffectual."[54]

Once the war intensified and American participation became fully committed, Sperry realized that he could no longer afford the luxury of one mind about it. He accepted the added weight of two minds, and ever afterward his theology had about it the exceptional quality of second thought. And this intersection of religious thought and social-political reality is the breakthrough of his significantly distinctive liberal Protestant outlook, distinguishable from his contemporaries not only for its Anglo-American attachments, but because he reached certain conclusions before any one else. In a letter to his sister one catches a glimpse of an unsettled mind shifting its earlier horizon to its eventual forefront:

> I am all over the place about the War. Half the time I think it must now be fought through to some kind of decisive military finish—that the world is in such a state of mind that no other argument is any longer possible or intelligible. The other half of the time I think no such decision can ever be reached and that cost what it may we had better stop now while the stopping is as good as it is. Half the time I think the conscientious objector is right in not having anything to do with the whole mess and the other half of the time I know he is wrong, and that any one who does anything to "help heal this open sore of the world" in Red Cross or Y.M.C.A. or what not is the only man who can make himself understood. In short the world has got all out of hand and there is *no longer any one program or any single way of conduct that is comprehensible enough to cover all the facts* [emphasis added].[55]

❦

After the War: Afterthoughts on God and Human Nature

Years later, when the events of 1914-1918 were no longer fresh, yet still present in his mind, Sperry expounded further on his two "half minds" which he discovered during the Great War, in saying that "it is, theoretically, easy enough to live in one of these worlds at a time; it is not easy to try to live in both worlds at the same time without suspecting oneself of cowardice or compromise."[56] Recognizing the difficulty of living in two worlds simultaneously, Sperry made his hard choice and keeping both hands on the plough without looking back, moved into the no-man's land of theological paradoxes.

On the single issue of pacifism, however, there is an added double irony that would again make Sperry quite distinguishable from his liberal contemporaries and counterparts. As Richard Hofstadter observes in *The Age of Reform*, "war has always been the nemesis of the liberal tradition."[57] In this troubling web of contradictions many of the "liberal" war preachers after the Armistice recanted their views on the efficacy of militaristic solutions. Reinhold Niebuhr, for instance, conceded that "every soldier, fighting for his country in simplicity of heart without asking many questions, was superior to those of us who served no better purpose than to increase or perpetuate the moral obfuscation of nations . . . The times of man's ignorance God may wink at, but now he calls us to repent. I am done with this business."[58] Niebuhr had been, prior to the Armistice, a proponent of William James's "moral equivalent of war" which was based on the premise that despite its indisputable brutality, war answered an ineradicable longing in the human heart for service, sacrifice and heroism. And unless something equivalent to war could be organized, nothing else had the same properties of national and communal cohesion. Not only are there traces of this line in Niebuhr's *Moral Man and Immoral Society*, still eighteen years in the future, but Niebuhr in struggling with his German background became, as moral compensation, a super American and during the war a militant spokesman for the patriotic second generation of Euro-Americans.[59] In fairness to Niebuhr's delicate national identity, however, he had thought as late as 1914 that the Christian pacifists were on the right track, but, according to his biographer "he remained skeptical about transcending the nation-state altogether" through mere idealism once it was apparent that war was not going to be abolished.[60] Niebuhr was never a serious advocate of pacifism, though for him a just war was the remedy of last resort.

Others of this war generation who also changed their minds after the Treaty of Versailles, but who did not have consciously to overcome suspicions as to their American loyalties as Niebuhr did, included Douglas Clyde Macintosh, Ralph W. Sockman, Halford E. Luccock and Ernest F. Tittle. They all renounced war. A more interesting case study on the impact of war upon liberal preachers is that of Harry Emerson Fosdick's complete reversal. During the war years Fosdick was compelled to advocate, then to extol America's participation in the war to end all wars. He did not spare his congregation the details of atrocities "with ruined women and butchered children. . . Mothers broken hearted. Widows desolate. Girls who will never be loved. Children who will never be born."[61]

Fosdick went from being a trumpeter of military doctrine during World War I, borne of sincere conviction, to being an unyielding opponent of war in the 1920s and a peace activist from then on. Writing in *The Christian Century* in 1928 he confessed, "I do not propose to bless war again, or support it, or expect from it any valuable thing." His declaration was sustained by the stimulus of a protracted conscience which pursued the ideal that "war's motives, methods and results are essentially anti-Christian; no device of argument or trick phrase can make war and Christian principles harmonious." The famous preacher quickly added, "I ought to know for I have tried hard enough to achieve that impossible task."[62]

Fosdick was equally impassioned against war the rest of his life as he was for war in 1918. His biographer states that "not a year passed in which Fosdick failed to make a strong statement" about his feelings: "I hate war. I hate it because I have seen it... I have seen them come in freshly gassed from the front trenches. I have watched the long trains loaded with their mutilated bodies. I have heard the raving of those who wanted to die and could not."[63]

The first irony in comparing liberal Protestants around the same reference point of war is that the pacifist position which Sperry first staked out, almost alone and under a cloud, was where many of them, like Fosdick, wound up years later. The second irony, moreover, is that while others moved towards Sperry's original position on this issue, he moved away from it. As others arrived tardy in the 1920s where Sperry had once been, they might have realized that he had gone back against the grain to new light which he found and followed between the extremes.

While Fosdick and Sperry on so many other themes looked like identical twins, on this matter of Christianity and war they became at best a strange ineluctable pair, more complementary, even polar, than twin-like. They shared the same views, for example, toward the rise of post-war fundamentalism. Not long after going to Harvard, Sperry was invited to preach at The First Presbyterian Church in New York City, from which Fosdick had only recently been forced to resign for his lack of orthodoxy. Sperry addressed his concern to Fosdick about their mutually inclusive theological positions that bound them like banyan roots in common soil:

> I am mildly amused and somewhat perplexed to know what I am to make of an invitation to preach in the pulpit which for theological reasons is closed to you. I have long half suspected that I am one of the few real fundamentalists left in America, and now I am sure of it.

My point is this. . . do you feel that I could be of any service there? If so, I will gladly go down, but I do not wish to dissociate myself in any way with your witness to freedom.[64]

And yet, on issues of war and peace in the 1930s Sperry and Fosdick were in two separate camps which vaguely shared some common ground. Fosdick had sent Sperry a sermon he had preached, entitled "Jesus' Ethical Message Confronts the World." It was the kind of sermon Sperry himself had once preached in 1915 and now Fosdick solicited his reaction. Sperry's mixed response in 1939 to Fosdick at a time when world conflict was becoming inevitable shows a changed and cautious mind:

It is heartening to find you clarifying and elaborating the position [pacifism] with which we have come to associate you.

I am pretty muddled at the moment. If you put me at the butt end of an anti-aircraft gun in Kent and then confronted me with a flock of German bombers overhead, I should be very hard put to it not to turn the crank, or whatever one does to the business end of such a machine. I should feel a good deal moral responsibility about letting them pass on unmolested to London. I feel the force of all you say, but it may be the unregenerate Adam in me that I kept decently suppressed from 1914-1918 is bound to have his innings before I shove off this mortal coil. . .

The real difficulty seems to me to be this, that the non-resistant doctrine is now confronted with the brute in man, thoroughly encased in an armor of reflective self-righteousness. We haven't any place on which to meet the minds of the dictators since they no longer pay even lip service to what used to be the common ethic of Christendom. I think the problem is vastly more complicated than it has ever been because none of our arguments or appeals can for a moment get through that armor. It may be that I am fleeing from Rome meeting you coming up the Appian Way in the other direction. I wish I could get a half hour to talk about these things because, having been [a] pretty consistent pacifist all through the Great War and getting into no little trouble on that account, I am a good deal less sure of what was then my doctrinary position than I am now, and this mercifully for my peace of mind without any sense of being especially impaired as a Christian. . .

P.S.: Here is a subsidiary theological problem. When I read selected parts of the New Testament I can see and feel, as I once did, the full force of the non-resistant position. That is, I can fit the historical Jesus into that mold, but when I try to imagine God, I find myself less certain. The difficulty is that he really does make his sun to rise on the evil and on the good. I am, for the moment, quite certain that the Christian religion is more comprehensive than any single brand of the Christian ethic, whether pacifist or military.[65]

Sperry's inter-war ambivalence was often clarified in his personal correspondence with his sister when on more than one occasion he deduced that "the sight of Mussolini's jaw is a bad tax on my pacifism. I want to hit it." And again he writes, "I must confess I am getting less Tolstoian as I get older. I feel like taking a pot shot at some one, and risking my fortunes at the Judgement Day." Still later, he says, "I am clear that anything like non-resistance, at the moment, is just an invitation to the juggernaut to run over you and squash you completely out."[66]

Sperry not only altered his private views on pacifism between the World Wars, but his published ones too. He rejected the idea, for instance, that the Second World War was merely a continuation of the First, that somehow both were parts of a single vast event. Rather, he insisted that the "feel" of 1939 was unlike that of 1914. In a major article for the ecumenical journal *Christendom*, he explains, "We cannot recover, either for better or for worse, the feelings of World War I for the needs of World War II." Furthermore, of the Second World War he made the distinction that "this is a scientist's war, not a poet's war." This being the case "the lines between orthodox militarism and pacifism have been somewhat blurred by recent events. The resources of conventional casuistry employed in defence of both the one and the other seem for the moment to be stalemated."[67]

In Sperry there was little discontinuity after post-war disillusionment in the 1920's and during the inter-war period of making corrections upon miscalculated liberal optimism. On the contrary, Sperry's programmatic religious thinking from that point forward was intimately connected to the First World War, and only his earlier pacifism detached itself from that emotional anchor. What was said in a soldier's proverb that "the war will last a hundred years—five years of fighting and ninety-five of winding up the barbed wire," has immediate bearing and application on how Sperry was affected intellectually by the Great War. If Oxford was the first major turning point in his life, then the lost generation of Oxford was the second, more sobering event to shape his subsequent theological views, which considered apart from war have been neglected, if not also underestimated in their progressive qualities at a time of retrenched liberalism and rising conservative alternatives in theology.

Evidence that the the Great War is a watershed experience in the development of Sperry's Protestant theology, which in some respects seemed ahead of its time, is transmitted perhaps in oblique ways, most notably in his literary biography of Wordsworth. It is worth noting, moreover, that it was not unusual for clergy to have such broad literary interests up to the time of Sperry's generation. Sperry, however, may have been the last of the breed who could function as an equal to many academics in the field of English literature. The association of romantic and philosophic poets with liberal religion was extracted most immediately and clearly from Matthew Arnold's view of the critic's function; the "clerisy" was to be a class of critics of unparalleled social stature. Clergy, particularly in the 19th century, were very often cultural arbiters who believed that Shakespeare, Browning and Wordsworth were valuable sources of religious expression. This phenomenon in part represented an adaptation to an environing culture that would otherwise leave the church behind in the wake of progress. Liberal Protestant preachers not only assisted in promoting popular knowledge of literary texts, but in acquiring an expertise about those texts they tried to sustain sentiments drawn from nostalgic references to pastoral and domestic ideals which were translated and applied to Victorian family life.

Within Sperry's book *Wordsworth's Anti-Climax* (published in 1935 and reissued in 1966) conscious parallels are drawn between Wordsworth's disillusionment during the interval between the French Revolution and the Reign of Terror and the author's own change of heart in the early 1920s. Sperry wrote in 1935 of Wordsworth that "he was no stranger to the idealism, the disillusionment, and the cynicism of a generation which has passed through a great war. Our extremity, matching his distress, makes him a friend of the modern mind."[68] Sperry pinpoints the idealistic period of Wordsworth's history as falling between 1787 and 1795, the years from his going up to Cambridge until his settlement at Racedown, during which time his love affair with and in France began and ended. Sperry next finds a resemblance between himself and Wordsworth which he cannot leave untouched, though expressed in the most cryptic autobiographical terms. Both had pleasant experiences as young men visiting a foreign land which fed an inner idealism, until the harsh external world placed a heavy claim on their memories. Sperry suggests of Wordsworth that

> . . . the case is not without modern parallels, and one could find among convinced pacifists suddenly confronted with August, 1914, suggestive counterparts; idealists who were driven by the brutal irrationality of a world war, first to attempt to get "above the battle," and then, as fact refused to be stared out of countenance, to cynicism and despair.

Wordsworth, to be understood, should be re-read in the terms of doctrinaire pacifism of the Great War. The mental suffering of the type can be very great and of such intensity that it obliterates all other lesser pains.[69]

Like Wordsworth, a world changing event interfused the thinking and emotions of Sperry so that his mind shifted rapidly, perhaps obviating a certain degree of psychic numbing which other, more systematic liberals felt. In the words of Leslie Stephen which Sperry had applied to Wordsworth's post-revolutionary despondency, Sperry himself "would rather face the inevitable with open eyes."[70]

The "calm and terrible strength" of Sperry's best work, which was between 1914 and 1939, was a result, first of the war experience which according to Randolph Bourne had "spiritually wasted" the whole era of American intellectuals, but secondly because of a prior method of thinking acquired at Oxford.[71] Second thought and open eyes brought Sperry not only back to Oxford mentally, but moved him beyond the horror and stupefaction of post-war society with greater celerity than other Protestant liberals out of an altogether different (German) liberal school. The reason for this ostensively is that Oxford practiced a *method* and did not impose a *system* upon intellectual discourse.

Benjamin Jowett's warning to his students that they not throw themselves unreservedly into any particular system of thought was typical of the Oxford mind in which Sperry had been inculcated. Jowett cautioned against "a metaphysical fanaticism" which was potentially as absorbing as religious dogmatism. He made no exceptions to his rule that modern thinkers must be "read like an ancient philosopher in whom there are many things absurd and many things of highest value."[72]

German liberalism, of course, was methodical, too, but it seemed to emphasize a method that was secondary to and not separate from a grand scheme. Ritschl, for example, undertook to establish Christian theology as an autonomous and systematic discipline, purging German thought of Pietism, Hegelian speculative theism and the pantheism of Schleiermacher. Depending heavily on Kantian categories, Ritschl worked out a system, for instance, whereby he accorded moral primacy to the community (the nation) over the individual.

Sperry's transformation is indicated when he says that to resolve the "spiritual problem" of a war "divided society" one must be rid of systematic approaches. Having a system is what dulled Wordsworth's sensibilities, leading to the anti-climax of the poet's career which had in its beginning the promise of long-term brilliance, instead of short-lived genius. In an important article which Ellery Sedgwick solicited for *The Atlantic Monthly*, Sperry says it is best to adopt a *method* of an infantryman than to be bothered by the *theory* of military strategy. He writes that "civilians with their system are born Platonists. The soldier is an Aristotelean. For better or worse, he has had to live with concrete facts."[73]

Sperry uses the stress of war and the collision of ideals as an analogy for decrying the mistaken perception that is "freshly obsessed with the need for more and better systems in religion and business and politics. The enemy [Germany] has proved to us the terrible power of a systematic theology once a people are indoctrinated with it." Systematic thinking "all but wrecked the world." What is worse, however, is that so far the "reaction from the terrible power of a dogmatic system... has seen no duty but the clear duty of offsetting this sinister dogmatism by other and liberal dogmas." For Sperry the kind of thinking most useful to the world in the aftermath of war will not be a preoccupation with systems which are "debilitating if not dangerous"; it will be instead "a mind which has no systems, but only a method. . . a frame of mind, a mental and moral method." This solitary inner discipline, not the superimposed consistencies of systematic correctness, "must be reborn into the process which is to meet sincerely and fearlessly the facts of the world in their confusion, contradiction and totality."[74]

In the context of "a mind which has no systems, but only a method," Sperry moved to the heart of the matter theologically, quarreling openly with the presuppositions of his own time. It took other liberals longer than it took Sperry to reach the same inevitable corrective position, checking unbridled optimism, brought on by added disillusionment because they had so much systematic baggage to discard. Meanwhile, in the early 1920s Sperry swiftly initiated revised doctrines of God, sin, suffering and salvation by returning to the sources of New England theology whose austerity had for a generation been "eluded." He ran through the brambles and thistles of Christology, ethics and apologetics, not in the pose of a hunter in search of new game, but in the attitude of a plough hand working over old soil and old terms with sharpened tools of modern criticism.

❦

The Paradox of Religion

William R. Hutchison in his seminal work, *The Modernist Impulse* (1976)
concludes that for liberal Protestant theology between the world wars, "the
immanence and accessibility of God was far and away the most persistent
note" of affirmation. In general, "liberals remained unwilling to make more
of discontinuity and alienation than of continuity between the divine and
the human—unwilling in anything like the Barthian sense to 'reinstate the
distance' between man and God." Hutchison cites Dean Willard L. Sperry
as an example of an unreconstructed liberal immanentist to support his
otherwise indisputable argument: "Sperry would not renounce the liberals'
stress upon divine immanence."[75] That is only true in part, because there
is more theological intricacy in Sperry than seen at first. Sperry was not an
unconditional immanentist as Hutchison supposes.

Furthermore, while large scale assaults of the twenties and thirties,
especially from the crisis theology and the neo-orthodox critique, had
identified erroneous liberal assumptions about human nature and God, not
all the prophetic discourse came from outside the liberal camp. Long before
neo-orthodoxy forced liberalism to concede the declining reputation of
human nature, the consummate liberal insider, Willard Sperry, was
engaged in an analysis that brought him into closer sympathy with what
the Niebuhrians were saying *before* they were saying it. Both Sperry's
consciousness of human sin and the theological paradox that could not
exclude a transcendent deity were characteristic of his thinking from the
early 1920s. And yet, by every yard stick of his day and every historical
measurement since, Sperry remained a liberal and never flirted at all with
neo-orthodoxy. Not only are the ideas which he expressed somewhat
atypical of the period, but so too is the timing of that expression. And in
this sense Sperry is particularly important in dating the transition that
Protestant liberalism ostensibly made in the 1930s to an earlier time, or at
least to a moment of ferment sooner than historians have thought.

As early as 1921 Sperry was calling for "a modern doctrine of original
sin"[76] and by the following year he was elaborating on a doctrine of God's
simultaneous immanence and transcendence.[77] These views were being
developed not under severe provocation from outside the liberal fold, but
on the contrary right within and part of that tradition as Sperry stood
directly in its path, catching its unspent momentum from the past. To the
extent that this quiet, internal response preceded attacks upon liberal

theology, such as that hatched by Walter Lippmann (*Preface to Morals*, 1929) by a few years may have helped liberalism make a softer landing in hostile territory than has thus far been acknowledged. In several instances it may indeed be arguable, but it will anyhow be strongly argued that Willard Sperry, chief among several, prepared the way for his generation of Protestant liberals to survive and soberly alter its thinking about redundant theological assumptions dating to the twilight of the Victorian age.

Those Victorian notions of the faith are given a representative voice in the final work of Lewis French Stearns, a professor of theology at the Bangor Theological Seminary, who told an English audience in 1891 that before the Civil War American religious thinkers "had been too exclusively concerned with the questions of scholastic Calvinism."[78] Since the Civil War and "for some time past now," Stearns noted a renewed interest in preaching that was not only practical, but theological, "that the time of our theological eclipse is drawing to a close. The reaction against [Calvinist] theology seems to have lost its force."[79] The doctrine of God that was regaining value, however, was not purely Calvinist, nor impurely Arminian. Stearns observed that residual Puritan consciousness was not entirely dulled by the God of the New England fathers, but was rather quickened by present theological tendencies "that we have corrected the old view of God which emphasisized His transcendence at the expense of His immanence, by giving due place to the latter element."[80]

The due place and "the sense of divine immanence" that was the major distinguishing feature of "the modernist impulse" as late as 1939, according to Hutchison, refused "to give much ground in the argument between immanent and transcendent conceptions of the nature and action of God."[81] This mistakenly oversimplifies the dialectic. The inter-war generation of religious thinkers may, in fact, have had more than a single choice between liberal and orthodox alternatives. Hegelian methodology, however, not only sets up a thesis (liberal and immanentist) and an antithesis (Barthian and transcendentalist), but seeks a synthesis. And with extreme care there is found in the liberal background of Willard Sperry an element of Barth before Barth, which points to that overlooked, but nevertheless attempted synthesis.

The epitome of a synthesized idea which had been a seed thought planted in a 1923 sermon on Abraham Lincoln, germinated in full discourse when

Sperry delivered the 1927 Hibbert Lectures on "The Paradox of Religion" before a general British public in Sheffield, Liverpool and Birmingham.

In the Hibbert Lectures, which L. P. Jacks had given over the previous four or five years and had helped arrange through the offices of William H. Drummond, Secretary of the Hibbert Trust, for Sperry to deliver over a mere few weeks, Sperry begins with the question, "How simple can religion become and yet remain religion?" Simplicity, he says, is a seductive idea which grants dogmatic iteration by the powerful force of reductionism. The problem with Thoreauvian simplicity, for example, is that after its initial appeal, "so lovely in its intention," it then "tends to degenerate into mental and moral mendicancy, a pauper content with the crumbs of contemporary achivement which fall from the tables spread by more resolute natures."

Sperry warns his audience against the raptures of oversimplification. Plainly, he says, one cannot reduce religion "to one set of ideas and concerns all of a kind and all bearing upon life from the same source. Religion requires more than one idea."[82] In other words, what is especially and supremely true of the Christian religion is that it must hold antithetical ideas, which means that this state of tension is not always comfortable or easy. Broadly speaking, the best religious thinkers must be found with outstretched minds and arms upon the contradiction of things in the effort to compass the paradox of God's nature. Sperry is saying that when a person succeeds in awakening the dual consciousness of self and God, and even the dual nature of each, within the compass of a single idea, then that person has that very intense reality which is religion.

Lest all this seems rather vague, Sperry restates the proposition concretely by bringing to mind the example of Abraham Lincoln. "Lincoln is not unique in having held to this double principle of necessity and freedom. . . He kept, to the end of his days, an agonized awareness of these two wills at work in him, and he tended to emphasize rather than minimize the possible discrepancies between them. He seems to have known intuitively. . . that he was safe in devotion to one of these wills only as he referred it to the supplement of the other." Sperry's inference here should not be mistaken as theological schizophrenia which otherwise suggests, in almost pathological terms, some affective behavior characterized by a *withdrawal* from reality. On the contrary, the goal of religion for Sperry was the meeting of and facing up to reality.

Sperry next carries this theme of Lincoln's record of unrelieved psychological tension into an appropriate theological analogy. Divided between the altars of two gods, Lincoln during the American Civil War worshipped first the God of the Battles. The in-dwelling immanent God is what Lincoln, naturally, found in his moral convictions of mature faith. Lincoln worshipped, in the second place, at the altar of the God above the Battle. "This transcendent Being was the constant possibility of a cosmic correction of his policies and purposes, the residual otherness which would remain when he had done his best." Lincoln required the affirming power of the first God and the detached perspective of the second, thereby incorporating simultaneously united doctrines of God's immanence and transcendence.[83]

Because Sperry's prior conviction is that theological ideas "are simply perceptions of an ultimate dissimilitude or similitude," that is the riddle of likeness and unlikeness which is created by the paradox of divine nature, religion has only two things to say. Either it is confessing humanity's tragic unlikeness to God, or it is giving joyful thanks for humanity's reassuring likeness to God. All else is derivative or it is irrelevant. There were occasions Sperry himself "couldn't find God in it at all" (i.e., the war and the aftermath in a troubled world). The only realizable possibility, therefore, is the paradox of religion which is not at all the sleight of hand it may seem. Sperry admits that "the man who habitually plays with paradoxes is too often suspected of doing intellectual parlour magic." It is, however, not to demonstrate dazzling theological card tricks that paradox is necessary to religon, but as the best means to an end for the person who is "hot after realities."[84]

In the spirit of being challenged by sober second thoughts, Sperry kept his initial immanentist theology alive by giving the tragic antithesis of his war experience full scope and by bearing in his own mind the tension of divided loyalties. This meant that he was giving balance to two competing ideas. He realized that the natural desire to keep religion simple would not bear examining until it was understood that all ideas about God finally resolve themselves into one or the other of the two great doctrines, the doctrine of the immanence of God and the doctrine of the transcendence of God.

Sperry consistently kept his balance by converging his senses and powers of reason upon the hub of all the concurrently gyrating theological wheels, inevitably yielding for him a paradoxical doctrine of God. One of those spinning wheels was being whirled by a Swiss theologian, Karl Barth, who had enormous impact on twentieth-century Protestant theology in America and abroad. If since Schleiermacher the tendency in continental theology was to put humanity at the center of theology, with God pushed to the periphery, Barth firmly placed revelation again at the center, thus not only coming into conflict with the liberal point of view, but also violently challenging it.

In 1939, more than ten years after the Hibbert Lectures, writing for *The Christian Century*, Sperry said, "Though much out of fashion at the moment, in view of Barth et al., I am disinclined to rest the case for religion in its entirety upon the Christian revelation alone."[85] This is only an implied immanentism which Hutchison takes to mean as a complete statement excluding "the God of perspective," which acknowledges a doctrine of transcendence. That hasty implication misrepresents Sperry's peculiar liberal theology, which is notably not unlike certain British theological revisions that were represented by Sperry's old Oxford acquaintance, William Temple, whose emphasis landed and focused upon the Incarnation. Temple's position concentrated on the assertion that the Incarnation was the supreme instance of "the immanence of the transcendent." Sperry parted company with Temple on the absolute necessity of the Incarnation, but stopped way short of following the once liberal and Ritschlian British theologian, P. T. Forsyth from a theology of immanence to radical transcendence. Again, there is recurrent evidence that the obvious, but overlooked aspects of Sperry's career are his British intellectual sources and connections.[86]

Further, with regard to continental influences at this time, Sperry let his mind be a kind of fulcrum— both at odds and at home with the intellectual trends of Germany. On the one hand, he finds himself accepting the terms put forward by Karl Barth, but on the other he wholly rejects the Barthian "thesis that in religion the mind is utterly useless."[87]

In his Essex Hall (British) Lecture for 1927 Sperry works over the theme of transcendence by recalling a comment William Wisner Adams made after preaching one day in Fall River. Apropos of nothing whatsoever, but typical of his manner, Adams said, "The longer I live the more I am impressed by the reticence of God." Sperry traces that idea back through his New England heritage to Calvin's *Institutes* and to the passage therein which says, "God treats sparingly of his essence. . . . His essence is indeed incomprehensible by us. . . . Wherefore let us willingly leave to God the knowledge of his own essence."[88]

Sperry next brings the idea forward to a new time and place for the efficacy of the doctrine of transcendence:

> If you have followed the comments upon the drift of Christian thought in contemporary Germany, you know that the very phrase, the *Deus Abscon-ditus* [the absent God, cf. Isaiah: "thou art a God that hidest thyself"], has been made again the cornerstone of the theology of those younger men who have been disillusioned by the events of the near past and who despair of the complacent humanities of liberal and critical Protestantism in the Germany of the last two generations. It is natural as it was inevitable that the whole doctrine of God and conception of religion should suffer there this change, that the divine reticence should succeed to a divine revelation. . . . Karl Barth and his followers may receive us all, each in his own way, into the communion of those who now wait upon the divine reticence.[89]

Ten years later Sperry expressed concern for Barth's doctrine being "righteous overmuch." He writes about the dangerous momentum of neo-orthodoxy that "if our first instinct is to lend ourselves in sympathy, and perhaps in actual practice, to such movements, our sober second thoughts must give us pause." Sperry thought that in one quarter the doctrine of transcendence was being foolishly over-emphasized, to the point of turning the clock back, "leaving it for posterity to travel again the same tedious path over which the freer spirit of religion has come in the last century and a half. . . Even if you wish to do so you cannot wipe out a century, particularly a century like that."

Sperry had in mind "the theology of Karl Barth" as being too "histori-cally conditioned," adding that "it is a natural comment upon the collapse of the dominant German theology of the old Imperial days." About the new German theology Sperry says facetiously, "It is useless for man to try to do anything. He must passively wait for God to speak and work. . . All the hereditary German skill in theology is now employed in demonstrating the futility of our every thought about God."

The irony of Barth, according to Sperry, is that therein "some rapier-like mind is bent upon proving the futility of thought." To put it differently, is it not strange how the human mind can be successfully used to demonstrate its own worthlessness? This is a paradox which "the apostles of irrationality in religion"—that only God can break through and transcend the world's meaning—have never resolved.[90]

By incorporating some sober notion of divine transcendence into his thinking, however, it is not surprising that Sperry also brought back into the theological domain the concept of grace, which had been, according to Horton Davies, "superannuated by liberalism in favor of the weaker and more anthropomorphic term of love."[91] Sperry called for a new Calvinism of sorts, "not from the Geneva of yesterday," but "some equivalent and contemporary statement of a doctrine of Grace and Freedom." This was urgent "if we are to be saved from subtle magic and sophisticated mysticism."[92] And in rediscovering soteriology which was endowed by the means of irresistible or persuasive grace, Sperry was pointing away from God the problem to man the sinner. He therefore proposed a modern doctrine of original sin, the very Augustinian concept that was still anathema to American liberal Protestants, especially to any liberals still claiming their Enlightenment heritage as late as 1921.

Having suggested the paradox of God's nature, Sperry concluded that "this dual aspect of God who is at one time revealed and at another time hidden indicates, not a truth about God, but a truth about man." A human being is a creature of two natures:

> The orthodox Christological account of the case in the Chalcedonian Definition holds good not only of Christ, but of all men. We are to seek and to find the two natures in the one person of every human being of us. Man is a chaos, a contradiction, prodigy, a paradox, he is the glory and the offscouring of the universe. His greatness and his littleness are the two most obvious facts of him. He is the stage, the scene, the victim of a civil warfare within his own person. His only hope of peace lies in carrying this civil war to some conclusion. . . . It is the part of wisdom, rather than of folly, to press these contrasts to the end.

For Sperry any valid doctrine of God had to have its complementary doctrine of human nature, for "in the presence of God we become increasingly aware both of the good in us and of the evil." Sounding very much like a distilled and updated Calvin, Sperry proposes that in the end it must be God who saves humanity as "a great transaction in the area of freedom, the freedom of the divine grace which knows the times and seasons of its own self-revelation, the freedom of the man who finds in the divine reticence his own religious occasion and opportunity."[93]

In the recoil of war, Western intellectual life, according to Sperry was "struggling to escape from the enervating and fundamentally vicious influence of a decadent Romanticism."[94] And as a result the theology which would interpret religion as the human pursuit of moral excellence was falling beneath the horizon while "the wholesome prophetic spirit of mankind" was again reasserting itself. But the irony of the reassertion, Sperry thought, was its new found source; it was coming from outside the Church through literary and scientific works. And what this cultural phenomenon represented, at least in inverse proportion, was the Church's too ready accommodation to modern humanity's satisfied self-image which was a betrayal of its own heritage and a major factor for "the apparent impotence of Christian religion in modern society."[95]

From the first, Sperry contends, Christianity was "an effort to roll away the heavy burden of sin and guilt from the bowed shoulders of the human conscience." Christianity competed successfully against the classical world's neoplatonism and mystery religions and it prevailed because "it proffered a sounder healing for the hurt" at the heart of the world. Now in the twentieth century nothing is plainer than "the indifference of the crowd to the traditional message of the Christian religion." And in thinking of Christ as some young beautiful Apollo in whose image the post-Victorian generation was remade, the "young Apollos have no hurt conscience, and in a time which thinks well of itself morally, the offices of Christianity seem superfluous and its central doctrine of salvation gratuitous."[96] To put it succinctly, the modern world feels that Adam has been a badly overworked character in human history and that he deserves some eternal sabbatical.

Sperry was not recommending a return to preliberal doctrines of original sin, nor was he implying an extension of an earlier moral individualism. To recite the verse "in Adam's fall we sinned all" would be to say nothing to modern men and women; and similarly, the church would only disparage itself if it returned to a petty notion of sin as "the sort of transgression which is confessed by the sower of wild oats at a Salvation Army mourners' bench." Sperry did not have in mind the man who fell asleep in church or who "lost his temper on Monday, or drank one too many mugs of mead on Tuesday, or cut too sharp a corner on Wednesday's horse trade." Rather, Sperry sought to restore a sense of the Calvinist's "agonized conscience" which was felt "not at the top, but deep down from inside." And only after the deeper aspects of the elder doctrine of original sin are candidly reexamined can one commend a "religion of salvation to the deeper want of the world." Sperry was not advocating the rehabilitation of the strict letter of the New England fathers, but he was expressing the desire "to enter with a more resourceful sympathy into the experience of the fathers."[97]

What needed to be recovered for the modern individual was the Calvinist's sensibility that the moral problem had not been "to keep his petty cash account with God balanced week by week. What haunted his soul was the knowledge that there was a mortgage on the whole business, and that if the moral order suddenly foreclosed. . . he would be found bankrupt, his few private profits on the moral venture counting for nothing against his heavy outstanding liabilities."[98]

For twentieth century Christianity the problem is two-fold: one of definition and one of articulation. Once the major issue is divested of minor personal peccadilloes, original sin must be perceived as "an early and inadequate effort to express the sense of personal participation in the corporate moral liabilities of humanity as a whole." And that must be the point of departure for the way ahead to be clear. But the tour guides, in Sperry's mind, are not necessarily to be found in the Protestant pulpits. "The true successors to the Calvinist with his agonized conscience and his initial dogma of original sin," writes Sperry in 1921, "are to be found to-day among the biologists, the psychologists, the novelists and dramatists."[99] In Sperry's view, scientists like T. H. Huxley, writers like George Bernard Shaw and H. G. Wells, while admittedly more social commentators than moral penitents, nonetheless, were offering to modern audiences the instinctive rudiments of a lapsed doctrine of original sin.

Sperry, of course, turned to the classics of Christian devotion for validation of the modern struggle with human nature. The *Confessions* of St. Augustine had particular appeal because it was an authentic transcript of an agonized conscience fighting for its next breath while "uniformly framed in a heavy black moulding of mature condemnation." The outcome for Augustine should somehow be matched to whatever sincerity and simplicity of thought that the modern world can achieve for itself.

> In the eyes of God there can be no distinction between little sins and great sins. The stuff of evil deeds is uniform and terribly sinister. It is the quality and connotation of the act, rather than its dimensions, which God abhors, and which, by inference, the Christian should condemn in himself. Varying shades of grey must be given the full value of that final blackness which they foretell. Augustine. . . is not writing of ethics as an empirical science, or dealing with the moral relativity which we discern in the mixed motives prompting most human acts; he is praying to God. The very word

"confession" carries with it the idea of praise to God for his work of grace.[100]

Sperry's "anthropology" was not a complete reversal of liberal presuppositions, as overestimated as they had become for him. What he thought warranted reexamination was what was beyond the picture, once one has finally succeeded in turning his eyes "from the black framework of condemnation to the innocent recollection of the original event." In achieving that through the reading of the *Confessions*, for example, one meets a person who is immediately recognized as a fellow creature. And all is not bleak and even the modern world is not completely sunk in a bottomless pit of iniquity. Sperry did not read the *Confessions* without possessing his characteristic two minds on the subject. "Personally," he admits, "I am inclined to believe that in this particular respect Augustine framed his picture so black that we are in danger of losing sight of its many redeeming lights."[101]

Sperry's life-long method of sober second thought aided in bringing the matter of human nature back to public mindfulness with constant and recurrent fine tuning. In fact, one may say about Sperry that he had second thoughts about his second thoughts. Near the end of his life he had occasion to review an essay by Howard L. Parsons, entitled "Rooted and Grounded in Love." Parson's article attempted to transcend the dichotomy between what is "essential" and what is "existential" about human nature using the tools and techniques of developmental psychology. Parsons identifies himself with a "liberalism which was the order of the day from the mid-eighteenth-century until the onset of World War I." And for Sperry encountering Parsons's optimistic revival of humanity's sullied reputation, "liberalism seems, in retrospect, a little too good to be true," which is not to discard entirely the liberal view like dated and remaindered inventory in the warehouse. What Sperry thought in the early twenties is confirmed by him in the early fifties:

> There is no doubt that our conventional liberalism, whether in politics or in theology, had overbid its hand. Even those of us who continue to call ourselves liberal, because we feel that this position has permanent values which cannot be destroyed by the tragic happenings in history, and that the position is worth holding against a better time, feel that our doctrinal overconfidence in man needs sober reconsideration and perhaps a more realistic restatement.[102]

This is essentially the same statement made after World War I as after World War II, though modified in expression and mellowed in tone. The difference, however, emerges in Sperry's use of Whitehead's dictum against the "vice of oversimplification." While he takes exception to Parson's very generous account of humanity's indigenous character, Sperry is not entirely unsympathetic to that position because he is "aware of a similar element of overstatement in the theological reaction of those who fall back, rather than fall forward, upon neo-orthodoxy." Sperry took equal exception to those who displayed "a kind of pathological glee in confessing our inherently sinful nature." Acts of penitence must not have a masochistic quality. Further, "the revival of the ancient idea of our innate sinfulness still seems to lack concrete moral content."[103]

Sperry ultimately came out on the issue of human nature where he had previously allowed his method to take him with the doctrine of God. Like Pascal discerning the greatness and littleness of humanity, Sperry rested his case in the baffling realm of paradox, which may not seem to make complete sense. But that is the point, human nature is not complete in the making. And paradox is curiously like human self-consciousness itself which, at least, escapes the sin of oversimplification, because it is always in the making, it is never made.

In 1939 Charles Clayton Morrison, the distinguished editor of *The Christian Century*, set about organizing a journalistic "testimony meeting" in the hopes of confirming that "a radical and significant change" had taken place in the thinking of Christian scholarship and leadership. Thirty-five authors, including Morrison himself, were asked to make submissions on the theme "How My Mind Has Changed in This Decade." Willard Sperry along with Karl Barth, Reinhold Niebuhr, Walter M. Horton and Halford Luccock were among the participants in the symposium.

Sperry, like many of the other contributors, mostly liberal with a token smattering of a half dozen neo-orthodox representatives, acknowledges that his generation had counted too much on human progress as "a fiat creation of the finished article." The liberal doctrine of human nature, writes Sperry, "had become so much a truism that we had ceased to examine it. Alas, man has not turned out to be the sort of being our tradition has assumed him to be." Sperry adds a confessional note, "I have not given up liberalism, but I begin to see what the error of liberalism has been."[104]

Sperry subscribed to the theory of the twice-born life. American life, generally speaking, up to the period between the world wars had been "optimistic, once-born, and resilient under adversity." Now in Sperry's opinion a new mood is required. And to explain his meaning he invokes the name of a curious but looming influence from a distant day and place:

> George Tyrrell used to say that the Christian religion is an ultimate optimism founded upon a provisional pessimism. Liberal American Christianity, until twenty-five years ago [ca. 1915], had been chronically wanting in provisional pessimism. We had instead a provisional optimism, with the result that we did not always grasp the full meaning of the ultimate optimism of our religion.[105]

Changed times are supposed to mature people. And the supposition of *The Christian Century's* year long discourse to gauge these changes of the 1930s indicate many minds were remade at a time of life they are supposed to be beyond remaking. Sperry grants, that as painful as it was, he exceeded the limitations suggested by William James that one has no new ideas after the age of twenty-five. *The Century* was right to invite Sperry's comments for its series, because his mind had changed considerably. It was wrong, however, to assume his mind had changed in the decade of the 1930s when most other Protestant thinkers ostensibly came to their senses.

The remarkable thing is that Sperry's mind had changed in the 1920s and the change was in the making at Oxford, in discovering the Catholic Modernist, Tyrrell, and in the remaking "with uncongenial actualities" of the world. In fact, Sperry's mind was made up by the 1930s—that God is real *and* reticent; that H. G. Wells' "damned fool" and Jonathan Edwards' "damned sinner" are only different names for the same thing.[106]

Finally, in his own words, Sperry's theological mind replaced its "youthful resilience" which was once his, with "a wealth of sober second thoughts." His theology came down to the proviso: "Any Christianity which perpetuates the original is a religion of the twice-born, and the process of being reborn presupposes some kind of disappointment with a prior once-born state."[107] His once-born society was changing radically before the eyes of the world, but for Sperry it was a preliminary recognition of the ultimate optimism that finds religion being expressed inside and outside the Church.

CHAPTER 4

Inside the Church

*"For the very beginning of [wisdom] is the desire of discipline; and
the care of discipline is love."*
—Wisdom of Solomon 6:17

SOMETIME IN APRIL of 1922 President A. Lawrence Lowell of Harvard
University offered Willard L. Sperry, a local Congregationalist minister and
part-time instructor of homiletics at Andover Theological Seminary, the
deanship of a new joint venture merging Andover with the Harvard
Divinity School. The novel academic enterprise thus formed was called
"The Theological School in Harvard University." The affiliation was meant
to strengthen the declining resources of both schools, combining faculty,
students, administration and conferring a Harvard degree.[1]

It was a bold move on President Lowell's part to appoint a young,
untested intellectual pastor who was not an academic to such an important
position, even though it was common up to the turn of the century for clergy
to serve as educators or as college presidents. The appointment carried the
charge of cementing in academic affiliation a relationship that already
carried a stormy history.

While Harvard has been a reference point for New England education
in general, sometimes a point of departure in the case of Yale's founding,
Harvard was similarly for Andover the earlier cause and necessity for a
theological alternative, to be located elsewhere, dating to the incipience of
the Unitarian Controversy in 1805. A proposed reunion in 1922 for Andover
with the very institution from which it had fled a century before was a move
that prompted a faculty wag to remark, "Jonah returns to the belly of the
whale."

Lowell's selection of Sperry was appropriate from the standpoint of
compromise. From the Andover side of the merger he was one of them, a
Congregationalist not a Unitarian. This was a significant gesture on the

part of Lowell given that Harvard Divinity School was led exclusively by Unitarians for more than a hundred years up to the point of the Sperry appointment. In resigning from his pastorate at Central Congregational Church on the 2nd of June 1922, Sperry told his congregation:

> The Andover tradition is one that is bred in the very stuff of me. My father was a Phillips Andover boy and an Andover seminary man. My mother was an Abbott Academy girl and later a teacher, and acting principal and trustee of the Andover School. "Andover" was one of the first words in my vocabulary.[2]

For Harvard, Sperry's candidacy for the deanship represented a liberal enough choice to offset any lingering resentment that he was not Unitarian. He was broadly sympathetic and that was more than satisfactory at the time and over the next thirty years. For Sperry, however, there were deep reservations about entering a community wherein by scholarly criteria he believed himself to be "the most illiterate." In a personal reflection he recalled, "I had always thought that had I gone on with theological studies after my years at Oxford and Yale I might have done a little something with scholarship, but I had been fifteen years in the parish ministry, occupied with unacademic matters, and that, whatever qualifications for scholarship I might once have had, my tools were now rusty and dull and it was too late to sharpen them up."[3]

Sperry, admitting his inadequacies to himself, responded to Lowell's proposal to become Dean of a joint faculty, some of whom were world renowned scholars, with concern over the perceived scholarship gap between pulpit and podium. Lowell's reply was to ask Sperry if he knew a scholar when he saw one. Sperry indicated that he indeed recognized a genuine scholar at first pass. And with characteristic New England abruptness, Lowell closed the matter by saying, "That's all a Dean has to know."

The experiment in a closer affiliation between the two schools ultimately failed to materialize. The relationship was dissolved by the Supreme Judicial Court of Massachusetts in a decision handed down on September 19, 1925, as the result of action brought against the plan by the Andover Board of Visitors. At the end of the academic year (June 1926) the connection with Harvard was severed. Andover subsequently moved to Newton, Massachusetts, and formed a corporate alliance with the Baptist Newton Theological Institution and began operating in 1931 and continues to this day as Andover- Newton Theological Seminary.[4]

Meanwhile, President Lowell asked Sperry to continue as Dean of Harvard Divinity School. Then in 1929 when Edward Caldwell Moore (brother of George Foot Moore) retired as Plummer Professor of Christian Morals and as Chairman of the Board of Preachers in the University, Dean Sperry succeeded him, thus doubling the load of responsibility to Harvard by incorporating the charge of the Divinity School with the religious program in the Yard. In essence, Sperry over time became the indispensable utility player through his efforts to preserve the uncertain life of the Divinity School while serving conjointly as minister of the college chapel. The college chapel (Appleton) would become transformed within the first few years of his leadership and guidance into the majestic architectural centerpiece of Harvard, The Memorial Church in the Harvard Yard, a building project to which he made many useful suggestions. After slightly more than thirty years as Dean of Harvard Divinity School, Sperry's colleagues on the faculty praised him generously for measuring up to more than one professional demand: "He gave to his School heightened morale, increased dimensions, and standards which could be the envy of more liberally endowed institutions. . . To the College Chapel (now the Harvard Memorial Church) he gave his leadership in difficult years and his incomparable preaching."[5]

When Sperry announced his decision to accept the opportunity at Harvard he openly confided his unexpected feelings and anxieties of separation from a congregation he had grown to love. He writes in his final editorial for his parish bulletin "that I am turning away from a Church and a work that I have come to care for more than I know, at a time when I am most reluctant to do so. It could not have been timed worse. We have had one year of harvesting after seven years of planting and tending our field."[6]

To leave Central Church at a time of institutional stability and gain for a larger possibility was not the sole reason for crossing the Charles River to take up life in Cambridge. Unconsciously, but not surprising psychologically, Sperry also measured his professional development and progress against his father's record. And in doing that he discovered a remarkable parallel which served as added impetus toward the decision to leave the parish. In reviewing the circumstances of his father's ministry he not only gained valuable perspective, but assuaged his doubts. In reflection he told his congregation that his father, "after exactly the same number of years in the parish ministry" that he himself had served, turned aside to become a college president. Sperry recalls his father's hesitation to leave the active ministry and that in his academic duties "he often turned back. . . to the thought of the work he first chose, with wistfulness." A career shift parallel to his father's caused the forty year old Sperry to ponder deeply:

> Perhaps all this has helped to clear my mind and give me a sense of comradeship with him in a deeper way. I have not felt quite so alone as otherwise I should have been. And I have realized that these choices and changes are no solitary incidents, but part of the life of ministers and churches together, all to be interpreted as best one can in the light of the total task of God's Kingdom and not of what we seek for ourselves merely, but of what we are called to do, when the call comes clear and plain as this has come to me. Few things in life have been as clear to me as this.[7]

Complementary Loyalties: Harvard and the Church

Sperry was not only becoming the Dean of Harvard Divinity School in order to advance his theological career or to continue and complete the unfinished work of his father, but he was entering the last stages of that genteel tradition which established ministers as the presiding officers of colleges and professional schools. What was a common arrangement in the nineteenth century, however, passed out of existence in Sperry's generation so that not only were church and state separate, but for the most part so, too, were church and academe, particularly in the older American private colleges and universities with Protestant roots. Sperry was joining university life, not from some other and prior academic subsistence, but like Henry van Dyke in the English faculty at Princeton, William Newton Clarke at Colgate and Francis Greenwood Peabody at Harvard from the parish ministry. By the 1920s higher education had been professionalized enough to have hatched its own rules of membership which removed most considerations of reciprocity between ministerial and professorial callings. The two worlds were not interchangeable, as once they were, but had drifted apart, which meant that if one were an "insider" with respect to a single sphere of influence, he was an "outsider" in the other.

While "culturally liberal," and by that he meant an "undogmatic" liberalism, Sperry was never considered in full measure an "insider" in terms of his status within the community of scholars at Harvard. He developed over the course of years many faculty friendships, especially becoming close to the eccentric, but scholarly Arthur Darby Nock, a noted expert in the field of classics and Patristic history. Outside his field of interest he enjoyed the comradeship of Howard Mumford Jones, Alfred Tozzer and Walter Clark among the Faculty of Arts and Sciences, and he touched with lasting influence and acclaim two generations of under-graduate and graduate students. Sperry was, however, in the view of the venerable Harvard raconteur, Mason Hammond, "an outsider tolerated at Harvard."[8] The role of a "ministry" among scholars has its transparent complications. Sperry recognized that "diversity of piety" himself and according to Charles Forman, a Sperry disciple and later a professor of religion, he would emphasize that the Memorial Church in the Harvard Yard "was not a faith community, but an intellectual one, it was not a covenanted church, but a preaching station."[9]

In leaving the parish ministry for an academic calling, Sperry remained an "insider" in the former world and became an "outsider" in the latter. And while "Jerusalem" and "Athens" were different places, Sperry's preferences for academic life were only intellectual, not institutional. He wrote near the end of his deanship, "I can only say that thirty years in a university have not made me think worse of churches... I am still a believer in our churches, and have had no sense of relief in exchanging a parish for an academic post."[10]

His "belief" in churches stems from a nearly birthright condition that made it impossible for him to surrender "insider" status, even if he had sought "naturalized" citizenship in the community of scholars. He was still travelling on the church's passport. A peculiar irony unfolds, nonetheless: rejected and rebuffed by denominational authorities in two instances as a ministerial stripling, Sperry coming back from England was a reluctant outsider trying to get in. Once in, he stays in, but not in a traditional way—he leaves the church to serve outside it in a secular community; while in that community his first loyalties are reinforced as a church "insider" with the outsider's self-consciousness and occasional isolation. In other words, like Emerson, Sperry left the church in order to continue in the ministry. But unlike Emerson, Sperry did not repudiate the culture and traditions which the church engendered. Unlike Emerson he did not leave a Back Bay church for negative reasons; his departure was not brought about by "disloyalty" or "indifference" and "the least shadow of criticism or disappointment toward the church." While at Harvard, while outside the community of scholars, or rather while never fully inside that privileged society, Sperry's mind and heart were at home inside the church, while outside it institutionally.

When Sperry went to Harvard he received from Alexander Meikljohn, long associated with Amherst College as its president, a one line note reading, "Another damned fool who has left a perfectly good job and gone into an office!"[11] For the next three decades at Harvard Sperry devoted himself mostly to religious thought in the context of church life and not, as one might have expected from a Harvard official, to the pedagogical precision of theological or philosophical inquiry for which academics are notorious. The reality of the Divinity School is that its mission has always been divided between training ministers and training scholars, often the emphasis being placed on the latter function. Sperry's commitment to the education of the ministry would be utterly appropriate were he the president of a theological seminary, independent of any university but not of a denominational body. A Divinity School, however, is a division of a university and must live at first-hand by the rules fashioned in a society of scholars.

Sperry may have been a dean in America's oldest university, but like a proper history which looks back beyond the founding of the Divinity School to an earlier Harvard College as it was before such professional differentiation was achieved, Sperry's own internal history was fixed in a prior relationship to the idea of the Church, of truth and virtue pursued with equal measure. As Dean of Harvard Divinity School Sperry described himself in 1939 for the readers of *The Christian Century* as not being "a technical theologian and have never claimed to be." He explained, "Professionally I have been more concerned... to intimate what I would like to say about God by means of worship and the prayers of churchgoers than by discussions of theism in the pulpit."[12]

Under President Lowell Sperry found Harvard congenial to a church insider. Lowell, after all, was the primary force behind the building of Memorial Church which was dedicated on November 11, 1932. And Sperry worked closely with Lowell in diffusing the controversy about also memorializing the Harvard war dead (of 1914-1918) who had died in service to their native Germany, an issue brought about by Lowell's own initial misgivings. Sperry was not only persuasive in defending his convictions that the Germans should not be excluded, he was also allowed to raise money for that memorial plaque, inscribed with words composed by

Arthur Darby Nock, *Academia Harvardiana Non Oblita Est Filiorum Suorum Qui Diversis Sub Signis Pro Patria Spiritum Reddiderunt* (Harvard has not forgotten its sons who under different flags gave their life for their country).

Meanwhile, Lowell's successor, James Bryant Conant, came to the Harvard presidency in 1933 with little interest in, let alone affection for religion as part of a major center of learning. The support Lowell accorded the Divinity School and Memorial Church was uniformly warm, but under the Conant administration it turned icy. Conant was a scientist (an important figure in the Manhattan Project of the early 1940s), whose emphases and beliefs about education precluded the necessity of religion in the process. About President Conant, Theodore H. White (Harvard '38) would extol that he was, compared to Eliot and Lowell as Harvard presidents, "greatest of them all... Conant wanted to make Harvard something more than a New England school; he wanted its faculty to be more than a gentlemen's club of courtly learned men, wanted its student body to be national in origin." And this insistence on excellence, on "a meritocracy in which students and professors vied for honors with little mercy or kindness" did not require the religious relics and divines of a Harvard past.[13]

Sperry and Conant maintained a professional relationship for twenty years that was in the memory of Lady Henrietta Wilson, Sperry's daughter, "civilized, but not cordial."[14] Conant's attitude toward religion at Harvard was openly known and well remembered past the retirement of both men in 1953. Conant's autobiography, *My Several Lives*, for instance, makes no mention of religion at Harvard, Memorial Church, the Divinity School, or Willard Sperry. There was even a time when Conant seriously contemplated closing the Divinity School, as he felt it to be a drain on Harvard's mission. Long after the Divinity School's future was secured under the Presidency of Nathan Marsh Pusey in the 1950s, Mason Hammond (Harvard '25) recalled in the summer of 1986 that "Conant thought the whole operation foolish," meaning the Divinity School primarily, but also Memorial Church.[15]

Paul G. Kuntz in an unpublished memoir pertaining to his Harvard years when he was Sperry's student assistant at Memorial Church asks rhetorically, "What was it that Conant objected to in Sperry?" Professor Kuntz speculates:

I imagine it was Sperry's care with expression, his literary fastidiousness that must have seemed artificial. Why not deal with the problem by reason and experiment and express it plainly? This Conant did. I know from several talks with Conant that he disliked subjects that carried all their history with them [like religion]. Once he asked me about what I was doing outside of all my courses. I told him I was reading in the history of science. "Why?" he asked, "all that is true in science, such as chemistry, is conveyed by recent summations, such as textbooks. All that is left behind is the false. Why study the false?" This was in the late '30s and the next decade saw Conant's recognition of the value of the history of science. I believe Conant himself later edited Boyle on *the Spring of Air*.[16]

Sperry survived the Conant years of hostile uninterest toward Memorial Church and momentary cold blasts of indifference aimed at the Divinity School, not only by making patience a virtue, and thereby demonstrating additional qualities of accepting the inevitable, but by being loyal from the first to something other than Harvard. If he could tolerate the silent assaults against the departments of university life he was charged with running by not taking it personally, it was also because the goads and kicks were absorbed by a deeper allegiance to the Church. And while Sperry was affected and at times wounded by Conant's indifference, the Dean, a church insider, and an academic outsider, must have found comfort in the adage that the Church for two thousand years had somehow outlived its detractors and "cultured despisers."

In spite of President Conant's occasional twitting of the Divinity School, implying that should it close it would not be missed by saying directly that the natural means of secular education were neither godless nor amoral,[17] Sperry found kindred spirits and supporters for the school among individual members of the Harvard faculty. Howard Mumford Jones was one of the school's chief nonpartisan advocates, believing that its purpose transcended the specificity in university departments. Jones put his thoughts down in a letter to Dean Sperry which privately endorsed the school's *raison d'etre* and its incommensurable adequacy to help the university cohere. Jones offered Sperry his findings after a year long survey of the conditions in American graduate education. The heavy emphasis on technical training convinced Jones that a serious defect existed stifling "the realm of human and spiritual values." Philosophy departments, for example, had abrogated their opportunity to become centers of such a realm by becoming instead technical schools in logical thought. As a result mature graduate students have nowhere to turn in search of ethical and spiritual values.

Jones argued strongly for a divinity school within the university because "by its existence, generously conceived," it is the only "source of ethical teaching at this high level other than literature and philosophy, and both of these present obstacles to the purpose in view." Furthermore, Jones reinforced the argument from intellectual necessity:

> Is it too much to suppose that the reaction of God and man is at least as serious an object of inquiry as the relation of sunlight to grass or the law of falling bodies to airplanes? And if the subject is important, surely it deserves at least equal rank in the hierarchy of knowledge.[18]

Sperry was not an obscurantist in his leadership of the Divinity School. He did not yearn for a past golden age, or begrudge the ascendancy of science in the twentieth century. It was quite clear early on in the years at Harvard, that what he wanted was an integrated theory of ministerial education applied and achieved with progressive means. Had he thought differently, his estimate of the universally beloved President Charles W. Eliot might have been expressed otherwise. Confiding to his sister, he wrote, "I always thought old Eliot too good to be true. He annoyed me frightfully, both in legend, and as I occasionally met him in fact the last few years. His world wasn't wild enough and dark enough to be faithful to the facts. Men are worse—and thus better—than he thought." Sperry goes on to give report of his own educational theory as being summarized in the Wisdom literature of the Apocrypha that "the beginning of wisdom is the desire of discipline." He continued in that general vein, "That's what's wrong with most modern education—it doesn't believe that. But look at life—musicians at endless practice, scientists at work in laboratories."[19] Sperry had enormous admiration for modern forms of discipline and trained thinking.

Sperry understood and respected Conant, at least in the abstract, but remained permanently at odds with the premise that religion was mostly psychology and not the exercise of real thought independent of some other discipline. In rejecting the presupposition which Conant brought to Harvard, Sperry stayed "above" the issue because he was never "inside" Harvard in the first place, and besides his public message was intended more for the Church at large than it was for the community confined by the brick wall of the Harvard Yard. While in Harvard he was simultaneously detached from it in some deeper and prior foundation. He had no illusions about Harvard, even before Conant arrived. In the late twenties he had come to the realization that

> the more I see of universities the better I think, in retrospect, of churches. Academic politics are as smalltown and nasty as any in the world. Why persons who indulge in them should parade themselves as intelligent and emancipated human beings I don't know. God save the world if it ever had to be run by the kind of people on faculties.[20]

The Divinity School may have fared better under any administration other than Conant's, but Sperry would in all likelihood have remained much the same, regardless of the adversary, living within a university environment, but also projecting his work outward from it and forward upon the inside of the Church. In this regard, then, the Divinity School had a life of its own, not necessarily serving either at the full pleasure of its host, nor failing to serve the chief recipient of its own generosity, namely the Church. Sperry once said, "The Divinity School, like Information Please, goes it[s] own unprepared and unpremeditated Way."[21]

In speculating about the prospects of the Divinity School without the presence or pressure of Conant, and all that Sperry had to push against for the school's survival, there were, on balance, other compensating forces than the Church which were also pulling at Sperry mentally and away from Harvard, but which never materialized. One can imagine a Divinity School without Conant, but what about Harvard without Sperry? Sperry developed an identity with Harvard that reached levels of mutual affection, but never was Sperry sentimental about Harvard to the extent that it was required to define him to himself and the outer world. He was not in his own mind even an adopted son of Harvard as many others coming from outside Harvard and New England have gladly and proudly become. Sperry gave his heart to his work, but he did not give it all to Harvard. His emotions for Harvard were spare enough so that he might comment upon a typical class reunion as being "just a bit pathetic and always rather liable to be ludicrous."[22]

Harvard was stimulating and rarified, but did not hold uppermost prestige in Sperry's mind. There is no doubt that Harvard enhanced Sperry's career as a public man and gave him status and ready access to publishers, but there is, nevertheless, the residual impression that, during most of his deanship from the late 1920s forward, Harvard needed him more than he needed Harvard. And if a door had ever opened to him at Oxford he might willingly have crossed its threshold.

If Sperry had in the words of George Meredith, "longings for the buried day" which served to keep Harvard in perspective beyond the iron gates of the Yard, it was Oxford that expressed his own feelings of the authentic self. After only a few years at Harvard he commented to his sister, Pauline, "I have never liked Cambridge as a place to live, much preferring Boston..." But what he preferred best of all is indicated in the same letter when "[L. P.] Jacks asked me if I wanted a job in Oxford and will undertake to get me one if I wish it. It is a problem with many angles, depending partly upon what opens up here [Harvard] for the future." He explained himself further by adding that "I am a bigamist in the matter of countries and can live in one quite as happily as the other... In many ways I should love nothing better than life in Oxford. As Jude Fawley says, 'It would just suit me'." About Harvard he felt that as his responsibilities advanced, "I get more and more restless with the red tape and typewriter ribbon web of administration that gets spun allround me like a huge spider's web, and as I know I have no gift for it and ought to be doing other things, writing increasingly, there's something to be said for the Oxford life."[23]

Like a first careless love that must yield to other, sensible matrimonial probabilities, Sperry's thoughts of succeeding L. P. Jacks as Principal of Manchester College, Oxford collapsed within a couple of years. He, therefore, remained at Harvard, all told, thirty-one years. Apparently, the possibility of succeeding Jacks waned because the College had "fallen into the hands of a militant Unitarian crowd," whom Jacks, himself a moderate Unitarian, had been "fighting off for ten years, and whose policies he deplores." Sperry was, in effect, labeled "damaged goods" because he was American in the first instance, but also because he was associated with a discredited patron.[24] According to Charles Forman, who went from Harvard at Sperry's urging to Oxford in the early 1950s, Sperry was eliminated from the running only because he was American, and not because he was, as a non-Unitarian Congregationalist, theologically unacceptable.[25]

By the time of President Lowell's retirement, the dedication of Memorial Church, followed a few years later by the Harvard Tercentary, Sperry was so intimately connected with Harvard that by custom and common sense he had nowhere else to go. He could not reasonably return to the parish, because it was like retiring to the farm after a sublime tour of

Paris, nor turn away from Harvard where he tasted the joy of alliance with critical thinking inside the university. But what he realized too was that intellectual life inside the Church could actually thrive in the atmosphere of the university, perhaps more so than in the parish. Paul Kuntz ruminates on his mentor's mind, mood and career:

> One of the curious aspects of Sperry's intellect was that it was so heavily literary and historical that he had almost nothing to say about philosophic issues directly. I think he could have devoted his attention to synthetic a priori propositions, or to the subsistence of universals, or the ontological argument for the necessity of God. But no man of common sense is concerned with such problems. Sperry was a man who prided himself in communication with the general public. If specialists communicate in jargon, so much the worse for them.[26]

❦

A Dean's Musing on the Ministry

It is clear that Sperry's chief intellectual aim throughout his Harvard career was to explore the experience of "God in the community," to teach others how to investigate that relationship broadly and to report his findings in intelligible prose and speech. Sperry's main concern at Harvard turned to the original purpose of the College's founding—to produce learned ministers able to communicate the issues of life to the general public. Sperry's task was to make a contribution that could be felt inside the church, and only secondarily would he consider whatever else he might add to scholarship. It is noteworthy that Sperry's first public address before the Harvard community, just before leaving the parish ministry, was on the Dudleian Foundation in which he lectured on "The Call to the Ministry." From that theme, which occupied much of his mind in its most productive years, are derived other subjects which Sperry discussed publicly in building up a national reputation as a thinker and writer on worship, prayer and preaching.

Sperry wrote near the end of his life a retrospective for a history of the Divinity School and considered the diverse aspects of the professional religious leader, "The ministers of a century ago, to use a crude metaphor, took the field with a rifle; the ministers of today carry a double-barreled shotgun, and their shot scatters widely."[27] This is suggestive, therefore, of those specific vehicles of religious expression which need to be examined under Sperry's generous conception of the ministry. After all, what goes on inside a church as conducted through the public office which the ministry bears is worship, prayer and preaching. It is along these lines that his thought divides to consider the attributes and deficiencies inside the Church. The validity and the work of the Church stem from the "sincerity" of the ministry and the "reality" of congregational worship which are finally guided by George Tyrrell's distinction: "God will not ask us, What sort of Church have you lived in? but, What sort of Church have you longed for?"[28] The latter inquiry lies deep in the background behind the life's work of Willard Sperry.

He was fond of a story illustrating the modern misconception about the Church being the home of lost causes which the ministry only perpetuates. Describing certain of the Oxford colleges which are built of a very soft limestone, he recalled that because of the acidic quality of the air in the upper Thames valley, "the fabric of these colleges looks to be in a state of imminent collapse." Two American women, wandering around Oxford as tourists, "ventured into one of these shabby sepulchers of 'lost causes', pushed their unabashed way up a stair in the back quad, and opened a door. They saw before them a much alive and entirely contemporary-looking boy, sprawled in his basket chair before a cheerful fire, filling the room with pipe smoke and his brains with Nicomachean Ethics. 'We beg your pardon, we didn't know that these ruins were inhabited'."[29]

Sperry would make the point that for those persons investigating the Church or even considering the ministry, it is worthwhile to say that the ruins are still inhabited. For the sincere person who is drawn to the specter of living in and among ruins Sperry recommended that careful delineation be drawn between the problem of personal and institutional religion, which are quite apart from each other. He had his students consider that before finally seeking ordination to the ministry that they remember the useful advice he had once received. "Just before I left Oxford, my tutor, Canon Streeter, said to me, 'You ought to consider seriously the question whether you can make your best contribution to the total cause of religion through the ordained ministry of a church, or as a layman—presumably as a teacher and a writer'."[30]

For those who prepare for the ministry and enter its calling, Sperry realized that the decision implied further perplexity and poignancy. If anything, merely answering the call settled nothing, because the claim upon the minister's life and time were such that another moral problem was created. Sperry called this "the double loyalty of the Christian minis-try." The fact that he chose the word "loyalty" to emphasize a complex idea rather than "dilemma," may point to an indebtedness that ends up owing Josiah Royce for the fractured concept about the main problem of the ministry. Sperry explained that a minister "has a loyalty, in the first place, to Christian truth, made known and to be made known to him in his own religious experience. And he has a second loyalty to his fellow human beings with whom he lives and works."[31]

Sperry by no means thought that the problem of reconciling loyalties was unique to the ministry as a calling. All the professional groups were subjected to similar pressures from within and without. The universal situation which Sperry brings to light is not a contest between good versus evil, which as a moral problem makes the solution a simple one. Rather, it embodies the essence of Greek tragedy whereby loyalties collide, each of which is good in itself, but which cannot be reconciled to the other in a given dilemma. An example of this for the minister is the inability to square one's duty as a preacher with a competing duty as a pastor. George Tyrrell, again, helped Sperry clarify and become increasingly conscious of a paradox in the ministry. Tyrrell's moral fervor and religious courage were cited "when he stood at the parting of the ways in his Modernist pilgrimage and said, 'I am driven by a fatality to follow the dominant interest of my life, though it should break half the heart of the world'."

The friction arising from the double loyalty of the ministry creates a potential tragedy to which Sperry proposed that ministers and seminaries give renewed thought. To its credit and academic worthiness, Sperry said, "liberal Protestantism is not a body of clearly defined belief and practice; it is distinctively a religious method, a way of thinking and meeting the world. The cardinal virtue of sincerity has with us supplanted the older ideal of an immutable orthodoxy. And our theological disciplines... look primarily to the perfecting of this inner integrity." The liability of the liberal position in being modern by admitting the scientific method is "to ignore and neglect the claim of the individual to be in himself a centre of spiritual value." Religion is other than singular ideas and formulations about "laws" of theological gravity and proofs of God's existence. Sperry explained, it is also as Balzac says of himself in his relation to his characters, that he wore their rags, walked in their tattered shoes, felt the pangs of their hunger and their warm, human tears pouring down his face.

Sperry identified the failure of clergy in the modern world as being far too one sided, first taking up "a scientific interest in the universal laws of the religious life to the neglect of individual values; and second... [viewing] the ministry as a kind of modern Hebrew prophecy calling for a moral detachment from society."

Sperry, however, much as might be expected, did not call for a compromise, or suggest a certain paring down of truth, compensated by the diluting of charitable acts or in his words, "a kind of inglorious muddy mean between truthfulness and time-service." What clergy are seeking is "an attitude which somehow grasps the two loyalties in a comprehensive vision, even though it may not reconcile them." It is not the business of religion to present hard and fast alternatives between "Either-Or," but to help a person say, "Both-And." At this juncture, Sperry's doctrine of the ministry was somewhat out of synch with the growing Neo-Orthodox influence which tended toward collectivizing a sense of urgent social concern, as a kind of theological New Deal. Sperry resisted the reshaping of the Social Gospel, which became the ambiguous goal of Neo-Orthodoxy in its more practical expressions, because such an aim was too doctrinaire. By cutting itself loose from the genteel tradition of caring for individual souls in favor of a utilitarian pastoral ethic, Neo-Orthodoxy put itself, in Sperry's view, in the grasp of an all or nothing dilemma.

Sperry is adamant about the necessary, though imperfect breadth and nonspecificity of the ministry, because,"the man who knows only one major loyalty of the ministry to a pitiless sincerity and whose ruling principle in every dilemma is 'All or Nothing' may find himself led... into futility as well as heartlessness." And moreover, if there be in a minister an attitude "toward the fallen and despicable world a touch of relenting, that relenting may take the form of moral pity." And pity, being a virtue only of aristocracy, has about it a tone of condescension ill-fitted to a democratic age and modern world.[32]

Sperry is once again describing a paradox in his feelings toward religion, particularly as it is encountered by its first line of defense, in the ranks of clergy. As for method of thought Sperry is showing a regular pattern of arguing on both sides of an issue. Philosophers would not dispute the value of looking both ways and noting the exception that usually makes dogmatic approaches to a problem invalid. Nietzsche was quick to point out that "It is good to express a matter in two ways simultaneously so as to give it both a right foot and left. Truth can stand on one leg, to be sure; but with two it can walk and get about."[33] The value of paradoxical thinking has its own immediate rewards, first of which is to escape systematic solutions and thinking. One must ask, however, having encountered paradox often enough in Sperry's thoughts, is there not, in effect, something systematic in walking consistently around ambiguity with both feet? Perhaps for Sperry it is more important that a proposition be dynamic than it be a fixed certainty, because contradictory views are not signs of error, just as lack of contradiction is not a sign of truth. Any philosophic or methodological system without its paradoxes is suspicious, but any paradox without some quality of pattern degenerates into hopeless complexity.

Sperry often conceded that liberal Protestantism was a religion which laid great stress on method, perhaps more than on result; for the latter will take care of itself if the former is trustworthy. In this respect Sperry invoked Darwin who once said that any success he had had as a scientist he owed to his cultivated mental habit of never letting an exception pass unnoticed. Sperry, in counterpoint, also said, "Very few of us have any closely articulated system of theology today. Certainly we have no system in liberalism comparable in its interior rigidity to Calvinism... The trouble with Calvinism was not its logic, but its premises. We believe it to have been a steel skyscraper built on sand. But we by contrast are building houses of cards on the rock. What we need eventually is the same kind of inner truthfulness in a system which Calvin had, on a better foundation than his."[34] Sperry found that inner truthfulness in paradox and unconsciously "systematized" it as a method.

In the face of paradox Sperry prescribed for the minister the strong drink of firsthand experience. He declared that secondhand study or the perfunctory sense of duty to the needy will in the end disappoint, as well as diminish the minister's effectiveness if one loyalty over the other is chosen or an ugly compromise is attempted. "The Christian minister should learn to enter into the lives of those to whom he ministers by taking the simpler and deeper experiences of his own life quite seriously, as not exceptions to the common lot but rather as a clue to what happens to men and women everywhere, always, to all."[35]

To achieve what Sperry proposed in theory for the ministry, he was compelled to be mindful of certain practicalities and limitations. These were factored into the transaction which tried to match training and purpose in such a way as to be germane, genuine and useful. To practice the art of the ministry meant taking "those aspects of human life which are at once the most important and yet the most difficult to define."

The life-work of the minister is to study the final questions of life from a firsthand perspective as they arise in that "human laboratory which is his parish." Preaching, for example, "is not re-echoing at second hand the thoughts of other men." Instead it is "primarily a process of thinking aloud about life" as it is discovered out of a vast fund of "inarticulate religion," religion which has "never really become conscious of itself, found itself, and got itself out in the open."

What constitutes the call to the ministry is largely an internal process. First, it is the "inner necessity" to get some answer to the question, what shall one do with life? "It is the moral command of circumstance." Then, also, it is "the necessity he feels to find out why he is here, what it all means, what he ought to do." Any person who feels this necessity and "hears these human voices has a sufficient call to the ministry." Beyond these major criteria, the minister is the person "who is trying to win the power and to give others the power to say 'God' in all the experiences of life." Here ministerial aptitude and training are paramount because "the minister must know the world's way of saying 'God' in broad outline, and must be prepared to reinterpret them in the light of present conditions."

Sperry allowed for no deception in celebrating the privileged call to the ministry. "It is drudgery, put it any way you will, and a wise man ends by accepting drudgery as an inevitable part of any serious life." The aim and end of the minister's discipline and hard work point toward knowing the lives of other human beings in detail, so that the minister "is in a position to help them when they really need help." In other words, broad impersonal schemes for social reform and human betterment are no substitute for the willingness to take time and trouble with individuals.

Taking up mundane concerns, Sperry pointed out that while clergy salaries are modest and often in direct conflict with ministers' "moral responsibility to provide adequate support for a home" and in contention with a felt duty not "to make the members of that home the victims of their inability to command a salary adequate for these needs," he assured many prospective ministers that "the Protestant churches as a whole are facing this problem seriously and propose to set their ministers beyond hardship and anxiety."[36]

The more abiding compensations of the ministry, ultimately, are to be reckoned among life's intangible rewards. The double compensation accrues from a prior double loyalty to living with great ideas on the one hand and with concrete human needs on the other. In its own coin, the ministry is its own best reward.[37] The currency of exchange inside the Church, moreover, is spent in the spiritual transactions that register in worship, prayer and preaching. Both in theory and practice these are areas where Sperry was able to make enormous and lasting contributions.

Defining the Significant Form of Worship

Herbert W. Schneider writing in *Religion in Twentieth Century America* (1967), says, "the dawn of the century found theology more conscious of its duty to science than to worship." This great erosion of interest in Protestant worship is explained by "a mutual estrangement between doctrine and cultus, doctrine fraternizing with science and philosophy, while cultus threw in its lot with social service." By mid-century both had discovered a mutual need for the other and this reconciliation had invigorated both aspects of religion, its thought and its practice of piety. Schneider believes that "the creation of this conscious will to worship is for Americans an achievement of the twentieth century and a product... of the agony of our times."[38]

More than any other American Protestant figure of the 1920s whose career spans the entire first half of the twentieth century, Willard Sperry is in large part responsible for this "achievement" of making American religious leaders conscious of public worship's supreme worth. Sperry saw a vacuum and rushed to fill it with probably his best book, *Reality in Worship: A Study of Public Worship and Private Religion* (1925).

He was more a cause than a symptom of interest in a doctrine of worship. His influence in the field is notable from a sampling of various opinions which succeeding authors on worship rendered. Albert W. Palmer in *Come Let Us Worship* (1941) considered Sperry's contribution a major reference work essential to any minister's library. Bernard Eugene Meland in *Modern Man's Worship* (1934) felt that "... no recent book on worship exceeds Sperry's." Albert W. Palmer came back to praising Sperry's treatment on worship in 1957 with the remark that it was "probably the best all-round book on worship yet written in America. [It] combines insight into the underlying philosophy of worship with practical wisdom born of sound experience and all fused together in a prose style of notable charm and power." A homiletics professor at Princeton, Andrew M. Blackwood, considered Sperry's *Reality in Worship* among "the best known books about theory" along with distinguished works by Evelyn Underhill, Friedrich Heiler and Rudolf Otto (*The Idea of the Holy*). Clarence Seidenspinner, author of *Form and Freedom* (1941) is highly dependent on Sperry's prior work and the result is a book which is obviously derivative from Sperry's work. Up through the late 1950s *Reality in Worship* enjoyed an excellent reputation and was still regarded as "the modern classic in the field."[39]

The background of this important contribution, naturally, shifts to England. It is from England that Sperry so often got his best perspective on America. In a long letter from Great Stones, Headington, to Edward Caldwell Moore, Sperry is struck by the growing impression that Oxford is "rather 'up in the wind' theologically:"

> I cannot find anything very important going on. Manchester College, and I suppose Mansfield, have been compelled to admit a good many ill-educated men who fall far short of the A.B. standard. But Nonconformity seems to me not to be in anywhere near as strong a position as it was twenty-five years ago. It lacks its outstanding preachers... The Church of England, on the other hand, seems much more active... The cathedrals have come wonderfully alive in many new and surprising ways. And the Anglo-Catholics are a vigorous and aggressive body, not to be put off by the plaintive protests of the old evangelical broad churchmen. The proposed revision of the Prayer Book [1928]... is said to be opening the wedge. On the other hand it is apparent that in its own way England is in reaction, as many churches on the continent are in reaction, against the subjective, humanistic, anthropocentric liberal theology of the past fifty years, and is in search of something more objective...It is rather odd that while in America we are still wrestling with the problem of subjective religiousness of the humanistic type, everybody over here wants some objective restatement of religion. I suppose this Anglo-Catholic business, although it was on its way before the war, has been greatly furthered by the reaction from the war.[40]

Dean Sperry attempted to fashion just "some objective restatement of religion" for an American church constituency, drawing upon his orientation and observations from England in order to suggest and, if not predict, hope for a coming shift in the winds of worship from across the Atlantic.

The quality of worship in every religion is usually determined by two things: the worshippers' prior conceptual framework of doctrine and the exterior ethos modified by the blowing currents of world news. As Sperry noted above, after World War I the earlier preference for (Non-Conformist and Modernist) immanentism, once given its impetus from theological and social pressures, collapsed in favor of "something more objective."

In a very large way the popular pulpiteer, R. J. Campbell, was not only symptomatic, but symbolic of this dramatic shift in England. Campbell was the most distinguished, if controversial, English exponent of "the subjective, humanistic, anthropocentric, liberal theology." Typical of his subjectivity is the often quoted epigram, "My God is my deeper self and yours too..." Campbell was minister of City Temple, the most powerful Free Church pulpit in London, whose theological iconoclasm went so far as to redefine sin as a blundering search for God. Campbell, however, after lamenting the chaos of his unorthodox reinterpretation, and shaken by Charles Gore's *The New Theology and the Old Religion* (1907), returned to the Church of England in which he was reared.[41]

Campbell's life, at least in its relationships to religious institutions, reflects in microcosm the movement of an entire English society as Sperry saw it and described it in the 1920s. And furthermore, what Campbell symbolized for England, Sperry himself, absent parallel fame and controversy, perhaps came to resemble in American post-war consciousness of religious forms. Sperry, like Campbell, and unlike contemporary American liberals, was drawn by the substance and intention of Roman and Anglo-Catholic affirmations. The difference between Sperry and Campbell is obvious and at once institutional. Sperry remained in form a Congregationalist (as Tyrrell, though excommunicated, remained a Catholic in his own mind) while Campbell, also transformed, merely transferred back to his Anglican roots. In substance, however, something notably similar occurred in each of their lives with different causes and results. Campbell may have been more robust intellectually and effusive rhetorically than Sperry ever could be. But in essence each against the background of his own national culture represented a movement that is traced in the relationship of worship and theology; and that movement, albeit subtle, presented itself in series, first in England, then in America.

Horton Davies argues that any weakness in worship is ultimately attributable to a defective theology. That in Sperry's view "the cathedrals have come wonderfully alive" can be ascribed culturally to a concomitant weakness in worship "of the humanistic type" as much as to "a very rigorous and aggressive" alternative, Davies's thesis is supported. The weakness in worship which was apparent on both sides of the Atlantic can be imputed to doctrine which Davies assesses as having three major defects due to "the utter dominance of immanental over the transcendental concept of God, so that the mystery, the majesty and the judgement of God were dissipated." First, "the imperatives of corporate ethics were aggrandized at the expense of the need for personal transformation and discipleship." Secondly, the kingdom of God was presented as much too evolutionary, thereby, "ignoring both the Divine initiative that brings in the Kingdom and in its transhistorical fulfillment." Finally, because liberal theology confused secular utopian solutions of the day with the historical image of the Kingdom, the Church has been "grievously undervalued" and with that, so too its "corporate discipline and sacramental life."[42] Sperry would concur completely with the premise that theology is prior to worship, writing in 1935, "the aesthetic problem in worship must always wait upon the theological problem."[43]

Sperry's work on the subject of worship was indeed a response to a bankruptcy of form as well as substance in post-war liberal theology, but it was also surprisingly representational of a broader American cultural phenomenon. Sperry might well come to be regarded, because of the English background and his subsequent breakthrough in American religious thought, as among elite American intellectuals who were something of a timely index of what T. J. Jackson Lears has called, "the rise of Catholic taste" in American culture from 1880 to 1920.

Sperry was not only influenced positively by "this Anglo-Catholic business" being "greatly furthered by the reaction from the war," but was immersed culturally in an America that had buried its Puritan past, first in the therapeutic preaching of Henry Ward Beecher ("more humanity, less divinity"), in favor of a "Protestant aestheticism" which led to "the fascination with Catholic forms."[44] In general, the American Protestant movement towards ritual may have been a result of a church culture rebounding from habits of introspection clouded over by an Emersonian haze that had lost sight of any supernatural sanction. That situation and the mood of the individual church-goer combined with vapid sermons steeped in sentimentalism suggest not only a growing deficiency in the stated purpose of worship, but "an embryonic uneasiness with liberal theology." Given the centrifugal tendencies of liberal culture, that is, "the center cannot hold," a certain recoil aimed at Catholic corporatism was not only natural but expected in hindsight. It was within this theological milieu that Sperry stepped forward to argue a strong case for "reality in worship." His work was in keeping with the judgment made by Lears that "the movement toward art and ritual, by elevating church atmosphere beyond mundane human affairs, suggested a reluctance to divinize human purpose and a longing for a deity who was wholly other."[45]

Sperry's writing on worship moves beyond historical and literary criticism which attempts to trace a liturgical form to its source. Also, Sperry is not particularly desirous of expanding the ample literature of "suggestive hints" as to appropriate discharge of Bible lessons, hymns and responsive readings. Sperry, instead, addresses a more thorough-going question than that of how to extend current liturgical research and pedagogy. He is asking of public worship the question of purpose, of cause and effect. He begins with the modern premise that "in a service of public worship both science and art come to the aid of personal religion, criticizing that individual experience, discovering its universal truth, and then giving to that truth significant form." And doing that, the Church does for the individual what science and art are charged with doing: to give "added clarity, fuller meaning, and adequate expression" to one's own personal religion.[46]

The first third of Sperry's book, *Reality in Worship*, retraces meditatively the familiar ground of what happens to a person when that individual "gets religion." The author restates the overarching intention of religion "in the forbidding phraseology of the theologian" that "man must seek his origin in a cosmology and his destiny in a teleology," which in a pedestrian vernacular means "life is one half a matter of where we come from, and the other half a matter of where we are going." The serious work of the Church is to represent itself as an interpreter of whence and whither life? "For whatsoever else religion may be, it is the formal organization of the constant major episodes of common human experience into a social whole" which is to show how individual experience is "a broad recapitulation of the history of the race."

Sperry makes the argument from the logic of necessity, not essence, that "the world seeks the church, uncritically, habitually, at those times when life matters most." Religion is in a perpetual state of being rediscovered

when young people, professing to have outgrown religion, seek the service
of matrimony, when parents, having drifted away, bring their children back
for baptism or when the church is requisitioned to speak God's name over
the dead, who in life were never uniformly burdened with that name.
Sperry contends that "in obedience to some deep unreasoned prompting"
people seek churches "when life is most real."

And yet, before people "need definition or ask instruction" that will
match their individual experience to a universal reality, "they seek expression," an outlet that will be sincere and not unwelcomed by the institution
in whose context that experience is being examined. Then, and only then,
out of the habit of "church-going," or what Harnack called "the sanctifying
power of blind custom," which is not necessarily piety telescoped "down
to a mechanical and unthinking life," are "economy of effort and margins
of strength" granted so that one feels part of a larger pattern, that there is
some substance and order of the spiritual life. If "such a habit is one of the
ways to perfect freedom," then one of the ways and signs in which such a
habit comes of age is to wonder, "Why are we here in church about these
offices of worship? What do our rituals and our symbols and our sacraments intend?"[47]

The abstract answer to the questions posed above is that worship
intends a religious consciousness, which "always involves consciousness
of the self, but never of the self alone, always of the self in relationship to
something else." Sounding slightly Socratic, Sperry explains that "the
better we know ourselves, the less self-sufficient we become and the deeper
our need and desire for this otherness of things. Religion is the quest for a
Real Other, and the transaction and communion between one's own self
and that other."[48]

Sperry enumerates the various "forerunners" to which this Real
Other is attached. Pleasure, for example, may very well be one of the
first heralds which the Real Other voices, still and small. However we
"succeed in losing our little selves and finding our larger selves in play
or work, in a science or an art... becoming one with this Other is the object
of our interest or loyalty" or pleasure. And in being taken out of ourselves, "we advance farther in our experience of religion's way, until
finally there comes a moment, when suddenly we say, 'Surely, God is in
this place and I knew it not'... And then it is that we see what religion is
all about."

Religious consciousness, as articulated by idealistic philosphers, will in maturity and discipline perhaps turn back upon itself to seek reality and to find satisfaction in the kingdom that is within; and when it does it will be pressed to define "the parabolic value of the antithesis between the self and the other." The definition of this antithesis, idealism accepts as a form of self-consciousness. And if that is troublesome, then Sperry reminds the reader that "the ascetic attempt to evade the self seems to have been singularly unsuccessful." The recalled force of St. Augustine's rhetoric hammers the issue with poignancy, "Whither could my heart flee from my heart? Whither could I flee from myself? Whither should I not follow myself?"

While mere self-reference and its antithesis do not completely fulfill the terms of a meaningful religious transaction, Sperry believed that "the idealistic philosophies which assert that the world and the individual are simply two aspects of a single reality, which can be compassed by self-consciousness, are probably better fitted to interpret man's experience of religion than are the pluralistic systems." Sperry's philosophic preferences not only give added evidence of his initial distrust of systems, but show how much he stressed "the practices of this interior piety" because self-consciousness yields to "a social self capable of dialogue and commerce and transaction within its own limits." The shorter version of this is to say that if religious consciousness suggests self-consciousness, then to find that self one has to lose that self. "And to lose yourself utterly there must be an otherness to things which for a time claims you. Unless we find that otherness, perhaps we should say unless that otherness finds us, we are condemned to the solitary confinement of unprofitable introspection."

Sperry elaborates the analogy of unlocking the imprisoned splendor of the individual soul in a related passage:

> The keys which open the door of our moody prison-cell are always in the keeping of some angel visitant who comes to us as the ambassador of the Real Other. Possibly, at some later time, we may return to the place of solitude to discover that we can make it a market place for the large commerce of a truly social self. But only actual experience can enable us to make a heaven of idealistic thinking out of the hell of our initial introspection. The God within is awakened into life at the call of the God without.[49]

It is not an accidental connection that Sperry ends the discussion on self-knowledge's priority (to religious knowledge) with a quoted passage from the British incarnationalist, Bishop B. F. Westcott, forerunner of Charles

Gore and William Temple,[50] both of whom typified (theologically) the England Sperry came to know and favor after World War I. Sperry uses Westcott's words to undergird his own argument and, one may further assume, to show his (Sperry's) sympathy for the high church position. What Westcott said was that Christianity "assumes as its foundation the existence of an Infinite Personal God and a finite human will. This antithesis is assumed not proved. No arguments can establish it," wrote the Bishop. "It is a primary intuition not a deduction... Each man for himself is supposed to be conscious of the existence of God and of his own existence. We can go no further."

Having distinguished the necessity of religion from the deeper intuition of religion's essence and then arranged the sequence of expression as necessity prior to essence, Sperry devotes the remaining two-thirds of *Reality in Worship* to "what these individual experiences mean when translated into a public office of worship." Otherwise, to paraphrase Josiah Royce, one would be left to sit in the isolated dungeon of self-consciousness to rot away unheeded and alone.

At this juncture Sperry attacks liberalism, by which he means, the general belief that society can safely be established on the self-directing power of personality. "Liberalism has been content to discover, to suggest, and to vindicate the inherent worth of the self without reference to any Other." Religion, however, "confronts the self with an alter ego" and "is concerned with the paradox and puzzle of likeness and unlikeness as between the self and the Real Other." Sperry argues that the real reason for the slow spread of the liberal temper in religion "and the answer to the otherwise insoluble problem, why a point of view which seems so right makes converts so slowly," is that "it does not direct attention to ideas apart from itself, and this doctrine of itself does not suffice for a religion." Liberalism has been too much an ethical rather than a religious movement. And contrary to its own assumptions, "liberalism cannot permanently shirk a description of an Ideal Other, and must invite men [and women] to the worship of that Other as real." Sperry adds a radical recommendation that liberalism's "moral seriousness and scrupulousness need now to be supplemented by a touch of mysticism."

It is for this reason that worship is its own end and is only to be enjoyed, not first comprehended as "useful." Liberalism needs to reintroduce the idea of the enjoyment of God as the chief end of humanity and not the mere glory of going onward and upward. Sperry reminds his readers of a British intellectual's premise that cathedrals are built "in those ages when men do beautiful, useless things for the sake of an idea."

In this line and connection Sperry builds his case for the spiritual efficacy of worship by contradicting the familiar account of Christianity "as a life of usefulness, void of enjoyment." Sperry suggests instead that "the paradox of life is such that the ultimate ability to do useful things constantly and well depends upon a prior courage to enjoy useless things."[51]

Furthermore, liberal Protestantism is out of touch with the whole Pauline conception of the Christian life, says Sperry, because "it is not accustomed to think of the initial commitments of the Christian life as above all else the quest for power, the power which saves us from ourselves and from the world and makes us, out of weakness, strong." What Sperry is saying here is that modern thinking expects religion to supply understanding—"a credible compound of historical knowledge, scientific information, philosophical speculation, and moral engineering"—whereas the initial truth of religion is that "it gives strength before it gives meaning or advice." Sperry cites Henry Adams's chapter about "The Dynamo and the Virgin" as "one of the most important accounts of religion in modern letters" because the realization is achieved that "all the steam in the world could not, like the Virgin build Chartres. Symbol or energy," wrote Adams, "the Virgin had acted as the greatest force the Western world ever felt."

After all the glories of human moral progress have been documented, "the fact remains," says Sperry, "that a man's religion is defined by that to which he gives his life and by that from which he draws power for living... What you do with the power you get from God is your responsibility." How one is spiritually strengthened is the purpose and occasion of public worship. Meanwhile, Sperry points out a kind of surprising pragmatism in that, in his mind, "mysticism is the parent of the pitiless and revolutionary practicality." By this he means that "the love of God tests itself and fulfills itself in the love of man. When we glorify God and enjoy him forever we are thereby put under bonds to treat our fellow human beings also as ends in themselves."[52] By making the moral justification of "the enjoyment of God," that is, of worship as an end in itself, Sperry came full circle back to his liberal roots and inclinations.

The idioms by which he has put place names upon the map of his mind are certainly novel for an American Protestant liberal of the twentieth century, but not original in the broader cultural context that fostered his thought. His references to mysticism and his general approval of the Catholic Mass, as examples of reality in worship, are not impulses toward a Victorian cultural ambivalence between "engagement and withdrawal," a pattern that Jackson Lears discusses in detail. Rather, for Sperry these models of religious experience are philosophically engaging and are not mere sensual anachronisms to be discarded as forms of pre-Enlightenment preferences.

Sperry is open to the possibilities of a liberal Protestantism "touched with mysticism" while "restoring some of the older objective material" similar to "accounts of divine reality and divine grace as concrete and dramatically moving as the Mass,"[53] because of being exposed to three weighty intellectual sources. These three which will be traced separately are, in the order of their consideration, an American aesthetic milieu in which he found himself, English theological trends and the Harvard Department of Philosophy.

Jackson Lears argues convincingly that part of the American "medieval unconscious" was a protest "against a desanctified, weightless universe" in a modern world. Not only was William James discussing mysticism in his Gifford Lectures on religious experience, but "by the turn of the century... Catholic mystics, like Catholic saints in general, laid unprecedented claim on the educated Protestant imagination."[54] The explanation for this grip upon American mainstream imaginations, contemplating a severe preparation for union with the divine, is speculative, but Lears thinks that the appeal reflected the general longing for intense experience. Also the mystic demonstrated powers of self-control lacking in the modern world while also affirming that there were yet measureless reaches of the soul which preserved some stress on the sense of boundless opportunity in the twentieth century.

This medieval mentality was manifested in the art, architecture, ritual and belief of American Protestant culture because, according to Lears, "the secularized postmillennialism pervading the churches" undermined "the task of illuminating a mysterious yet providentially ordered universe." Religious aesthetic sensibilities were elevated in order "to rekindle a sense of transcendence... and to recapture a vanishing, God-centered world view."[55] Lears is quick to note the problematic nature of shifting aesthetic tastes, no matter how valid the intention may have been to stimulate

"unconscious realms of vitality." He writes that "for Protestants who were
adrift from older theological moorings and still clinging to liberal formulas,
the encounter with premodern art and ritual engendered confusion and
even despair."[56] Sperry is a figure who stepped in to mediate the confusion
at a time when American culture, in the vivid image of Walter Lippmann,
was mostly "drift without mastery."

Sperry's thinking in this "milieu" not only turned to the problem of
worship, but because Memorial Church in the Harvard Yard was conceived
while he was there, he also took up in theory the matter of proper church
design. While Memorial Church is colonnaded and transparently Georgian,
and thus the epitome of New England from its exterior inward, there are
qualities about the building which are unmistakably and distinctly
medieval and in keeping with the broad aesthetic themes of which Sperry
was part. His views were solicited for the proposed chapel and his sense of
form, function and propriety led him to conclude that "an adequate and
beautiful building is of itself a tremendous help to the services held in it."
He especially admired the chapels at Groton, St. Marks and Williams
College, all of which are generally classified as neo-Gothic. The problem at
Harvard is "to provide first an adequate architectural witness to the part
which real religion plays in the more serious life of the University itself...
Every great religious building is a matter of 'record' before it is an attempt
to meet a demand. Its primary influence is as a record and not merely as a
utility."[57] In this vein Sperry issued a warning against what he called "the
decoration-heresy" as an altogether "pathetic failure" to enrich the sacred
spaces set aside for public worship.[58]

When it came time in the course of the project to consider the details
and drawings, Sperry's advice was again requested. In particular, Sperry
suggested how a smaller chapel for Morning Prayers could be integrated
with a large, adjacent, and except on Sundays, empty sanctuary. First of all
Sperry remarked of the problem "that this ought to be treated as a cathedral
choir, proper... by increasing the length of the chapel or 'apse' to twice the
length shown on the architect's drawing." Then Sperry proposed in front
of the choir a "a chancel proper, with altar, lectern, desk and a couple of
seats behind a rail." The cathedral intention is apparent in the resulting
edifice because the chancel is divided longitudinally and the pulpit is not
in the center, but upon an "hour glass" to the left as faced from the narthex
forward. The choir would be divided across the rear of the chancel by a

screen behind which the organ console would be set. The combined arrangement of a choir and backstalls for daily prayers and a church or nave proper on the other side of the screen was the design adopted and has functioned ever since as Sperry had first proposed "as a cathedral."[59]

Next and probably equal in influence on Sperry, after the general American "fascination with Catholic forms," was the rediscovery of mysticism in English theology. Sperry found the medieval mentality helpful in reviving a doctrine of Protestant worship through the writings of William Ralph Inge (1860-1954), once characterized in the oxymoron as "a right wing liberal" with no special liking for immanentism. To some extent the letters and works of Baron Friederich von Hügel were also consulted, but definitely not the writings of Evelyn Underhill who was of the same mystic genre. Sperry passed on his interest in these authors to his students with regularity. James Luther Adams recounts his intellectual journey in the 1930s as a Unitarian minister, "My own interest in von Hügel I owe, like many another fruit-bearing seed, to Dean Willard Sperry of Harvard Divinity School. Von Hügel's philosophy of critical realism," explains Adams, "his emphasis on the role of the body, history, and institutions in religion, his attack (along with Maritain's) on the 'pure spirituality' of unhistorical, noninstitutional, nonincarnational religion became determinative for my conception of religion."[60]

Sperry was drawn to this corner of English theology because religion is, for the mystic, essentially the adoration of God and worship is the corporate expression of adoration. Sperry always cautioned himself and others about the hyper-individualism of mysticism which is too often reduced to an extreme personal malevolence falling into a kind of spiritual masochism that digs out the deep roots of self-love with the knife of self-hatred.[61] At other levels void of disturbing psychology, Sperry found mysticism much more ecumenical in spirit than other channels, able to bring Catholics and Protestants onto some common ground. This in turn opened up on both Catholic and Protestant sides a common literature of Christian classics of devotion, a genre which Sperry examined and commended in his considerable work, *Strangers and Pilgrims* (1939), developed from a course he had taught for many years. In that book he drew character studies of a disparate group of otherwise unrelated devotionalists such as St. Augustine, St. Francis of Assisi, Thomas à Kempis, Brother Lawrence and John Woolman.

Furthermore, the twentieth-century exponents of mysticism in England were intellectually credible, "not intemperate enthusiasts or hotheads, but historical and critical scholars of... spiritual depth and discernment." But most importantly, Sperry found in Inge especially, as he would in von Hügel and Underhill had he consulted them more frequently on the point, a sense of paradox and second thought, which for "each of these authors insisted as strongly on the transcendence of God as on His immanence, and thus correlated the inevitable subjectivity of an exclusive assertion of Divine immanence."[62]

Mysticism did not have to be totally indifferent to the paradox of God's nature. While both God and persons are by definition necessary to religion, Sperry is neither subtle about this emphasis nor willing to let the typology of paradox go, for in the passing of paradox the reality which is religion disappears, too. Religion cannot be real when taken from the extremes of magic or mysticism, though Sperry emphasizes that "mysticism is an altogether nobler and more adequate account of religion than magic." The problem of religion should not be overlooked on this basis, says Sperry, because "magic tends to get rid of God; mysticism tends to get rid of man... The magician kills his God; the mystic sacrifices himself." Most difficulties in religion arise from this source: "Either the object is absorbed by a too powerful subject, or the subject is absorbed by a too powerful object."[63]

Sperry was careful to keep clear of too mechanical accounts of religion for fear of falling below the level of the best of human experience, and instead relied on "paradox as a faith in the independent actuality and worth, of both God and man."[64] Various accounts of the religious relationship (including mysticism) which enables one to meet these two requirements of actuality and worth were up through the 1930s examined by the earlier Harvard philosophers to whom Sperry also owed a major intellectual debt. Statements by William James reinforced Sperry's doctrine of intuition that pointed toward seminal discussions on mysticism:

> Whatever things have intimate and continuous connection with my life are things whose reality I cannot doubt. Whatever things fail to establish this connection are things which are practically no better for me than if they existed not at all.[65]

Josiah Royce, the idealist and counterpart to the spokesman for pragmatism, William James, refuted "private individual devotion" as an adequate means to interpret reality, even the intense and real union of the

human and the divine. For that Royce insisted that a community of interpretation was imperative and he argued in *The Problem of Christianity* (1918):

> mystical piety can never either exhaust or express the whole Christian
> doctrine of life. . . As a fact, the mystical tendency in religion is not the last,
> the mature, result, not yet the last refuge, of piety. Mysticism is always
> young, it is the childlike, it is the essentially immature aspect of the deeper
> religious life. . . Mature religion of the Christian type... takes the form of
> loyalty... by living in the community.[66]

Regarding these and other American philosophers with an interest in
religious experience, Sperry paid the highest compliment when writing to
his friend, the philosopher William Ernest Hocking that "this succession
from William James through yourself had had more influence on the
religious thought of America than any other single such group in the
country, and in the name of Harvard had been more influential than our
own Divinity Faculty has been."[67] Numerous points of intellectual contact
existed between Sperry and Hocking, not to mention a mutual connection
to Charles A. Bennett, Sperry's brother-in-law and Hocking's close friend.
Sperry and Hocking also shared a mutually keen interest in Memorial
Church to which Hocking transferred his church membership in 1932 from
Old South (Congregational) in Boston.[68]

What Sperry found so stimulating and useful about Hocking's work is
perhaps explained by a long section from *The Meaning of God in Human
Experience* (1912) where Hocking outlined a modern understanding of
mysticism and linked that particularly heightened personal experience
with worship. In everyday practical experience, Hocking explains, we are
not spared the details, but must attend these "parts" of our work; in
worship our attention shifts to "the whole," the big picture which is implied
by our dealings with parts of which we cannot be fully aware while
working. In Hocking Sperry finds reasonable justification for arguing that
worship is an end in and of itself, and not a means to some other "moral"
or utilitarian end.

To counteract this difficulty which undermines the thinking of and
working with one's "whole-idea," instead of setting upon its isolated
"parts," it is necessary first to recognize the symptoms of alienation in "the
over-prepared, over-equipped, over-trained person, with his eye habitually
fixed on some future moment of his action, [who] is indeed prepared for
everything except the judgement, 'Now is the time'; so the soul over-
steeped in actual work loses capacity to believe in the presence of the good

worked for." What needs greater scope of practice, according to Hocking, is something generally akin to the mystic's attitude of fusion, for "whatever recovers the worth of living by recovering the natural vigor of the whole-idea is worship, or part of worship... Worship, we may say, is the self-conscious part of the natural recovery of value; it is that part, therefore, which assigns all other parts their place and meaning."

Hocking anticipates Sperry's sense of paradox in also warning that religion, through the practice of piety, cannot be an all or nothing experience. The mystic's ability to concentrate on some objective whole is a most useful paradigm for worship, but only up to a point, because, "the worshipper who persists in his contemplation of the whole, thinking to establish himself permanently in the immediate presence of God, becomes an automaton, precisely as the determined worker becomes a machine."[69] To Sperry's thinking, consequently, worship must not be self-defeating or artificial, but real, an experience in balance as it shifts from "week-day self-assertion to Sunday self- abasement," a kind of quasi-mystical exercise of faith.

Sperry's Queens College roommate and brother-in-law, Charles A. Bennett had meanwhile gone to Yale, eventually taking his doctorate there, as well as a teaching position. He had been greatly stirred by the lectures of Josiah Royce who was, near the time of Bennett's arrival from England, visiting Yale. But also, more importantly, Bennett had befriended Hocking at that time. Under Hocking's guidance Bennett produced a book which went into two printings, entitled, A Philosophical Study of Mysticism (1923). Bennett's poor health led to an untimely premature death at the age of forty four (1930), and it was Hocking who stepped into Bennett's unfinished work which eventually was issued in a posthumous publication as The Dilemma of Religious Knowledge (1931).

If mysticism (and "the medieval mentality") was something of a philosophical rage in the 1920s, Hocking notes a changed environment by the time of Bennett's swan song and death, and perhaps this, in turn, signalled also the anti-climax of Sperry-styled liberal theology. Hocking writes in the Preface to Bennett's book which he assembled and edited that the mood of the day encouraged the evasion of religious thought. He notes that prior reflection which shaped old theologies had the merit of seeking hard-won answers to the serious questions of human destiny. Questions about the self surviving death, about theodicy and justice, about the divine foundations of ethics had permeated the discourse of an earlier time. Hocking was dismayed that by the 1930s these important questions were being supplanted by a falsely urgent concern, "How can we know?" He laments this failure of nerve which travels under the name of agnosticism because sophisticated thinkers err when they "are inclined to dodge the dilemma by eliminating the 'metaphysical' or 'supernatural' from religion." By doing this and by retranslating all religious language so that it will apply only to what is demonstrable in human affairs and the human mind they commit an act of cowardice, in Hocking's opinion, if not an act of betrayal.[70]

Consequently, epistemology became a substitute for theology, or at least a philosophy of religious experience. And by taking the form of humanism, these "erosions" shape Bennett's argument in the book, echoing much of the material preceding it in Sperry's *Reality in Worship*. Hocking wrote that Bennett's "conviction is, and he carries his point, that all such naturalizings of religion denature it and lose its essence. They would turn religious landscape into a metaphor, an analogy: but they are themselves mere analogies of religion." In other words, metaphor subordinates explanation, "the resemblance is taken for the substance of the original fact." Bennett, like the generic mystic, assumes that "faith in God is not a hypothesis, but a fact of immediate intuitive conviction."[71] Bennett's "cognitive compass," while absent quotation and citation in Sperry's footnotes, cannot be other than a positive indicator of where Sperry's mind was headed in discussing the makings of valid worship.

The dichotomy of subjective and objective worship was taken up by Sperry, especially in his treatment of symbolism which was also a matter clearly giving his brother-in-law pause in the face of overly subjective interpretations of religion. According to Sperry's view symbols are merely indicative of their objects, they are revelatory as a means of making the divine a present reality. The value of worship is its ability to extend one consciously into the presence of God. "The reality required in worship is double in nature. There will be first of all the objective truthfulness of the propositions and transactions of the act of worship. Then there will be our sincere subjective response to this truth."[72]

Sperry was all for the idea behind Clive Bell's term, "significant form," but found himself departing from the Protestantism of the previous century which had been "predominantly subjective in its interest and method,

relatively indifferent to the religious implications of the outer world."
Worship had to be more than decorated humanitarianism to satisfy its
purpose. "If religion seeks and finds God in the outer world worship will
be an act objectively conceived. If religion proposes self-consciousness as
the way to God worship will be subjectively conceived."[73] Worship must
mediate these two alternatives through symbols of significant form. What
Sperry means at this pivotal place is contained in a frank disclosure written
in reply to an inquiry made by a Presbyterian minister:

> My own theory of the ideal church is one which should supplement
> Quaker theology and mysticism by some outward and visible symbolism
> as beautiful as Roman Catholicism at its best. I only know that for a man
> less than a saint some objective forms are necessary as a "means of grace."[74]

Secondary to the role of preaching, traditionally the heart of Protestant
worship, Sperry indicated that the whole issue comes down in the end to
the question whether "a service of worship has objective worth apart from
the dimensions of subjective profit."[75] And in this regard, Sperry occasionally saw his views acknowledged and vindicated in letters from
sympathetic correspondents such as the young W. Norman Pittenger, an
Episcopalian theologian:

> The Catholic tradition is so much more substantial, so much more
> profound, and as Baron von Hügel has said, so much nearer to the truth
> by its refusal to simplify religion in the fashion of the ultra-liberal Protes-
> tants, that it must appeal strongly to men who are opposed to Christianity
> on other grounds [like H. L. Mencken, Joseph Wood Krutch and Walter
> Lippmann].[76]

Moreover, the emphasis on the objective Other in worship set Sperry
apart from the prevailing trends in American Protestantism of the liberal
tradition. Sperry never actually repudiated liberal theology because, in his
view, for all of its flaws it was still the best equipped relgious thinking to
deal with the modern scientific world. But he turned to the British Incar-
nationalists, a mystical liberalism, which was uncommon in America,
especially for New England Congregationalists and Unitarians, rather than
the dominant ethical-subjectivist liberalism of the Ritschlian school.

Sperry became more like his Puritan forebears and less like his liberal
contemporaries. The best parallel for making this case is probably Jonathan
Edwards for whom "the leading category of religious experience became
not salvation but beauty." As for Edwards, so for Sperry that, according to

William Clebsch, "true religion is not to achieve moral goodness but to receive holy beauty." Sperry shared in the legacy of Edwards which was, in a word, "to let one's life become an act of beauty." The ethical quest for human virtue became Edwards's aesthetic enjoyment of divine beauty— and that, as it seemed to Sperry, was an objective reality. The irony in making this connection is that Edwards's theological protégés (Joseph Bellamy, Samuel Hopkins and Jonathan Edwards, Jr.) conveyed "the real property, as it were, from the estate of Edwards's religious thought" to such unlikely successors as the modern fundamentalists, and not twentieth-century ethically conscious liberals.[77]

In seeking exceptions among Edwards's intellectual heirs, one discovers that Sperry rightfully claimed his Puritan lineage while most liberals were willing to forsake their birthrights. For Sperry religious reality grew toward beauty which then infused religious responsibility with a sense of moral duty and not vice versa, the usual way of arranging liberal priorities. Within Protestant liberalism, then, Sperry was something of a voice crying in the wilderness. Most liberals had relativized aesthetic sensibilities, thereby turning liberal theology into liberal reform, an altogether different emphasis than the plea Sperry was making in defense of his doctrine of worship.

To make operable what he proposed in theory, Sperry found the pattern of Isaiah 6 to be the most expressive model of worship's goal, alternating between correlative ideas—thesis, antithesis and synthesis. In the form which Isaiah furnishes one finds four simple ideas comprehended: 1. a vision and adoration of God; 2. a confession of creaturehood; 3. a perception of redeeming and reconciling energy; and 4. a reaffirmation of God's glory and a rededication of the self.[78] The order of service is thus ideally constituted to meet these criteria. And the role of the minister in the conduct of public worship is to efface himself or herself as an individual so that a congregation may express themselves under his or her leadership in and through that service.

❦

We Prophesy in Part: Preaching
One of the two tests and measures of sincerity as a minister is public prayer, the other being the sermon. Sperry writes that the minister's task "is to habituate himself to the spirit of prayer and then to discipline himself in

the best forms of prayer."[79] Before immersing himself in the "forms" of prayer, Sperry's definition begins with what prayer is not, and then having made that qualification, stipulates its demanding habit as facing up to inner realities:

> Prayer is not primarily a magical device by which we get what we privately want, at the cost of the reliability of the natural order or of the common good. Prayer is an intellectual discipline in truthfulness and a moral discipline in unselfishness. It is the endeavor to find what is true and right and then to conform to these realities.[80]

Sperry remarked in a lecture of unknown date or place of delivery that prayer cannot begin in too advanced solemnity:

> I have often found myself sitting in a kind of vacant pious brown study before a service, attempting to muster up the proper degree of contemplative spirit, and realizing that I should do better to follow Phillips Brooks' lead and hunt up a half dozen children to play horse or bear. Those moments of attempted recollection are apt to be too self-conscious to be genuine. What is needed is a simple and honest touch of the world outside, to give a few moments later to the world inside, its naturalness and felt piety.
>
> The permanent health of the soul, then lies in keeping the two lives and worlds, the inner and outer in some kind of close and constant relation. One rather than the other will be our native approach and that must be trusted to carry us as far as it will. But since it will not take us all the way we must supplement its insights by conscious acts of discipline in the other field. By such a life we come at least within sight of the mature conviction that "To Work is to Pray and to Pray is to Work."[81]

Where liberal Protestantism missed the mark, according to Sperry's sequel lecture called "Christian Prayer," is in its predominant temper that prayer "is a device for improving ourselves, for giving life fuller and better self-expression." That is one of the expected consequences of prayer, but not "from the Biblical standpoint, the occasion for prayer in the first instance." Sperry claimed that all of this "is a matter of nuances, of subtle emphases rather than of exact definition," but cast in the overall terms of "some modern loyalty and program" prayer "is a concern for God's plan for the world" more than for one's own tangible self-improvement:

> It is of course a desire to so order our lives that they may conform to that plan. But since our human powers are limited, it is also a passionate desire that, whether with our help or without it, God's great plan may go forward. There's a work to be done in history, a purpose to be expressed, an end to

be realized. Prayer is in the prophetic sense our human concern that history shall not be frustrated, that civilization shall issue in the Kingdom of God.[82]

As to the nature of preaching Sperry broke no new ground, except perhaps in conceiving the sermon as a particular vehicle for Christian apologetics to reach the world outside the church. In mediating religion to art and science respectively and to each other as secular counterparts, the sermon took on for Sperry a literary form with a definite, if unconventional, part to play in American culture. From inside the church, the relationship of preaching to worship must be more "didactic than the preaching of the past. Perhaps the sermon should never cease to be a vehicle for teaching." Further, explained Sperry, "the sermon is part of a service of worship, not something appended to the service as a prolonged after-thought."[83]

Sperry shared some of these somewhat contrary notions about preaching, contrary from the usual liberal Protestant perspective, with a companion college chaplain, Yale's Elmore M. McKee:

> My experiences as a college preacher have persuaded me that the service of worship in the college chapel is as important, or more important than the sermon, and that we ought to be giving some consideration to the question of the ideal kind of service for college chapels...[84]

These convictions that "good preaching is more important today than great preaching"[85] for the edification of the church, did not keep Sperry off the celebrated national preaching circuit of the 1930s, nor did it stop him from inviting to Memorial Church famous pulpiteers like Fosdick and Niebuhr. That Sperry noted a decline in the pulpit's prestige would not be especially significant from the outside, as the church and the ministry were subjected to constant journalistic iconoclasm, except that Sperry observed a trend too subtle but for an insider to notice. In his Lyman Beecher Lectures of 1938 at Yale, he said:

> A strong feeling for sacraments is characteristic of persons and societies mature enough to have outgrown the hope of ever putting their faith into verbal formulas. All such prefer to have spiritual realities intimated by symbols rather than mutilated by words. A kindred preference for symbolism is found among those whose interests are predominantly aesthetic, or whose daily life is so much a matter of signs that the sacrament is religiously more congenial than anything spoken from a pulpit.

For the sermon to be a present means and help at interpretation, prior to its potential by-product of inspiration, "the preacher's true task might be defined as a response to the trite demand of the gospel hymn, 'Tell me the old, old story'." Consequently, Sperry recommended that it is wise for the craft of preaching to begin and to continue with "the candid admission that sermons cannot be permanently unpatterned utterances." Like an order of worship in which context a sermon flourishes and depends for "survival value," it cannot stand insincerity and it cannot neglect the pattern of which it is part. Sperry maintains that a sermon cannot stand alone nor carry more than its own weight of what worship intends because such conscious artifice not only carries within it "an ineradicable germ of insincerity,"[86] but also the guarantee that confidence in a preacher is subtly and finally destroyed. Sperry did not deliberately overload his expectations of what a sermon must convey, though in practice "he put into one sermon what would have served many a man for three."[87]

While Sperry's ideal sermon was "less formal, more simple and direct, than that of a generation ago," he was himself most conscientious about the task of preaching responsibly "to living men and women where they are as they are." The form of the sermon should be simple and understandable, but its substance, in the words of Alfred North Whitehead, must "render to popular understanding some eternal greatness in the passage of temporal fact." And to achieve that end "the theory that a sermon which we find it easy to hear has been easy to prepare is false."[88]

Moving from theory to praxis, the best of Sperry's own sermons carried a single metaphor all the way through to fix a controlling image in the listener's mind. He was particularly fond of images from the sea— a coast line, a narrow strait, a passenger ship, a storm at mid-voyage (cf. *Rebuilding Our World*, 1943). Several years before delivering his Beecher Lectures on preaching, Sperry had been invited by Joseph Fort Newton to submit a chapter on sermon preparation for a book entitled, *If I Had Only One Sermon to Prepare* (1932). He was a manuscript preacher, often working over a draft two or three times until it had "direction and continuity." He made known his purpose, stylistic preferences and methodology in his contribution called "Priestly Preaching":

> In general I conceive of preaching under modern conditions as being a kind of experimental thinking-out-loud for the puzzled people in the pews. I do not believe in preaching at people, hardly in preaching to them. I believe in preaching with them and for them. By a kind of paradox, I think that much modern preaching is therefore priestly rather than prophetic.[89]

In preparing a sermon for delivery Sperry went on to say that such sermons which are most satisfactory are generally suggested by some concrete sight or fact. The worst form of the medium is the sermon which begins from an abstract idea and then finds illustrations to defend it. In Sperry's view the better sermons always develop as a metaphorical truth drawn from some aspect of nature, or some human situation which can be universalized. Sperry advised that a pictorial statement of the metaphor begin a sermon, but must be sustained throughout the text. He warned, in addition, that "the fact suggesting the metaphor shall have been clearly seen and deeply felt."

He also recalled how his mind worked inductively at the task of writing sermons. Never able to make a full outline in advance, for fear of assembling something mechanical, Sperry would start thinking and writing with a general idea of his point of arrival, but with no clear notion just how he would get there.

Sperry declared that his intention as a mature preacher, having been at the craft for twenty-five years, was to preach for people which stood in slight contrast to Fosdick's admitted motivation of "preaching for a decision." The difference between them at this point is perhaps that found between two forms of persuasion—description and dialectic, one seeking resonance, the other metanoia. Sperry explained that his final conviction about a sermon is that preaching is not "a direct product, but a by-product of one's own inner history." Put differently, a sermon is the result of what spills over from a brimming cup, and is not something dipped out of a tepid reservoir. Over a course of twenty years Sperry came to realize that it is foolish to make life a business of preparing to preach, but rather it is best to live in the world and then incidentally preach to both purge the system of ideas and to help people who find themselves in similar need and perplexity. Sperry recommended his method because there is an enormous gap "between the sermon which aloofly says it to them and the sermon which sympathetically says if for them."[90]

Sperry communicated best what he believed the challenge of preaching to be (as "the most characteristic and individual" of a minister's public acts) in a frank letter to his sister in the late 1930s:

> If you want my job preaching the Christian religion as an already proven matter-of-fact you can have it. I never had so puzzling a time in which to try to preach, and yet never one when it seemed so worth while to try to

talk long range common sense—which I think a fair definition of Christianity. It is common sense, but it is never a "close-up" common sense.[91]

To understand how Sperry chose to contribute his intellect to public
theology, to sample the various fruits of his thinking is to discover also a
person who defies ready classification, except in how he lived, served and
thought inside the church. Outside of that context he makes no sense to the
academic world in which he dwelled for most of his adult life. Moreover,
he does not always fit the "religious" times of his day in which he is doing
his most creative work. Disseminating "long range common sense" rather
than applying his mind to some specific scholarly problem, person, method
or tradition was a close-up commitment which superseded his depth of
knowledge and his lifelong hunger for learning.

The attraction Sperry held for "long range common sense" as opposed
to a more technical field has raised questions about Sperry's own form
being significant. His wife was known to be his sternest critic, not letting
him get away with any sloppy thinking whatsoever. And, in spite of "a
fierce quick temper and a sharp tongue, which made her enemies,"[92] he
valued her judgments enormously, dedicating his last book "To Muriel B.
Sperry, My favorite Critic, Generous, Just and Always Affectionate."
Muriel, nonetheless, according to the Sperrys' daughter, Lady Henrietta
Wilson, "in the last years at Harvard... upbraided him, unfairly, for not
being a scholar. This he bore without remark or riposte."[93]

Others have expressed similar disappointment in Sperry's career. Paul
Kuntz has wondered, "Was Sperry a tragic character?" Was he "a man of
superb natural talents who had wasted his time on Protestant liberal
theological themes?"[94] In part Sperry represents the larger liberal disposition in revolt against scholastic and exact systematic exploration of theory
or dogma, but he carried this work of common sense to a far more sophisticated level than what other liberals collectively were capable of attaining,
except those outside the church, if Walter Lippmann, for instance, can be
called a companion and kindred spirit of the late 1920s. On this minor note
of comparison, Sperry had thought favorably of Lippmann's controversial
work *A Preface to Morals* (1929) and expressed his approbation in the *The
Yale Review* for which Lippmann was grateful and even made known his
appreciation to the Dean. Sperry once said of Lippmann, "As I understand
humanism he is not a humanist at all, but belongs with the mystics who
were very often frankly agnostic up to a point." Unlike Harry Emerson

Fosdick, Sperry accepted Lippmann's "humanistic" orientation and criticism of liberal Protestantism, because Lippmann also respected significant and objective form in the practice of piety.[95]

Of course, the premise of Kuntz's question is disputable, if not plainly wrong, because it deals with a hypothetical issue of what Sperry would have been had he not worked from the "inside" to improve the rhetorical and popular position of liberal Protestantism. It is true that he dealt with many "big messy topics" (Kuntz's description) such as worship, but as Kuntz realizes in the midst of his puzzlement, Sperry "had an idea that the layman had to be served. It was the man and woman in the pew who had to be helped through life and death. This was a responsibility a professor no longer satisfied."[96]

Sperry's career at Harvard was very much awake and alive to the criticisms fairly passed upon the corporate life and thought of the Church at the time. There were discrepancies and perils which he tried to overcome and bridge in bringing Jerusalem and Athens closer together in his work, but to abandon one for the other was to run the deep narrow rut of professional singularity, a contradiction in moral terms, if not the nature of his personality and thought. This seemed so to him because the ultimate purity of the gospel idea also depends on the "imperfectly irreligious" to succeed. Here then is a great paradox, to which Sperry was loyal, never haughty, but loyal in the way Royce meant loyalty, loyalty that transcends "lost causes."[97] In comprehending Sperry's ostensibly misapplied talents, the internal evidence is most convincing as to why he remained inside the church even while the door was left open, "an effectual," for him to leave:

> I have greater respect for the Christian religion than I ever had before. There must be something to it or it would not survive the treatment of mixed sentimentality and assumed omniscience that it gets at the hands of its most famous public interpreters![98]

CHAPTER 5

Outside the Church

The knowledge both of the Poet and the Man of science is
pleasure.... Poetry is the breath and finer spirit of all knowledge; it
is the impassioned expression which is in the countenance of all
science.
—William Wordsworth[1]

Fresh Sources Of Calvinism

James Luther Adams, the Unitarian theologian who taught at Harvard Divinity School for more than ten years until 1968, recalls a story that Dean Sperry used to tell about his first evening at the graduate school in Yale in the fall of 1907. For his dinner Sperry went to the Common Room, and at the table he was joined by a stranger sitting by his side. Upholding the customary social graces of the long table, Sperry began the conversation in a friendly manner, saying to his dinner companion and fellow student, "My field is New Testament Greek, what is yours?" The stranger replied, "Mine is mathematics." Thereupon the conversation abruptly and quietly ebbed.[2]

In Sperry's theological career the episode took on symbolic meaning, for the general situation that existed outside the church was a perplexing culture highly charged with impulses from literature and science. Sperry lamented not only the separation of the sciences from the humanities, and not only abhorred the segregated expertise that prevented communication, but he himself turned to those very areas of specialized thought with an admiration tempered by a dilettante's humility, for what they could teach theology.

This move was not a peace offering, nor was it any kind of concession acknowledging the superiority of an outside discipline. Rather, Sperry sought understanding, if not intellectual unity, at a time when "most of us are unable to believe that our religion can hold out indefinitely against the siege of scientific realism." Born in the same year that Charles Darwin died, Sperry's childhood and youth paralleled the birth of a wholly scientific age and by the 1920s he had long realized that "many an American Galileo may

151

recant before the change comes, but even in his recantation he knows that the traditional theory of God 'moves for all that'."[3]

Writing for *The Yale Review* in 1928 Sperry recognized and identified a serious bifurcation in modern religion and culture whereby people "are eager for new knowledge when it supplements their interests and augments their comforts," but "they are not habitually eager for new knowledge which compels them to reconsider the very axioms of their living." Sperry went on to emphasize that "nevertheless, a doctrine of God adequate to the cosmic facts and to vindicated processes in nature and history is now in the making."[4] The implication is that theology will indeed be left behind so long as it ignores the major intellectual and creative activities of the day. Despite the cold shoulder that the budding mathematician turned to the novice theologian at dinner, Sperry carried no hard feelings because he thought modern religion must face the task of arriving at its doctrines, particularly the doctrine of human nature, "derived from biology, history, psychology, and the social sciences." The solution, Sperry asserted, "no longer lies with either the Puritan or the pagan but with the more dispassionate person whom we know as the man of science."[5]

Since those doctrines of God and human nature were in the making anyway (or the "remaking" in the philosopher William Ernest Hocking's phrase) Sperry insisted to a church audience that some of the best help in thinking out these theological issues and "axioms" of living will be found outside the church. To his way of thinking the years after the Great War were no time to remain an isolated church "insider," culturally provincial. In the backwash of war, the Fundamentalist challenge and the frequent retreat to sentimentality of mainline Protestants, Sperry was convinced by the early 1920s that ministers needed the help of secular thinkers in ridding themselves of their illusions. He sympathized with much "unchurched idealism" because it became apparent to him that "Romanticism and its bastard child Sentimentalism" had decayed beyond recognition or recall. Sperry pronounced that the majestic nineteenth century romantic movement, having displayed its Victorian vigor, had by 1914, if not sooner, begun "to putrefy" into decadence—in a crashing descent from Wordsworth to Oscar Wilde. And yet, maintained Sperry, "the wholesome prophetic spirit" of humanity was once again reasserting itself, "struggling to escape from the enervating and fundamentally vicious influence of a decadent Romanticism." The reassertion "from the rebel realists of life and letters," however, was coming from outside the church.[6]

Sperry struck the posture of a liberal self-critic whose deeper attitude was reflected in the prescient observation that "it is not the flood tide of familiar ecclesiastical apologetic which interests serious-minded men and women to-day, no matter whether they be inside or outside the Church." Sperry boldly declared his suspicions of those who were jealous of the "unecclesiastical quarters." Rather, he confessed, "It is still hard for the church mind to believe that any good can come out of these Galilees and Nazareths. The theologian scents the minor heresy of the novelist, the dramatist, the radical. He misses their major passion for a new world."[7]

Sperry argued that the most notable developments of religious life in the years after 1914 were the utterances of the unchurched mind concerning the message of Jesus. The thoughts of George Bernard Shaw and H. G. Wells "are far more significant signs of the religious times than the cumuli of conventional apologetic always piled up in the heaven by the trade winds of habitual ecclesiasticism." People, normally unattached to the church, such as "free-lance" philosophers, turned "to the gospel of Galilee with a renewed interest because the gospel of Manchester has proved such a shabby substitute." Further, "this desire of the modern mind to see Jesus has its origins in no academic or ecclesiastical interest, but in the sorrows, the frustration, the perplexity of the present hour."[8]

The problem which faced the modern church, according to Sperry, was "to find the equivalent forms of the agonized conscience of Calvinism in the thought of our own time." In so far as these forms of expression were evident, Sperry believed that "the true successors to the Calvinist... are to be found among the biologists, the psychologists, the novelists and the dramatists."[9]

Scientists such as Thomas H. Huxley and literary figures such as George Bernard Shaw were invaluable sources outside the church, whom church insiders dismissed at their own peril, in Sperry's estimation. Sperry recognized that Shaw, for instance, "is the last of the moderns whom we should suspect of being enmeshed in the cobwebs of a dogmatic system or committed to a professional apologia for Christianity, yet this same heretical Irishman... is essentially a spokesman for the ethical realism of the Calvinist outlook on life."[10]

In Sperry's first major theological book, *The Disciplines of Liberty* (1921), Shaw's serious morality plays, *Major Barbara, Androcles and the Lion, Widower's House* and *Mrs. Warren's Profession* are discussed at considerable length because Shaw "forces us in these plays into the dilemma where he can wheel about upon us and say,'Thou art the man!' "[11]

Sperry devoted equal attention to "perhaps the most important and epoch-making utterance in the realm of biological science since Darwin's *Origin of Species*," Thomas Huxley's *Romanes Lectures on Evolution and Ethics*, given at Oxford in 1893. While it was a series of addresses delivered a full generation before Sperry flourished, he regarded Huxley as "before his time," able to turn "state's evidence against the overhopeful ethical deductions drawn by [Herbert] Spencer [*First Principles*] and John Fiske [*The Ascent of Man*] and Henry Drummond [*The Natural Law in the Spiritual World*] from the theory of natural selection."[12]

On this point about Huxley Sperry hooks up informally with the tail-end of the post-Darwinian controversies and the Protestant reactions to science's intellectual and cultural prominence. Sperry's own rhetoric about religion holding out "against the siege of scientific realism" continues the military metaphor which has often created the conflict between religion and science where little or none actually existed. Huxley, in particular, perhaps unbeknownst to Sperry, was largely responsible for the provocative imagery of warfare which persisted well past his time in historical interpretation. James R. Moore in a complex and brilliant study, *The Post-Darwinian Controversies* (1979) which traces the Protestant struggle to come to terms with Darwin in Great Britain and America between 1870 and 1900, argues convincingly that not only was Huxley "the arch-antagonist of faith and certainly one of the most colorful contributors to the Victorian 'conflict' between science and religion," but "his irrepressible onslaught is rather a deception." Moore adds epigrammatically, "Too easily historians and contemporaries alike have mistaken the prominent for the prevalent and the outspoken for the ordinary."

Sperry probably overestimated the importance of Huxley's "epoch-making utterance." His "Huxley," derived from a popular image, is not the same as the "Huxley" of Moore's revisionism. The Huxley of the warrior motif, according to Moore, was something of a fallacy. That Huxley commanded an "army of science" was "thoroughly misleading," in Moore's view: "A dispute is not comprehended merely when one has heard from its loudest or its least learned partisans, entertaining though it may be."[13] If Sperry felt that religion and science were still at war it was a passing fancy directly traceable, like the many errant assumptions in the post-Darwinian controversies, to a variety of Huxley's polemical discharges, having to do more with stylized zealotry than an indication of another major battle forming between faith and reason.

Sperry also makes the claim that "the significance of the Romanes Lecture for the religious thinker lies in the fact that it aligned Huxley with Calvinism, and that he knew it and was content to stand there." In other words, Sperry made of Huxley a Christian apologist who "felt that the science of biology had revealed in some new and terrible way the moral liability of every child of man, a liability reaching back of the mythical Garden of Eden..."[14] This interpretation now requires the warning and revision of recent historical discernments.

That Huxley, according to Moore, frequently fell victim to his own passions meant that his later followers most likely did, too, which goes far to explain how Sperry at first needed to "see" Protestant doctrine masked as secular science. It was simply more exciting than the impassioned, but dated Enfield sermon of Jonathan Edwards. As one scholar has stated the comparison, "it is not surprising that [Huxley's] language again and again suggests the stark words of the old Puritans."[15] This parallel alone, although misleading, held enormous appeal to the seekers of an intellectually rejuvenated Protestantism such as that of Willard Sperry. In partially projecting a theological agenda upon the verbal pyrotechnics of Huxley, Sperry was lucky not to have severely burned his fingers. His use of Huxley might be considered dangerous on at least two points.

First, as James R. Moore asserts, "the military metaphor [with which Huxley is associated] must be abandoned by those who wish to achieve historical understanding." Moore demonstrates that the martial imagery was a fabrication and short-lived. He uses, instead, Leon Festinger's model (1959) of cognitive dissonance to interpret the actual course of conflict resolution in the post-Darwinian controversy. By identifying the "cognitive elements" of conflict, decision, dissonance and dissonance resolution, Moore urges the historian's avoidance of labeling negative reactions to Huxley "vulgar" anti-Darwinianism.[16]

Whatever initial dissonance he may have felt toward science (the result of perceived tension between theology and materialism), Sperry eventually softened his tone, perhaps unconsciously (after all, he studied biology in college), to more amicable approaches than the image of a "siege," thus confirming Moore's thesis that Huxley was at most a weekend warrior who also, and more importanly, represented the theological affinities of Darwinism. Much of Sperry's mature writing on the relationship of religion and science abandoned the idea of martial conflict between them. Rather, science when "pure" was a paradigm of discipline for religion to follow, at least up to a point, and to the extent of implying that religion needed the critical tools of science to uphold its intellectual integrity.

The second problem Sperry skirted, though coming close to the edge of it, was the expectation that "scientists surely were not free to be scientists without being at least amateur theologians."[17] This added scientific function of prophesy, if continued beyond the turn of the century, would have been disastrous for theology, thereby oversimplifying the whole doctrine in the modern age with metaphors drawn from the mechanical and materialistic thinking of the field and laboratory. Sperry never transferred the responsibility of theology to the amateurs, even though in his opinion some of the best minds of the day were in the sciences.

Sperry, however, was right in viewing Huxley as an intercessor of "scientific Calvinism" and if he had made of Huxley a defender of scientific liberalism he would have been wrong. Sperry quotes a passage from Huxley writing to a friend which James R. Moore has, coincidentally, also excerpted:

> It is the superiority of the best theological teachers to the majority of their opponents that they substantially recognize the reality of things, however strange the forms in which they clothe their conceptions. The doctrines of predestination, original sin, of the innate depravity of man and the evil fate of the greater part of the race, of the primacy of Satan in this world, of the essential vileness of matter appear to me vastly nearer the truth than the liberal popular illusion that babies are all born good, that is given to everybody to realize his ethical ideal if he will only try, that all partial evil is universal good and other optimistic figments which bid us believe that everything will come right at the last.[18]

As Sperry undoubtedly realized, Huxley's words may not have been pure orthodoxy, but they were by no means representative of liberalism as Sperry's generation had inherited it from the late nineteenth century. As Moore states emphatically, "If Huxley... had anything to say, there could be little doubt as to what kind of theology was best equipped to come to terms with Darwin."[19] Darwin, and thus Huxley, were not compatible with liberalism of the romantic period. The kind of liberalism Sperry attacked was indeed in the same form which Huxley in his day had also opposed. As Daniel Day Williams points out in his *The Andover Liberals: A Study in American Theology* (1941), "Darwinism applied to human life might have been made the basis of a radical Calvinism or other theology of human sin."[20] This is exactly what Huxley proposed and Sperry accepted in the 1920s. Williams goes on to say just before American involvement in World War II, that "the liberals tended to forget Darwinism, and to use the idea of evolution as an undergirding idea of progress in which emphasis is not upon human failure, but upon an increasing human achievement of moral worth." Furthermore, Williams says, "Many of the present difficulties of liberalism are explainable by the fact that in the nineteenth century special theories of development were accepted as final which have later had doubt thrown upon them or have been rejected altogether."[21]

Some liberal theologians such as Harvard's Dean Sperry were spared this embarrassing reversal of fortune because they did not "cut themselves off from Darwin's world and from resources by which, if Darwinism were true, it could be kept a Christian world."[22] Because Sperry went outside the church to sources such as Huxley he maintained a liberalism that did not finally resort to neo-orthodoxy at a time when a deeper realism was recommended for a Protestantism, which if simply "left to the devices of modernity" was captive to "concepts of divine immanence, human goodness, and social religious progress, only to have evolutionary speculations... undermined by future turn of events."[23] In identifying Sperry's voice in the clamor of theological contention, it is most significant that he saw himself as a "tough- minded" liberal who did not need Barth to correct his cultural and "scientific" waywardness. In reaching towards Wordsworth later, his tough-mindedness would yet be stamped upon him, notwithstanding the paradox of his renewed liberal sentimentality.

Secular Models of Theology
Sperry justified and made valid the necessity for turning toward "theological" sources outside the church in at least three particular ways. While the general body of English literature, such as poetry, novels and plays may be viewed as outside the church proper, it is a corpus not as far

outside as science. For that reason the church insiders have usually recognized literature to be more embraceable than science. Sperry has been in his own time and since rightly assessed as an excellent judge of the theological value contained in literary sources. He was, for example, invited to join the prestigious committee of scholars assembled by Yale's Luther A. Weigle charged to produce the *Revised Standard Version of the Bible* as a consultant on English literary and stylistic matters.

What sets him apart from many others inside the church, who were also well informed on matters of prose and verse, was his additional willingness to grant science an equal channel of influence as modern culture washed over and poured into, rather than out of the life and the mind of the church. In Sperry's view, "this old idea of the selfless love of God finds its best modern exemplar in the scientist's unmercenary love of Truth. This is the major contribution of the scientific spirit to contemporary Christianity... In this respect," opines Sperry, "modern science stands in sharp contrast to the self-regarding and generally mercenary spirit of much of our apologia for present-day Christianity."[24]

The first among the three reasons for Sperry feeling this way about the merits of science *vis-à-vis* the church, is theological. Sperry's central premise in the making of doctrine is that method must come before results. If the method of thought is trustworthy, then the eventual conclusion will be, too. For Sperry the experimental quality of Protestantism distinguished it from any other form of religion that emphasized the authority and infallibility of its conclusions. This did not mean that the community of interest shared by science and religion required at any given moment in their individual histories either consensus or hegemony. Instead, the liberal tradition in religion, "whatever its denomination, is primarily a matter of method rather than of results. Liberalism is confidence in a way of thinking," wrote Sperry in 1935, "and not an advance determination to arrive at predetermined findings. It believes that no important result can be reached by wrong or vicious methods; hence its initial concern for the ways in which we think and act."[25]

Sperry found rich religious meaning in the quality of spirit which Huxley once described in his famous correspondence with Charles Kingsley:

> Science seems to me to teach in the highest and strangest manner the great truth which is embodied in the Christian conception of entire surrender to

the will of God. Sit down before facts as a little child, be prepared to give up every preconceived notion follow humbly wherever and to whatever abysses nature leads or you shall learn nothing.[26]

Along the lines of Huxley's scientific approach to a problem, Sperry as a theologian peeked over the wall to find exhibited therein on the other side a selfless love of truth and an almost childlike humility so that "in the quality of scientific thinking at its best," there is "a strong strain of real saintliness," comparable to any personality met in Christian hagiography. Sperry was an exceptional churchman in noting that there "are indubitable signs of religion... to be found in modern science perhaps more clearly than in modern ecclesiasticism."[27] Religion cannot become the exclusive property of a narrowly sectarian church, but quite as likely belongs in the laboratory as anywhere else.

Sperry would not lose his grip on the point while risking controversy, but tightened it in the face of counterargument from the early 1920s through the 1930s. At a time when sharp divisions were being drawn between Christ and culture, the sacred and the profane, church life and secular society, Sperry found the mystical spirit, wanting in popular religion, in an unlikely place. He said, whether we like to admit it or not, "we have looked to science to contribute to religion a mystical correction."

The source of these convictions can be traced to Sperry's intimate exposure to Anglican liberalism at Oxford right at the peak of the Victorian Platonic revival. Benjamin Jowett, his colleagues and his successors at Oxford, "for almost three intellectual generations," ascribed to Plato the role of the best non-Christian philosopher to have asserted the necessity for positing the presence of unseen entities or forces without which this world and all that lives in it would lack meaning or perhaps existence. As Frank M. Turner points out in *The Greek Heritage in Victorian Britain* (1981), Anglo-Catholic philosophy in the early twentieth century "transformed the *Republic* into a Hellenic *Pilgrim's Progress*." This prophetic interpretation of the *Republic* in mainstream British Christianity and among university intellectuals became "sufficiently liberal, free of bibliolatry and concern with personal sin, and imbued with a concept of divine immanence to be seriously and philosophically equated with Platonism." This was the undergirding placement, for instance, of William Temple's incarnationalism (he had studied with Edward Caird, an important Plato revivalist) and much of the renewed emphasis on mystical components of Christianity.

Not only was Plato used to inculcate a new sense of moral duty (i.e., the Idea of the Good) leading to social justice and reform, but he was also supplying the deeper intellectual reserve justifying religious experience that included mystical focus.[28] On these grounds of British Platonism Sperry rooted his whole premise connecting scientific discovery with the qualities of mysticism. Just as Plato was willing to exclude poets from the Republic, Sperry was unwilling to exclude scientists from the Kingdom.

Sperry argued consistently for more than twenty years that

> at least one of the vital and contemporary equivalents of medieval mysticism, which remains a signal achievement of religion, has been the modern research laboratory. The material employed has been different, but the moral method followed has been the same. The quality of thinking required for pure scientific research is not peculiar to science and peripheral with religion. It is central for all religion which is mystically-minded, it is the moral will to put self-vindication out of the picture, to lose oneself in the objective reality.

> In this sense of the word science at its level best has often manifested a spiritual excellence which popular religion has lacked.[29]

The second reason which Sperry supported for turning to sources outside the church, in order to fortify religious thought in broad terms, was historical. One must recall that Sperry stood in a long line of succession to the New England theology. His first theological instincts were projected backwards to a Calvinism straining forward in a fading, winding path from long ago. Instead of continuity with a theological tradition, Sperry had to break out of that refracted projection, because Calvinism was in a state of discontinuity with American Protestantism by the time it reached Sperry in the early twentieth century.

Bruce Kuklick notes in *Churchmen and Philosophers* (1985) that "the collapse of Calvinist theology was merely the last and least consequential of a series of events... and these events were rooted in a decisive social, as opposed to intellectual, transformation." Kuklick advances the argument that "the substance of religion changed earlier... as a response to industrialization and urbanization. Theology was simply the ideological husk of religion."[30] As a consequence, philosophy triumphed over theology in America from the late nineteenth century to the 1930s, which is the major point of Kuklick's book. The path from Jonathan Edwards to John Dewey represents a shift in primacy from theology to philosophy that was in some measure irrevocable, except for "the revitalized theology of the period inspired by Richard and Reinhold Niebuhr and Paul Tillich."[31]

While John Dewey "offered powerful arguments for the superiority of the scientific credo," Reinhold Niebuhr "urged that the reliance on science was naive; and to some Dewey was incautiously hopeful about the sciences of man."[32] Within the community of celebrated religious thinkers, Sperry took decidedly the minority position and sided with Dewey on the ultimate efficacy of scientific method. Quoting Ralph Barton Perry's *Present Conflict of Ideals* (1918), which shared Dewey's vision, Sperry believed that "scientific method has come, therefore, to signify a respect of facts, in the sense of that which is independent of all human wishes. It has come to signify a conforming of judgement to things as they are, regardless of likes and dislikes, hopes or fears..."[33] It stands to reason, therefore, that Sperry, according to James Ward Smith, would be willing to "de-theologize Christianity," in order to accentuate Christianity as a quality of life rather than a fixed system of doctrine. This was in keeping with the kindred spirit of modern science.[34]

Kuklick supposes that "Niebuhr was a successful theological counter-revolutionary who defended the symbols of Calvinism," but who nonetheless "also believed in a mysterious and transcendent God whose purposes were controlling." The "ineradicable" conflict, therefore, that Niebuhr pinned on Dewey's advocacy of scientific instrumentalism had to do "with the sentimentally optimistic belief that science could trust society's spiritual dilemmas." These symptoms of an intellectual crisis and the transformation of American thought, however, have too often in the historical interpretation assumed Niebuhr's continuity with Jonathan Edwards and underestimated the continuities of Dewey's position.[35] Kuklick implies that Niebuhr's connection with an American theological tradition is more figurative than substantive. And on this latter point what needs to be stressed here is that Willard Sperry turned to scientific method for the same reason Niebuhr turned away from it—to protect Calvinism from being totally obliterated from religious consciousness.

Sperry, in fact, opposed what Niebuhr had criticized in Dewey. After the publication of *Moral Man and Immoral Society* (1932) and Dewey's retort, *A Common Faith* (1934), Sperry staked out a position much closer to the philosopher than the theologian. Sperry did not acquiesce to the fashionable winds of trade blowing in from the Continent, knowing full

well "that most of the recent and more arresting movements in theology...
have wittingly abandoned the liberal premise, and are determinately illiberal." Sperry is quite specific in his concern that "the Barthian movement
in Germany, and the wider tendencies which it represents in other lands,
are seeking to universalize religion by divorcing it from secularism, and by
departmentalizing it."[36] For Sperry neo-orthodoxy was breaking faith with
its Calvinist heritage which scientific method could protect better than
merely preserving, as a theologically counter-revolutionary action, the
symbols of Calvinism. In a way, therefore, Sperry's position conflated the
method of Dewey with the sensibility of Niebuhr.

In the early 1920s Sperry looked outside the church to defend what was
left on the inside after a period of searing self-doubt: "The problem which
faces the modern preacher who still has a message of salvation and redemp-
tion to preach to the world is to find the equivalent forms of the agonized
conscience of Calvinism in the thought of our own time."[37] Kuklick's
conclusion after analyzing the problem is not only in keeping with Sperry's
modernism, but using Dewey as the vehicle it demonstrates a continuity
with the New England theology from which Sperry is intellectually and
temperamentally derived, and to which he is also doggedly loyal. Kuklick,
in effect, paraphrases Sperry in writing, "If we give up the scientific method
in human affairs, we leave decisions to habit, authority or chance. Unless
we do nothing, what alternative do we have to the patient and systematic
investigation of phenomena and the exploration of causes and consequences?"[38]

Third, Sperry looked outside the church for apologetic reasons which
seemed to belie the internal weaknesses that only other venues of thought
and discipline could repair and sustain. He considered, in particular, the
growing debility of the pulpit as a sign of an apologetic crisis. He proposed
that exemplary lives and model ideas outside the church might remedy and
rehabilitate the troubled pulpit better than anything inside the church. Not
only in his writing, but also in his preaching, Sperry complained of the gap
between modern intellectual standards and the existing state of Christian
apologetics. In a sermon preached at King's Chapel in Boston during the
winter of 1930, Sperry admonished current standards of preaching and
prayers for "how careless and inexact most of our religious talk is." He
painfully recollected,

President Tucker of Dartmouth used to say that given two men of equal ability, one of whom went into the law and the other into the ministry, at the end of twenty years the lawyer would probably be the stronger man, for the reason that the minister's arguments were never criticized to his face, while the lawyer had to face searching criticism of his facts, his citations and his argument every time he went into court.[39]

What Sperry thought to be a worthy pursuit of both ministers and congregations was the hunt for "the power of self-criticism." The important part of a faith to be learned outside the church was to avoid looking only at the favorable aspects of one's work and thought, for if that side of things is the only view taken, then self-deception, the worst of all deceptions, is the natural consequence. General religion, in Sperry's opinion, cannot afford "its habitual neglect" of precisely that quality of mind and character which is the core of the scientist's life. Sperry's strong feelings are summarized by a pointed remark from his sermon that "religion, of course, operates in an area where emotions are employed and where feelings run high. Religion is at present more like politics than science, at least in its popular manifestations. But the religion of the future will have to be less like politics and more like science, if it is to command men's respect."[40]

Sperry was disturbed by two complementary circumstances which indicated a serious problem in modern Protestant apologetics. First, he stated late in his career to a largely British audience that "the liberal churches, at least in America, have not been conspicuously successful in enlisting the support of our scientists. They are puzzled by their failure to do so." He offered an explanation about the failure, being "due to the discrepancy between the romanticism of the non-orthodox churches and the reservations which the sciences of biology and psychology have as to the inherent excellence of human nature."[41]

At other and earlier times, Sperry's explanation specified not just how science reacted to religion, creating the first bothersome condition of being at odds, but secondly, how cavalier and sloppy ministers were in the face of scientific example and method. In the early 1920s Sperry asked, "How often does one meet in the modern preacher these outstanding qualities of the scientific mind?" He unabashedly decried "the sorry heritage of the traditional 'apologetic' temper in the pulpit," which "makes most preachers mere eclectic observers of fact and incident, gathering together out of the vast chaos of things... without the austere fearlessness and candor of the scientific mind."[42] Sperry emphatically recommended that "we need in the Christian pulpit to-day a full and candid use of all that modern science and modern literature have done to restate" the historic theological doctrines "in intelligible and credible terms."[43]

Nearly twenty years later in his Beecher Lectures at Yale, he lamented much the same thing, telling his audience, "I suspect that they [artists and scientists] are discouraged about church-going because, on their occasional visits to churches, they do not meet in the person of the preacher a mind of precision equal to their own. They do not expect to find an identical mind; they do wish to recognize a kindred mind."[44]

Sperry not only gave preliminary and broad consideration to his proposed remedy drawing from external prescriptions, but explored philosophically the whole proposition of apologetics using the conveyances of science and poetry; or put differently, he tested the theory that thought existing independent of the church might rescue the efficacy of apologetics in the making and the defending of doctrine. Sperry's work on themes outside the church had a purpose. By improving the quality of apologetics, borrowing from the models of scientific reason and poetic insight, Sperry came, over the course of his career, full circle back to two important and difficult doctrines, namely, the Christological idea and immortality.

❧

Contra Accommodation

Writing for *The Atlantic Monthly* in 1924 at the request of the venerable Ellery Sedgwick, who was still using various authors perceived to be from the Protestant elites, Sperry conceived that the chief cultural dilemma of the day was "that far too much is done for us by the pioneers in the natural sciences and far too little is asked of us by way of cooperative creation." For religion, "once the inherent necessity for interpretation is allowed, the occasion for creation is present and the joy of the creator is known." How to use the method and the findings of scientific criticism as occasions for creation is the modern test of a credible religion. And until its house of the Interpreter was put in order, "liberalism must grapple with the cultural menace of life forever on the side lines before it finds itself."[45]

The deeper problem of interpretation, which, once resolved, leads to the desirable occasion of "creation," was for Sperry traceable to a certain German theologian of the mid-eighteenth century, Johann Semler, whom Albert Schweitzer called "the father of the 'yes, but' theology." The devious mental process of the formula, "yes, but-," is carried down to the twentieth century whenever religion, because of some growing discrepancy with culture, must accommodate itself to new knowledge or else become anachronistic. The necessary periodic restatement of religion may not fully impair the faith which is old, but the cumulative effect is never satisfactory, "since there lingers about it a hint of casuistry in the process and of compromise in the conclusion. The religious mind does not like to qualify its beliefs and the scientific mind does not care to qualify its truths."[46]

In terms of conscious standing in the modern world religion is more likely than not to become a second-class citizen because, as Sperry perceives, "the new ideas, which religion admits after a long period of timidity, have been for years the commonplaces of knowledge, and the outside world does not see that religion deserves any credit for grudgingly conceding at a late date truths which it should have gladly welcomed from the first."[47]

William R. Hutchison has formulated several criteria to define modernism which came to mean "first and most visibly... the conscious, intended adaptation of religious ideas to modern culture."[48] Evidence abounds that this was so. Hutchison may also be correct in concluding that "adaptationism and the sense of divine immanence. . . remain with us not as historical curiosities but as main elements of a controversial, still-vital heritage from the decades of modernist enthusiasm."[49] A portion of this statement warrants challenging, particularly since Hutchison considers Sperry among "the most forceful and prominent" of the modernists advocating adaptation to new secular insights.

Just as Sperry was found not to be the immanentist Hutchison had cited in holding up one leg of his definition of a modernist, Sperry, on closer examination, was not as enthusiastic about cultural adaptation as Hutchison in part presumes. In fact, Sperry's enthusiasm was suspect long before the decline and criticism of modernism began in the 1920s, culminating in the assault by neo-orthodoxy in the 1930s. Hutchison miscalculated a portion of Sperry's contribution because the Dean was indeed not "unequivocal in stating the necessity for religious liberalism to turn to the novelists, the philosophers, and certain of the scientists for help in interpreting their own religious tradition."[50]

Sperry, no doubt, discerned great value in understanding the work that goes on outside the church, but he carefully qualified his endorsements of science and art with substantial reservations before the close of the modernist era as Hutchison has dated it (*circa* 1933-1935). Sperry wrote in 1931, "All that is bold and honest in us responds to the unequivocal 'yes' of pure science and is increasingly irked by the cautious theological 'but' which at present is used to save religion." Sperry explicated his receding enthusiasm for "unequivocal" cultural accommodation in the realization that "there are, however, some values which escape the meshes of the scientific net, and the traditional Christian is not without a case."[51]

Sperry shared the scorn of L. P. Jacks for the attitude of self-defense which constantly places religion behind the bulwarks of modern culture. About the prophets, Jesus and the makers of ancient creeds Jacks had written with Sperry's nodding ascent, "theirs was not the spirit of spurious open-mindedness, so much in fashion nowadays, which worships a note of interrogation—the timidity which dares commit itself to nothing.... The lines have fallen to us in a highly apologetic age... How can the world fail to despise a religion which is accompanied by a perpetual excuse for its own existence?"[52]

The dilemma of Christian apologetics, Sperry gauged, was held in constant store for the believer who feels "increasingly left out of the tasks that the world is working hardest at," like finding world peace or the cause and cure of cancer, which "throws him more and more onto the defensive in behalf of his faith." Before long, imagined Sperry, a religionist "cannot escape a certain natural resentment that his type of mind seems so superfluous." And if that defensive apologetic continues for long, the consequences are probably a total and reckless abandonment of religion and the creation of the cynic. Sperry pondered, "May it be, not that religion is outworn nor that the environing world is wicked, but that the man who professes religion today is not in the right relation to religion and to his world?" Here Sperry is questioning a very basic premise of what modernism is about, but without surrendering a liberal position to a neo-orthodox one.

Having already invoked the words of one British theologian, L. P. Jacks, Sperry reinforces his revised premise of what for too long had been the conventional, defensive Christian apologetic via adaptation and "the vicious formula" of 'yes, but-,' by calling upon a suggestion made by his former Oxford tutor, Canon B. H. Streeter. Sperry writes about Streeter's volume, *Reality:*

He says that as he looks back over his life he sees that for years he has been asking the wrong question; he has asked, "Is Christianity true?" The fixed habit of approaching religion through this question, he goes on to say, has put him in an entirely mistaken relation to all that should be meant by religion, since it implies that Christianity is itself a question, whereas it was at first intended to be and ought still to be the answer to a question.

Sperry proposed, therefore, that "the modern Christian, having begun by asking the wrong question, or by putting the question in the wrong place, has become a defender of the faith" and gotten himself in the poor rhetorical position of 'yes, but-.' Citing the example of Streeter, Sperry advocated departure from "the whole science of apologetics" because so long as cultural adjustments are required along the defensive lines of 'yes, but-,' it is a no-win situation. Rather, with Streeter, Sperry thought it preferable, though harder, to make "no attempt either to vindicate or to defend Christianity." This was an argument from the weight of self-evidence.

Sperry's criticism of the bankruptcy of the conventional and modern apologetics was more constructive than merely barbed. As a counter-measure he suggested that "contemporary Christianity, if it is ever to be rid of the timidity betrayed by its apologetic tempers, needs a realistic doctrine of the Spirit. We must believe," he continued, "that wherever men are honestly trying to find out what was so or what is so, there we are to discern the promptings of the indwelling Word of God. There is no reason to qualify this faith with any cautious 'but-'." On balance he added, "that particular inquiries within restricted scientific areas are often wholly untheological in their premises and tentatively agnostic in their conclusions, ... is no reason for fearing or ignoring them." What Sperry was after ultimately as a defender of the faith was Carlyle's "everlasting yea" or as he said, the sublime moment when believers "in the presence of the fact or truth... speak an unequivocal 'yes'." Moreover, Sperry's sense that "there is a Holy Spirit which leads men into all truth" is proved, he said, "wherever this high transaction of truth-seeking and truth-finding takes place, if only we had the courage to believe it, [as being] also 'the mind of Christ'."[53]

Whereas other modernists, such as Harry Emerson Fosdick, declared "we must go beyond modernism," Sperry inserted his own firm suggestion to "refinance" or restructure a bankrupt apologetic; and whereas Walter Marshall Horton and John C. Bennett were speculating on the theme "After

Liberalism," Sperry was asking in his book *Yes, But*, "Whither Liberalism?" assuming it still had some place forward to go.

Sperry placed the blame for poor Christian apologetics on bad habits of rhetoric other than "yes, but-" logic. In addition, a problem of perception arose among defenders of the faith because "religion nowadays seldom appears alone in public; it is habitually in company with some other human concern." Consequently, religion is coupled almost unnaturally with other departments of society as Religion and Science, Religion and Art, Religion and State. In thinking of religion with these other interests one detects a disguise for the old apologetic, "yes, but-" which is poorly concealed with phrase-making and the mistaken trust in "the power of those phrases to solve all mysteries." Despite "its cheerful intimations," and its "attempt to get back of the age of specialization to the lost unity of human life," the phrase "religion, and-," in Sperry's critique, "has a specious note of promise." The assumption is that "religion is best qualified to serve as the liaison officer" between widely diverse specializations.

Sperry warned against liberal Protestantism being taken in by this culturally mediating role of religion because "the full implications of the formula 'religion, and-' are by no means reassuring." To the contrary, Sperry thought that "the words plainly imply that matters have been going none too well with religion itself and that a suitable marriage of convenience with some other substantial interest would be desirable..., yet we should not be too hastily betrayed," he urged, "by the seductive theory, which remains to be vindicated in experience, that it is cheaper for two poor persons to live together than apart."[54]

Holding up to liberal Protestantism the truly unexpected example of the Roman Catholic Modernist and their practice of piety toward a focused, "subsistent quality" of religion, Sperry recommended as "the most faithful account of the facts" the recovery and built-in proof of "the intense vitality of the gospel" as being simultaneously modern and religious. To apologize for religion in the modern world with artificial mechanisms and random particles of speech, such as "but" and "and," "by which we try to relate religion to the world," Sperry says should suggest to us, "qualifying or minimizing turns of mind which are alien to the spiritual principle we wish to affirm." This is the very contradictory situation which, in spite of well meaning intentions, has disparaged the reputation of religion in a modern culture. Sperry argued instead, that

Surely this word "religion" is an imperial word that should stand alone, needing no props. The attempt to compound it with other words succeeds only in compromising it. Should we not cultivate the power to think and say this word in its singleness, since this of all words in the language should be no stranger to the "self-sufficing power of solitude"?[55]

Hutchison's general interpretation is not easily disputed, for his point is substantially documented and carries the argument about liberal trends. What is correct in kind, however, still leaves open the potential for errors in degree. And this is where Hutchison can be slightly revised. The author says Sperry "followed the logic" of modernism "faithfully" and the result was, ironically, a revision of the "reverently hopeful interpretation of the immanence of God in culture."[56]

Hutchison, particularly in the case of Sperry, might have pressed the point fuller seeing that not only were some modernists beginning to minimize their theological heritage of divine immanence, but they were also declaring independence from "the so-called secular culture." All of which calls a degree of finer distinction into Hutchison's assessment that "modernist enthusiasm" for adaptationism remained vital after the revision of the doctrine of God's immanence; a conclusion not entirely feasible after that doctrine had been tried and found wanting by several of the modernists themselves who encountered scant evidence of God's presence in the world of war, depression and suffering.

Sperry may indeed be the exceptional liberal, but nonetheless, in one of the major players of the modernist impulse a much more serious challenge to "the so-called secular society" than has thus far been acknowledged needs to be noted. Because Hutchison and other historians have allowed neo-orthodoxy to overshadow all other theological activity of the 1930s, or to dismiss that other activity as anachronistic, it is, of course reasonable to assume that for all other non-neo-orthodox thinkers "renewed cordiality toward culture and secularity remained... a sober acceptance."[57] This categorization does not fit Sperry who was seeking "a way for religion to do its own talking" independent of external descriptions that are historical, psychological and sociological.[58]

❦

The Illiberal Liberal

Sperry recognized that his day was torn by contradictions. Religion could not ignore science, for example, because "there is probably far more genuine mysticism in the research laboratories of our universities and great industries than is to be found in psychological classrooms where we study mysticism or in sentimental religious groups where we play at being mystics."[59] And yet, religion could not be so objective as science and still be religion. In this motif of comparisons Sperry wrote:

> The major contradiction of modern thought is that between the objective mind and the subjective mind. The former is intent upon discovering the truth of the outer world, irrespective of any human uses to which that truth may be turned; the latter is bent upon knowing human nature thoroughly and bettering human conditions as rapidly as possible. Neither of these minds, when about its daily business, makes habitual use of the language of theology, yet each of these minds is engaged ultimately on a religious quest, since the findings of both are relevant to any adequate modern religion. The fact that we have these two types of mind at work at the same time need not disturb us; there is indeed much cause for reassurance in this situation, since both are necessary to religion. What troubles us is their failure to understand each other.[60]

Sperry pulled the issue out of the context of theology against culture, which has been, as James R. Moore makes clear, too often the source of "warfare," and said, "everyone of us needs correction at this point, toward a greater subjectivity or a greater objectivity of interest." In reorganizing the problem around a different model, Sperry, in effect, enlarged "the mind of Christ" toward which all thought, scientific or poetic, must eventually point. In other words, the religious task is to affirm the objective and subjective work of the world as "the two shields of one reality." Sperry saw the gravest danger for the Protestant mind in "the apologetic business of fitting random items of late truth into the conventional mosaic of traditional theology," which led to the kind of conflict Huxley stirred. To avoid that peril Sperry propounded "the exciting task of trying to prophesy the revival of religion which may follow if we can get these two types of mind well introduced to each other and require them to compound or equate their dual interest fairly." Sperry thought that religion should neither be a diversion from the work of the world nor an adversary of that work, but that in the name of religion the scientist and the poet could find grounds for mutual understanding. Theology may be at odds with modern thought and expression, but religion insists that the specialized departments of society get on with their work unencumbered by each other or by the practice of piety. Sperry emphasizes that theologies ought to change, but when they do, it is not the signal of religion's demise, but rather of its vitality.

What Sperry had argued, beginning with the emptiness of apologetics, one might almost envisage as a kind of hyper-adaptationism, whereby everything secular can be found imbued with religious content, thus confirming Hutchison's supposition of the "still-vital heritage from the decades of modernist enthusiasm." One might also put forward the argument coming from the other side of the same coin, that it was immanentism run amok. Rather, it seems more persuasive to judge Sperry's position on the variety of religious relationships existing outside the church, as being expressed initially with fine degrees of subtlety, infused with the tradition of British philosophic erudition and prudence, which in combined form finally rejects the ultimate necessity of religion's adaptation to culture. Sperry deduced that rather than adapting, religion should be perceived as a constant, and if it varies at all in the eyes of secular society, religion varies in its presence by an inverse proportion to "its prominence in speech." He said, making something complicated sound simple, "the less religious we are the more necessary it becomes to talk about religion." And since Sperry would have it that religion is "the wiring between modern minds," this is saying something very different from the argument from cultural accommodation which suggests religion is merely another circuit added to the secular transformer. It bewildered Sperry, for example that Charles Darwin reportedly read very little poetry and seldom listened to music. How was religion, then, to mediate the double facing of culture, that is connecting science and art while also looking inside and outside the church for the best properties of conduction and resistance? The church was something of a cultural junction box for Sperry.[61]

To carry the metaphor another step, Sperry might have said that religion is the line through which an "electrical" energy runs in order to project the amplification of saying "God" in the midst of all the work done in the world outside the church. This "wiring" runs contrary to many popular assumptions Sperry judged as inadequate. It is, for instance, simply inappropriate to cross and to overload wires connecting what is inside to what is outside the church so that, by such reworking, culture is, thus, somehow pulling the voltage religion was designed to convey in the first instance. Religion must not occupy a subjugated role in culture, but like a large electrical system, must encompass, and, at times, transcend, the culture that it spans. To clarify a sticking point, Sperry devised a paradoxical reconciliation between the world at work and what Huxley called "the passionless impersonality of the unknown and the unknowable." For the modern liberal to remain "plugged in" religiously without passing into humanism and incomplete philosophies of self-reliance, one must recast, according to Sperry, other possibilites because the moral and intellectual discipline of liberalism had exhausted itself in "trying to tie up the loose ends of liberal thought and to bring its affairs to something like a decent conclusion." Sperry's concept widens rather than narrows the possibilities of religion outside the church: "The hope of a religious revival in the near future lies, then, neither with the elder orthodoxy, nor with the traditional liberal; it lies with that person whom we must describe as the illiberal liberal."[62]

In denying the older orthodoxy and the traditional liberalism with the same sweeping gesture, Sperry admits the "illiberal liberal" is a heretical creature. And the heresy of such a hybrid "in our day will be therefore a doubt as to man's right to happiness." Citing his friend, L. P. Jacks, as an example of the illiberal liberal, Sperry writes whimsically, "Orthodox Christians in England have long known that L. P. Jacks would undoubtedly 'perish everlastingly', in accordance with the damnatory conclusion to the Athanasian Creed. But now conventional liberals find that he does not hold the pure faith of their persuasion, either." Jacks had been taking public exception to "the kind of nonsense talked by Rousseau and in the preamble to the American Declaration of Independence." Jacks had come to believe that most of the problems and cruelties of the world "have their source in some fool's 'secret of happiness'." Jacks contended that "nobody has any such right.... no human being is fitted for such an existence." Furthermore, "any God, or Universe, which offered them that [right to happiness] as the end-all and goal of their existence, would be a God not worthy of worship, and a universe not worth living in," because it would then be a life without meaning, value and beauty, being at best a fool's paradise.[63]

What Sperry admired about Jacks was that, like himself, he was "the type of person who in his heredity and experience has passed clean through the discipline of the liberalism of the last two centuries, has seen it finally formulated in the dogmatic theology of humanism, and who has no mind to be put off with a dogmatic theology instead of a living religion." Sperry goes on to say, "This illiberal liberal is a person with deeply humane sympathies and humanitarian hopes, who despairs of ever fully expressing those sympathies or realizing those hopes unless this be also the cosmic intention." For him the vindication of the liberal's faithful insistence upon the dignity and worth of the individual with the concomitant right to happiness is not enough without going beyond humanism to other realities. "Either we are involved in and with the universe or religion is the ultimate delusion."

Sperry summarizes the course of the "illiberal liberal" in recalling that "it took our liberal forefathers a century to learn to say 'man' plainly and fully. They had to fumble with the word at first and found its meanings and promises slowly." Meanwhile, during a modern interlude of "a waiting agnosticism, an agnosticism which is expectant rather than despairing" the new goal of the liberal is to say "God" and mean something by it. Thus, the illiberal strategy is to seek and gain newer and truer meaning for the idea of God because "this is the one word above all others which any religion must utter."[64]

Sperry illustrated the sense of the illiberal liberal "at once religiously mature and modern" with Pascal's doctrine of human greatness and littleness. Sperry explained that "whatever the universe might do to him, Pascal knew that he could always be his own man. Yet it was in the presence of the infinities that he learned the sober lesson of his littleness. This side of Pascal is patently illiberal, since it is entirely wanting in any humanistic self-confidence or self-congratulation."[65] Sperry was interested in demonstrating that in both the sciences and the arts there are parallels to the religion of the illiberal liberal, such as Pascal, who does not refute his humanism "as set in final relation to the universe" nor question the mature judgment of human greatness found not in a forthright humanism, but in something far afield from that humanism.

Sperry thought that a symptom of liberalism's chronic weakness and the deficiency of romanticism and humanism was in the growing popular literature about astronomy. He submitted that "it is because humanitarianism and humanism are not enough to satisfy all the capacities of the human mind, and that these popular accounts of vast and mysterious matters minister to an actual spiritual need in our souls." Simply put, Sperry added to this assessment that we people "are not enough for ourselves."[66]

To the list of Jacks and Pascal, Sperry also placed the names of William Wordsworth and Albert Einstein as illiberal liberals, for it was their same sense of an unresolved contradiction which ran through their work to give them each a peculiar religious quality outside the church. Sperry admits befuddlement about the subtleties of the theory of relativity, but says, "what I can understand is Einstein's simple account of his religious faith." By his own confession Einstein believed in what he called "cosmic religion," whereby the individual feels the puniness of human aims and ends while realizing "the nobility of the marvellous orders which are revealed in nature and in the world of thought." Einstein is compared to Pascal in Sperry's sense of context that "the greatness of man who is thus little lies in his power to lay his mind faithfully alongside the universe that is infinite; this is his only greatness." Sperry rounds off the thought:

> Einstein says that this highest religious experience is found only among the heretics of all ages; be that as it may, "cosmic religion" must be for the modern humanist what Modernism itself was for the Catholic Church, not merely a heresy, but "the sum of all heresies." Einstein's mind has nothing in common with religious liberalism and humanism, being at the crucial point utterly and consistently illiberal. Yet I venture to say that he catches our attention and stirs our imagination... precisely because there is more in us than can be satisfied by a purely humanistic religion.[67]

In the spring of 1935 Sperry gave an address at the University of Chicago on "Religion in an Age of Science." From the theological "left" his talk was glowingly received. Henry N. Wieman wrote him in the most flattering terms:

> I have never heard a lecture on Religion and Science, nor any other subject, for which I have felt so profoundly as I do for the lecture I heard you deliver in Breasted Hall. I think no word is more urgently needed than what you spoke.[68]

The urgent word which Sperry spoke began with the premise that "science serves in our day as the concrete representative of that total secular world which always environs religion in history, and toward which religion must forever redefine its relation."[69] As Sperry points out in Harnack's phrase, "the acute secularizing of Christianity" began long before the age of science. Meanwhile, in Sperry's estimation,

> the modern theologian, theoretically committed to the reconciliation of religion and science, has not been a very convincing figure. As some one said not long ago, the arguments of Modernism, whether Catholic or

Protestant, may be a valid reason for staying in the church if you are already there; they are not a reason for coming into the church if you are not there. This reversal of the roles has made modern science the aggressor and has thrown traditional religion on the defensive.[70]

Sperry implies that where religion can offer superior guidance to science is in the moral responsibility which must "reckon with the fact that findings of pure science, when 'applied', might be turned to sinister account."[71] But Sperry warned that religion, in turn, must not leap to conclusions of instant equality or superiority in its relationship with the sciences, the "impatient desire to have science yield at all points the verdict which religion has previously announced." Sperry insisted that "we of the religious side, should beware of exploiting the present findings of science for our own wishful thinking. And we should beware of treating religious faith as though it were a pious advance guard of science, determining the direction in which science is to move and prophesying the conclusions at which it must arrive." Religion must not be too eager for science to rescue it. "It is not the office of theology to draw from the work of sciences direct inferences which the scientists themselves are unable to draw." Sperry advised instead that "we should shun the fashion too prevalent among our kind of leaping to the conclusion that Einstein is already among the prophets." Too much "vicarious science," thought Sperry, is practiced by theologians who had not passed beyond elementary physics and chemistry. Finally, "modern liberalism, in its impatience to effect a reconciliation of science and religion, must be careful not to go farther in these directions, in the name of religion, than the sciences themselves are prepared to go."[72]

Sperry was not trying to bring science inside the church, but on the contrary, defended the necessity of science to remain outside the church. This is not to say that in terms of method religion lacks "an affinity if not a moral identity with pure science." Sperry believed that safer ground for each could be shared not in terms of mutual results, but in similar methods, a consistent message of Sperry's thirty year discourse of relgious topics. In short, strict definitions of faith based on scientific results will never satisfy, for, in Sperry's words, "we must learn not to be afraid of a tentative agnosticism," because "the illiberal liberal may not always understand the new physics or the new astronomy of our day, but he trusts the direction in which such a mind faces."[73] One such illiberal liberal of the modern world whom Sperry trusted outside the church was Walter Lippmann.

Lippmann's *A Preface to Morals* (1929) illuminated the perplexities of a generation that had passed beyond the high ground of optimism in motifs of Progressivist reform to the provisional pessimism of the twenties, one which "having ceased to believe without ceasing to be credulous, hangs, as it were between heaven and earth, and is at rest nowhere." What Lippmann graphically described as "the acids of modernity" had already consumed much religious faith, while science had spilled its own caustic solutions over belief, and Freud had trespassed on the sanctity of the human soul. Where people had once lived securely with a sense of order and continuity, there were now "brave and brilliant atheists who have defied the Methodist God, and have become very nervous." Furthermore, women have "emancipated themselves from the tyranny of fathers, husbands and homes, and with the intermittent but expensive help of a psychoanalyst, are now enduring liberty as interior decorators." Young people at twenty-two are "world- weary" and overdosed on the cult of pleasure who "ought to be very happy." Instead, "they stagger out into trackless space under a blinding sun."[74]

As Ronald Steel makes abundantly clear in his biography of Lippmann, the prescribed antidote was neither a return to the church nor a separate peace with secular expertise. Authority was absent in each. Lippmann suggested that since the modern person could not expect to find security and serenity in institutions, that person would have to look inward—to adapt to the world as it was and discover some internal, personal resources for dealing with it. Such a person would have to become distanced from it emotionally and be "disinterested." The new system of morals would not be designed on the models of revelation or of science— both of which were inadequate—but on humanism and emotional self-control.[75]

"When men can no longer be theists, they must, if they are civilized, become humanists." Lippmann was, of course, pointing to something "deeper and more poignant... than churchmen suppose." His goal was to fulfill Bacon's aphorism, that "a little philosophy inclineth man's mind to atheism, but depth in philosophy bringeth men's minds about to religion." Lippmann decided that the choice was peremptorily a personal one and the only way he saw fit to transcend the difficulties was through a "religion of the spirit," which "does not depend upon creeds and cosmologies; it has no vested interest in any particular truth. It is concerned not with the organization of matter, but with the quality of human desire."[76]

The humanism Lippmann proposed rested on detachment, more a mode of conduct than a philosophical principle. Many of Lippmann's critics viewed his sense of detachment as "only a fine name for disillusionment." No matter how brave the author, it was marked by a "certain unreality," said another, a discourse that only masked an apology for disappointment.[77] Sperry's own view actually takes little exception to Lippmann's thesis because he has, perhaps inadvertently, fashioned a secular equivalent to "the truth of the rarer mysticism of the past." Sperry sees the problem with Lippmann as one of misinterpreting his use of the word "humanism":

> No man with as strong a feeling as Mr. Lippmann has for outer reality, or with as much concern as he discloses for disinterested correspondence with a reality-not-ourselves, can be called a humanist in the stricter sense of the word. The designation that he needs has yet to be discovered or coined, meanwhile his profound conception of life as correspondence with reality is the substance of a religion at once older and newer than that of most contemporary humanism.[78]

Sperry considered *A Preface to Morals* "more a treatise on theology than a tract on ethics." It was a journey from "pure science to high religion." And when Lippmann set his face towards the high religion of the future he saw that the core of it was an attitude of disinterestedness, like that of pure science, or to Sperry like that of L. P. Jacks's "heresy" (i.e., being dispassionate about happiness as a human right).[79] Although Sperry realized that Lippmann's book "was dismissed with impatience by most conventionally religious persons, because such persons are more interested in religious results than in religious methods," he nevertheless stood by his first impressions of the work which appeared in *The Yale Review* and, subsequently, in *Yes, But* and in his Chicago lecture on religion and science. Sperry agreed wholeheartedly with Lippmann about the central significance of disinterestedness. For Sperry at the time of the early thirties and beyond, Lippmann "identified the one important community of interest between religion, at least liberal religion, and science."[80]

Sperry is not generally troubled by Lippmann's lack of effort "to formulate rules for the application of this moral principle which receives the sanctions of high religion." Instead of specific prescriptions for the moral problem along the lines of "elder sanctions," Lippmann substituted "austerer sanctions, and the 'civilized asceticism'...[which] requires a self-discipline that overcomes the moral immaturity of the natural man at a cost that only heroes can pay."[81]

It is ironic, however, that when Sperry looked for the illiberal liberal among the modern poets, as he had among the modern scientists, he was disturbed by an excess of asceticism and, therefore, turned to Wordsworth for the proper balance between human greatness and littleness. The modern poets, in a word, were not illiberal liberals, but just liberal or just illiberal. In a 1933 article for *The Atlantic Monthly*, entitled "The New Asceticism," Sperry expressed serious reservations about any wholesale return to an intellectual stoicism found in the literary mood of the 1920s. Sperry raised a question around the Protestant premise of "trying to rid religion of its stubborn traffic in intellectual self-indulgence." The continuation of this premise, dating from the time of the Reformation, is that through "the newer knowledge of the devious ways of the human mind" eventually one begins to "suspect his own wishful thinking as being an escape from reality rather than the gateway to reality." As a consequence, Sperry, cautioning against a premature celebration by the arts community of its "civilized asceticism," tempered his view because "the truth is that most of us moderns are comfortable only when listening to religion's uncomfortable words."[82]

Sperry is not opposed to the kind of ascetic discipline offered by the scientific mind, but in turning the coin over, it reveals a basic religious axiom "that the truth of poetry cannot be falsehoods for science." In part this plea is a form of pietistic conservatism hearkening back to another function for poetry, but it is also a call for intellectual honesty in the poet. Too much literature was inflating a cult of despair when it was not always warranted. Literature, says Sperry, had not been as comprehensive as science. In fact, for modern authors and poets the ascetic impulse had been in the twentieth century "too highly selective to carry the whole consent of candor, however it may stir the emotion of pity."[83]

Sperry's point picks up the main thread of Lippmann's theme of disinterestedness. Artistic selectivity goes against the pattern of scientific objectivity so that "the pain which the modern mind has accepted in the name of scientific candor is one thing, but that which it has voluntarily selected in the name of art is another and far more dubious thing." Sperry's usage of the term "asceticism" requires clarification because by it he means a deliberately planned and specific experience in hardship calculated to

exercise one's soul in honest, if, at times, unnatural, ways. This particular
literary trend which Sperry had spotted possessed a specificity in the
premise of its exponents that was not disinterested enough to be "objective," and therefore it became for him an affectation.

This kind of isolated "intellectual asceticism," concludes Sperry, "is fast
becoming an anachronism" because "where dispassionateness prevails,
there self-inflicted pain, whether addressed to the body or to the mind, falls
out of bounds." The poets must be real, they cannot be unfair in order to
"escape from this newest form of the old ascetic delusion." Finally, Sperry
resolved to "look to the candor of science rather than the comforts of
religion to dispel the intellectual asceticism of our time" which is not a
contradiction in terms because, as he framed the question rhetorically, "Is
not the candor of science part of the ultimate comfort of religon?"[84]

Sperry's article drew the fire of T. S. Eliot who was addressing a clergy
association somewhere in Boston shortly after it was published and circulated. This "amused" the Dean in replying to the Rector of Christ Church,
Cambridge (Massachusetts), who had reported Eliot's adverse reaction to
"The New Asceticism," because "knowing his frame of mind I suspect he
did not like it much."[85] Earlier in a book review from 1930 Sperry had
seemingly praised Eliot for being an advocate of supernatural humanism,
"a successful gospeller... of a mild Anglo-Catholicism, as a cure for the pride
of modernity."[86] For Sperry it was not wrong that Eliot had had second
thoughts about religion, but that he and other authors carried them too far
ascetically.

Sperry also drew criticism from less visible personalities than T. S. Eliot
and took the time to respond thoughtfully, in one instance to points raised
by an unknown camp director in Tennessee:

> As to the whole question at stake I cannot help feeling that the human mind
> has been too much occupied in recent years with the civil affairs of the race.
> Indeed, I think a good many of the deeper moral difficulties of the times
> are due to the lack of a state department in our thinking. That is a constant
> reference to the universe around us. We have become too self conscious
> and self centered. On the other hand, I stand by my point that the arts have
> carried this ascetic tendency too far. [e.g., Eugene O'Neill's play *Mourning
> Becomes Electra*].
>
> My article came after a long dose of this ascetic literature in novels, plays
> and the like. Somehow, suddenly, they seemed to me to cease to be true to
> life, and I suspected the doctrinaire in them... I suppose that living in a
> rather sophisticated corner [of America] where there is a good deal of

ascetic posing among people interested in the arts I suspect the honesty of the pose.[87]

Although Sperry was interested in the war poets and Francis Thompson, about whom he lectured at a Harvard English Colloquium, William Wordsworth epitomized for him, more than any other literary figure, the illiberal liberal from that side of the religious equation which the arts represented. And for a time Wordsworth had "the possibility of becoming one of the great spokesmen for humanism, but with his disillusionment as to 'social man' his religion of humanity died slowly away."[88] Sperry's choice of Wordsworth as his poet, a seemingly old-fashioned selection for a toughened liberal (who was unwilling to yield an inch to Barthian doctrines of revelation), deserves more than mere passing identification. It warrants analysis, even the setting down of suspicions. For someone who once railed against liberal sentimentality in the 1920s (cf. *The Disciplines of Liberty*) the turn to a romantic poet whom even Keats dismissed seems patently absurd. In the winter of 1923 Sperry had a house guest who arrived with certain mawkish suppositions about poetry and departed with his views significantly altered. Sperry told his sister Pauline of the incident:

> Ernest Guthrie [a Boston clergyman who was later Director of the Chicago Congregational Union] has been here for a few days with us. He is just out of hospital after a very heavy operation— kidney stone. He is left rather knocked down. All went well until the last evening when he rashly advanced the theory at about ten p.m. of the final evening of his visit, that Tennyson was a poet. I gathered up his remains at about two a.m. after Muriel had finished with him, and put them to bed. He went home the next day more of a wreck than he was when he left the hospital. Having Tennyson out is worse than having a kidney stone out.[89]

While Sperry once excised sentimentality from his own tastes, he never acquired much liking for the modern realists. What turned Sperry away from T. S. Eliot, for instance, was that Eliot's poetry was a forced austerity that was ultimately too selective to be genuine, no matter how pure the poet's asceticism. What led Sperry to Wordsworth, however, is likely a combination of factors.

First, Sperry, a foremost product of middle-class Victorian America whose Protestant parents were born in antebellum New England, experienced directly the coming and the going of a particularly privileged literary function for clergy. It is no coincidence that poets such as Longfellow, Whittier, James Russell Lowell and Oliver Wendell Holmes had their verses set to Protestant hymn tunes straight through the middle of the twentieth century. The boundaries between Victorian literature and Victorian hymnody are at times so blurred as to be indistinguishable, but nonetheless, it is symptomatic of an important link, exemplified by clergy, which united church and culture. Clergy were steeped in the poets of their day and their fathers' day, able to quote verse extensively in sermons and pamphlets, produce literary biographies and occasionally attempt a novel (e.g., Henry Ward Beecher). Clergy were, before the rise of critics and academics, the respectable arbiters of literary culture. Eventually, Matthew Arnold pointed the way for revision in his hope of establishing a new professional class of "clerisy," the literati who would bring religion to the people through their writings. Teachers of literature would revive what had become dead and defunct in conventional religion. It is not surprising, therefore, that Sperry, a child of the Victorian manse, knew some Browning and Wordsworth and accepted the Arnoldian concept of literature's saving properties. Further, it should not be at all astonishing that his first expectations of the ministry were the filling of a culturally mediating role. He was reading Carlyle before he was reading any historic theology. This, after all, was his lineage which he proudly claimed from the generation of clergy which begat him. To him Wordsworth was a natural outgrowth of his personal history and his professional heritage.

If the Arnoldian garment woven on his behalf was a fitting mantle, it is probably the main context of Sperry's decision to cast his mind with literary affirmations from an earlier day. This would seem anachronistic and even contradictory, given Sperry's point of attack within liberalism during the advent of the sobering 1920s. He pointed a straight finger at the intoxicated sentimentalists who had carried liberalism's banner before 1914. While other liberal Protestant preachers in the 1930s often quoted in their pulpits Browning, Shelley, Keats or Wordsworth as taken from a corpus of vaguely religious expression, it was Sperry alone who made more than a bowing gesture to a romantic anthology. He embraced Wordsworth, and it is not just clear why he became a Wordsworthian when he did.

There may be a subtext at work here which holds the key to the double doors that opened a way to Wordsworth for Sperry, namely science and America. Just as Sperry had had his fill of "the new asceticism" in modern artists, perhaps in turning to the Lake District he was beginning to question the soul of science and the discrepancies of materialism. Sperry is reminiscent of John Stuart Mill who described in his autobiography a personal transformation after a long period of dejection about his "fabric of happiness" and his despair as a Benthamite over a growing scientism that could not meet the material needs of a population in spite of prevailing boasts of social prosperity. Mill discovers Wordsworth for the first time and this became a turning point in his spirit. Wordsworth suited him because

> In the first place, these poems addressed themselves powerfully to one of the strongest of my pleasurable susceptibilities, the love for rural objects and natural scenery; to which I had been in debted... for relief from one of my longest relapses into depression... What made Wordsworth's poems a medicine for my state of mind, was that they expressed, not mere outward beauty, but states of feeling... the very culture of feelings, which I was in quest of.[90]

One can argue that for Sperry "modernity" was ending in a "terrible headache" for which Wordsworth was the strongest analgesic. As it was for Mill, a distant and disinterested "preface to morals" was not enough to suit a caring, interested soul who took the world and its problems seriously. If Sperry were growing weary of a culture where the power of scientific analysis had somehow outrun the means of moral knowledge and spiritual experience and had meanwhile become too ascetic in its expressions, Wordsworth was not only compensation, but sanctuary, an alternative to overly rationalized liberal theories of society and the thoroughly mechanized scientific world view. He had already rejected the Barthian alternative, where else could he turn except to the older, romantic liberalism?

Secondly, if Sperry were troubled by a sensory fatigue related to the influence of science, then his peculiar English background against an American foreground posed a contrast that also accounts for his Wordsworthian preferences. In fact, his difficulty with what science had come to symbolize and his impatience with American literary trends were not only negative factors, but were complementary, working in concert to push Sperry in the direction of romanticism. Anglo-American differences were clearly and constantly at play in Sperry's psyche and by adopting, arguably the greatest of the romantics, Wordsworth, Sperry was yielding to his British loyalties over his American ties. The recurrent double facing in Sperry's thought of competing British and American intellectual forces was conclusively pointing toward resolution in voting for Wordsworth. But more than on-going casual differences between the two nations, Sperry believed that there were deeper cross purposes emerging borne of dissimilar experiences in the Great War. To Sperry America of the early 1930s represented humanism while England typified romanticism.

In reviewing simultaneously two books for a distinguished literary journal, one American and the other British, Sperry discovered he could not assimilate a pair of opposites because one celebrated humanism and the other romanticism. Sperry understood humanism as it was advocated by American authors under review to mean that

> its central maxim is "nothing too much," it is not concerned with the extremes, but contents itself with life at the middle level. It aims to achieve the harmonious development of all man's faculties in this world. In so doing it reaffirms the centrality, for man, of his own affairs, insights, and moral judgements. As a way of life the will-to-refrain, which the romantic movement discarded, is to be rediscovered.[91]

Over against romanticism, Sperry writes, these humanists, "will allow no emotional or moral liaison with nature," which was hardly acceptable to a Wordsworthian. And yet, Sperry detects that, with the exception of humanist Irving Babbitt, who is the best of the lot in the reviewer's opinion, it is still a tradition which "seems to betray some want of final immunity against the virus of romanticism."[92] And in levelling that criticism at American humanism, it is right to suppose that Sperry is also being autobiographical. This conclusion comes by evidence of what follows in the review when Sperry is discussing positively the new romanticism from England.

If American humanism is merely residual Puritanism, then, according to Sperry's review, a reminder need be added that "England never had to make a permanent culture out of this Puritan half-truth; it always had the Cavalier correction." This contrasting history points to the conclusion, as Sperry understood it through British author Hugh Fausset's book, *The Proving of Psyche*, under review, that "the aristocratic morality of Puritanism has proved to be incompatible with the democratic expansiveness of America, and therefore the American humanist, who was from the first a cultural accident, is now the soldier of a forlorn hope." The choice offered in the Anglo-American literary dichotomy is between creative and critical individualism, or in Sperry's terms the will-to-refrain (humanism and America) and the will-to-live (romanticism and Britain).

Sperry believed the division could be traced to the Great War as an obvious truth: "England was hurt, terribly hurt, by the war; America remained relatively unhurt." Consequently, Sperry came to the realization that there were basic differences: Americans "are still left with margins enough of strength and goods to employ profitably the critical method;" the British, "to whom the lines have fallen in a strait place," have no such reserve and "can afford no such luxury of criticism, and must affirm the creative instinct as the will-to-live," rather than the will-to-refrain.[93]

This, finally, is the best clue behind Sperry's intellectual migration not only back across the Atlantic, but to the time and source of romantic intimations of immortality. Through his sympathies for England, therefore, Sperry justified his seemingly incongruous alliance with Wordsworth. While trying not to be a romantic liberal for a long time, Sperry's critical powers in part gave way to that in him stirred by sentimental liberalism just when his fascination with Wordsworth blossomed. Sperry may have joined the ranks of Sentimentalists, or at least entered into a half-way covenant with them, but he was not a sentimental fool, being especially wise to Wordsworth's limitations. "[A]s it is," he writes, "we have a dogged consistency which was both Wordsworth's making and unmaking... Possibly Wordsworth realized his defects better than we can. His self-knowledge was more acute than is commonly supposed."[94] And by inference, Sperry was also saying that liberalism renewed by romanticism stood a better chance of gaining self-knowledge than liberalism censured by humanism or counterblasted by neo-orthodoxy.

Ironically, Sperry points out that humanism never had a finer statement than in the last lines of the sonnet to Touissaint L'Ouverture, "...Thou has great allies,/ Thy friends are exultations, agonies,/ And love, and man's unconquerable mind." Like most liberals since, Wordsworth had never doubted or denied a doctrine of divine immanence, that "the divine which is deeply interfused in things dwells 'in the mind of man'." Sperry noted the exception in Wordsworth as a liberal, because "his liberalism was constantly turning illiberal, for he could not escape the conviction that this something far more deeply interfused dwells also in 'The light of setting suns.... And rolls through all things'."[95] Like Pascal, like Einstein, Wordsworth came to his mature faith so that "Our destiny, our being's heart and home/ Is with infinitude and only there."

Wordsworth looked at some of the lovely, large and constant facts of nature and found his "central peace" in a binding "natural piety." Sperry claimed that Wordsworth "did not gain this religious reassurance by introspection; he learned it from the outer world of which he became newly aware in maturity and with which he believed himself to be in some vital way identified."[96] The lack of natural piety in the modern liberal is precisely what commends Wordsworth to liberalism, even though it risks possible drubbing by critics using the anathema of sentimentalism.

Wordsworth, according to Sperry, was only a nominal churchman and by virtue of his emphasis upon "solitariness" indifferent to matters pertaining to the inside of the church except in how the continuity of the English nation was guaranteed. For that reason alone, Wordsworth loved the Church of England. In the religious sense, however, Sperry saw the futility of measuring with precision the Christianity, theism or pantheism of his verse. Sperry writes, "Wordsworth seems to me to be religious at that deeper, undifferentiated level where distinctions hardly obtain." In this respect he regarded Wordsworth as one who manifested "the elemental genius of all religion and of any religion,"[97] which insofar as it is self-serving of a liberal to make such a claim, it is also sheer "Religious Romanticism."

Much paradox exists in Wordsworth, according to Sperry's analysis of his religion. "In practice Wordsworth used loneliness as a device for discovering his kinship with the natural world... For better or for worse Wordsworth's religion was a commerce with some imaginative principle of things at once and greater than himself, unlike him and yet like him."[98] Wordsworth himself has explained in the "Prefaces" his conception of the poet and, therefore, of his own spirit as a man pleased with his own passions and volitions, and who rejoices more than other men in the spirit of life that is in him."[99]

Wordsworth was careful "... to keep/ In wholesome separation the two natures,/ The one that feels, the other that observes." Whether in pure science or high religion the transaction of poetry has its equivalent with both because there is

> A balance, an ennobling interchange
> Of action from within and from without;
> The excellence, pure spirit, and best power
> Both of the object seen, and the eye that sees.

Theological Outlines of Immortality

With Wordsworth, whose traffic with the world furnished "endless occupation for the soul," Sperry happened to belong to the company of those who believe that "Our destiny, our nature, and our home/ Is with infinitude, and only there."[100] Being able to speak of infinity either in pure science or high poetry was indicative of the illiberal liberal's sense of religious authority outside the church, but when translated back into church vernacular it became for Sperry "the mind of Christ,"[101] a concept he was using as early as 1922.

Sperry advised that "the whole weight of Christian argument in this matter points in one direction. What was true in Jesus and of Jesus ought to be true in us and of us."[102] And this, for purposes of living and not only defending religious faith, raises the specter of the ultimate question, "If a man die, shall he live again?" (Job 14:14). A modern consideration of immortality for Sperry presented the mutual aims of science and poetry in a theological context. Both branches of knowledge were by nature interested in where humanity had been and where it is going ultimately; thus they turn with theology to an abiding question.

During the late thirties and through the war years, Sperry wrote touching and frank letters to his daughter in London about world affairs and intimate religious problems, the latter often prompted by a challenging query, perhaps because of the context of those uncertain world affairs. In one such revealing moment he offered how difficult he had found "preaching the Christian religion" to be, especially in locating its proper direction, being either earthward or heavenward:

> Unless, indeed, we say that the Christian religion is concerned solely with "heaven." That is a point of view—and is of course the strength of Roman Catholicism. I have to admit that Liberal Protestantism in reducing Christianity to a two-dimensional matter—i.e., the immediate structure of human society has complicated its problem and lessened its ultimate [effect]. Historic Christianity has never—until our time— restricted its view of life to this life. I feel that rather strongly. But I am quite aware of the difficulties which arise when you allow religion to become an "escape mechanism." The standard example is the Negro spiritual about heaven—since then this life of slavery offered no hope.[103]

Sperry addressed the issue of life beyond this life frequently in public through lectures, seminars and sermons exactly for reasons as he indicated to his daughter in private, because "historic Christianity has never restricted its view of life to this life." Preaching at Princeton in the spring of 1935, he began dramatically with the average modern view of the oldest Christian creed, the Apostle's Creed, going over it point by point in an imagined running dialogue: "I believe in God the Father Almighty." - "I suppose so, though it is by no means clear and cannot be proved." "...Suffered under Pontius Pilate, was crucified, dead and buried." - "Yes, certainly. If anything in this creed is certain, that is certain." "...the third day he rose again from the dead, and ascended into heaven, and sitteth on the right hand of God the father, whence he shall come to judge the quick and the dead." - "Well, that all depends on what those words rising and ascending and coming mean. I certainly don't believe the letter of those words as the writers meant them." "...And in the resurrection of the body." - "No, when the body's dead, it's dead and that's all there is to that." "And in the life everlasting. Amen." -"I don't know. I wish I did know. To tell the truth I don't think about it much."

Sperry builds his case for approaching the idea of immortality around the common perception that "this creed, like a well written sonnet or a good piece of music is intended to come to a climax in its last clause ...but for the average man today, the creed ends, if not with an anti-climax, at least on an inconclusive and puzzled note." Sperry wonders, that in the presence of one of the great ideas of religion, the immortality of the human soul, why the modern times have "entered into this conspiracy of silence," this indifference that no longer thinks much about it. Sperry admits the utter inadequacy of all the old symbols and notes how wanting the times are for other symbols to take their place. He admits that immortality has been the vehicle for exploiting people in the past, "giving the hope of heaven to underpaid workers in mill towns and mining camps." Immortality is a "drug that will keep them quiet under social injustice." Another reason for the "conspiracy of silence" is the false bravado that God could not be bothered with a man or woman forever. Sperry called that the "affectation of unimportance," an exaggerrated false modesty that bravely, but unnaturally denied the thought of immortality on grounds it was the mere preservation of selfishness. Still another reason for the idea of immortality to be greeted coldly was due to "our want of realism in the presence of the fact of death." Sperry suggests here sardonically that "death is an intrusion, almost a thing of bad taste, a kind of social error. It's not good form to die." On this Sperry replies, "until you are a realist about death you will never feel the true occasion for faith in a life after death."[104]

While some of the motives behind modern indifference to the doctrine of immortality were to Sperry intelligible, and at times laudable, none of them really settled the question. Found in Sperry's lecture notes are phrases and incomplete sentences which are not at all disjointed in meaning or logic for the reiteration intended: "Preacher should avoid the common error of saying that a man who does not believe in immortality has no sufficient motive for a good and moral life, or cannot live a good life. Plain fact that it is not so." Aside from the universalism that creeps into this sentiment, that believes in the final harmony of all souls regardless of the moral life on earth, it shows Sperry interested in a neglected doctrine, but also that he was not interested in being doctrinaire. In dealing with the resurrection of Jesus one finds in note form an indication that for Sperry the answer there was not going to satisfy completely one's modern sensibilities:

> If these stories proved it beyond all question of a doubt why are we still discussing it. Why an open question.

> We believe what we believe about his immortality because of some previous conviction regarding Jesus, we do not believe in Jesus because of the resurrection stories.

> The resurrection stories have meaning and worth to those who are disciples of Jesus, those who are not his disciples [are] unaffected as to immortality by the story.[105]

Sperry's considerations and arguments moved away from texts to experience and reflection about that experience. In the Garvin Lecture for 1947 at Lancaster, Pennsylvania and the Ingersoll Lecture at Harvard for 1953, his last major address to the Harvard community, Sperry in both instances made it clear that immortality cannot be taught separately from a doctrine of God; if it is construed independent of a prior theology, it is utterly worthless. Immortality rests on the antecedent doctrine of God, an argument derived from Emerson's "The Over-Soul" which states, "The specifically religious desire for Immortality begins, not with immortality, but with God; it rests upon God, and it ends in God."

It follows, therefore, that the soul does not seek, find or assume its own immortality which, in turn becomes the equivalent to seeking, finding and assuming God. That would be presumptious. What is at stake is "the probability or the assurance that personality shall persist, and the test case is the survival of self-consciousness and of memory. Can we still go on saying 'I' of a consecutive experience? Are we going to know one another again, shall we recognize one another?" Sperry was not, obviously, willing to reduce his conception of immortality to impersonality. Rather, because "individuality is always in process of being enlarged and supplemented" the qualitatively different life after this life is perhaps contained in the immortal hope that an individual is forever in the process of becoming more of a person. In this respect Sperry is in agreement with Kirsopp Lake who preceded him as an Ingersoll Lecturer. Lake said at that similar and earlier occasion that immortality will probably be one's chance to learn to say "we" instead of "I."[106]

Finally, taking Wordsworth's best image of divine attributes to heart, Sperry concluded with reasoned conviction, part instinct, part discipline:

> For myself, I find it increasingly difficult to divorce human thought from the "eternity of thought." The former is framed within the latter. And so I find it hard to believe that human minds and hearts and wills can come to the maturity and the splendor that the race achieves so constantly, only to be snuffed out and thus to end the process in nothingness. It seems more probable that the process that initiated these lives of ours must make provision for their conservation.[107]

Sperry's argument for a doctrine of immortality can be placed in the scope of "recapitulation theories" described by John Hick. In general, this view of human immortality suggests the eternal presence of human earthly life within the divine memory. Hick cites Miguel de Unamuno and Paul Tillich as examples of a divine accounting system to which Sperry is also attached theologically. In the case of Unamuno there is the dual assumption of a Supreme Consciousness and every human being as an idea in that universal mind. Unamuno argues the impossibility of any "idea" ever being blotted out or forgotten in the mind of God. Tillich in his work, *Systematic Theology*, similarly develops the concept of "eternal memory," not without some inconsistencies around the secondary issue of self-consciousness after death. Sperry, however, does not bog down in speculative details which inevitably become entangled as contradictions. Rather, Sperry possesses a high threshold of paradox and a disinclination to the kind of systematic thought represented in Tillich.[108]

In yoking "human thought" and the "eternity of thought" Sperry was pulled into a homeland of the mind and spirit which he explored consciously inside and outside the church. And yet, early, late and throughout his active intellectual journey he adopted and reaffirmed the prescient mood of George Matheson, the blind poet and hymn writer of late nineteenth-century Scotland, who expressed for him what it is like to follow religiously "the object of aspiration even more than of memory":

Son of Man, whenever I doubt of life, I think of Thee. Nothing is so impossible as that Thou shouldest be dead. I can imagine the hills to dissolve in vapor and the stars to melt in smoke... but I feel no limit in Thee... Thou art not obsolete. Thou art abreast of all the centuries. I have never come up with Thee, modern as I am...[109]

EPILOGUE

A student who plumbs the core of Willard L. Sperry's career of religious thought inevitably falls into something of an elegiac mood. Sperry is a maverick with the insider's sensibilities of liberal Protestantism; many contradictions are discovered about him, which make his story not just intriguing but also a commemoration of one who had to accord constantly the themes of life's antitheses. Sperry is a troubled liberal of the modern era, yet ironically finds an outlet in the "untroubled" Wordsworth who believed "... brightest things are wont to draw / Sad opposites out of the inner heart." Sperry's life is representative of the middle ground, troubled not by ambiguity, but by systematic solutions posed throughout theology and disciplines outside theology.

Even more striking, however, is his persistence, his success in discovering and displaying the processes of irony and paradox that somehow sustain people through and in spite of that very recognition of protracted discord. Sperry recognized honestly and precisely the problem confronting his life, which makes him instantly an attractive person to study because of his acute self-awareness.

By the mid-1940s he sensed the incongruity of his thought with his times, telling his daughter, "I have felt for the last ten years that all the graces and dignities and refinements of an Upper Common Room in Oxford were *fin de siècle*—as though I were seeing a period dying before my eyes."[1]

His feelings about the changes coming at Oxford extended naturally to the American liberal Protestant scene he had observed critically for a half century. Looking across those years Sperry recalled the comment of Kirsopp Lake, a renowned New Testament scholar at Harvard, who said to him in the early 1920s, "The men whom you and I knew in Oxford are tired—mentally and emotionally tired."[2] While the context of Sperry's recollection was in comparing England and America, it is unavoidable to assume that what was true of Oxford became true of Sperry, in that he sensed that he was at the end of an important era and that he was tired.

While Oxford, according to George Santayana in *The Last Puritan* (1936), "seemed a compromise, a sort of lingering sunset: the classics and the poets, Platonism and Christianity, illuminating beautifully, for the old world, the approach of night," it could also be portrayed as something else. Santayana continues, "The most antiquated things in it were revivals. If the place seemed dedicated to recollection and fidelity, that was because here the seminal principles were still living which could give form to a wise man."[3] The situation at Oxford by the forties not only spoke to Sperry's intellectual condition in America, but its role, as depicted, by Santayana, seemed also to be the pattern of Sperry's thought within American Protestantism because his "seminal principles," derived from a time before 1914, "were still living." By the forties Sperry was "dedicated to recollection and fidelity" and the chief way it was manifested was in his attempt to "revive" the problem of the historical Jesus that was first introduced to him at Oxford, just before the older, middling liberalism grew tired.

Two other passages from *The Last Puritan* are suggestive of Sperry's milieu and anti-climax. When Santayana's protagonist, Oliver Alden, goes to live in Divinity Hall at Harvard he is somewhat secretive about his lodgings. He is finally pressed about his living arrangements and Oliver tells his inquirer, "I live in Divinity." "Not possible? Isn't that somewhere beyond Memorial? Never heard of anybody living there," came the reply, with the afterthought, "That remote region had one clear meaning... it meant poverty."

Santayana's second description of that part of Harvard comes on a near page: "Opposite Divinity, behind the trees, rose a vast factory-like, red-brick edifice, then half-finished, the Chemical Laboratory; and in its shadow the old Theological School seemed absolutely derelict and overpowered."[4] From these tandem impressions some of Sperry's occasional asides to his correspondents are confirmed as a deeper, inevitable consciousness at work in him. First, the "poverty" of the Divinity School was constantly symbolic in his mind of a bankrupt liberal theology, and secondly, the coexistence of religion and science was emblematic of a disturbing, unequal cultural status between them. Consequently, Sperry's career must be evaluated in light of the declining reputation of what he represented and of how he tried to restore a sense that the brave struggle of the older liberalism still had purpose.

Sperry again and again tried to avoid a sentimental compromise between the world he inherited and the world he saw disappear. Typical of the way his mind worked toward the synthesis of opposites, he tried to reconcile an acceptance of both worldviews, each in its unvarnished reality.

As he perhaps expected, the outcome was at best a moral victory, the last heroic, but bewildered effort of a liberal mind with "roots struck before 1914." One of the roots was a doctrine of the mind of Christ.

Sperry thought that science and art were daily vindicating the religious intuition that, through the central realities of the vast world, the mystery is singular and not many, and that it is order and not chaos. The equivalent to a deepened sense of the interrelatedness of things that characterizes the illiberal liberal's outlook on life is, as Sperry posits, a doctrine of Logos. Noting that Darwin once raised eighty seedlings from a single clod of dirt taken from a bird's foot, a parable of interdependence, Sperry granted, "It is hard for the modern Christian to believe that he counts, and God cares for him individually and needs him." On the contrary, within "the mind of Christ" exists knowledge of how all the detailed parts work together for the sake of a whole greater than their sum. One of the vaguest of all liberal clichés, however, was "the mind of Christ," which became a shorthand for an ambiguous Logos doctrine. It bracketed the many paradoxes that liberals in a modern world had to defend.

In his Commencement Address at the Newton Theological Institution, delivered June 6, 1922, Sperry in contemplating the ultimate oneness of things, said, "This sense of the interrelatedness of all things, and of the value of each component item, which is so characteristic of the Mind of Christ and yet so hard for the modern disciple to grasp, is perhaps the most distinctive contribution which modern Science is making to a simple Christian faith."[5]

Sperry, in working his way forward, Christ-ward, or from outside the church inward, not only located epistemological authority within such an encompassing mind, but spiritual authority, too. He explains in *The Disciplines of Liberty*, "Each man gathers out of the record what is congenial to his own nature and circumstance and then reconstructs a figure from whom he draws authority for his own living." It is a mind too broad to describe or measure: "What there is of authority in this figure comes not as a clear, final, sufficient statement of the things men are to believe and to do, but as a stimulus to freedom and a source of unfailing spiritual energy." It is apprehending, not comprehending this omniscient mind that yields the fierce loyalty of Christ's devoted followers:

Our devotion to him is merely our consent to the clearest of all those earnests of nature and history which give us courage to believe that the

Universe is friendly, that the Veiled Being is no passionless object of our unrequited desire, but is in very truth the Eternal Goodness. It is to all such farther and final considerations that the authority of Jesus leads the human mind on into the central energy of all religion, man's friendship with God.[6]

Sperry saw the work of the world outside the church as following the oft-cited sequence of relationships that Whitehead insisted was natural and constant. Sperry endorsed the symmetry proposed by Whitehead that religion must move from God the void to God the enemy, and from God the enemy to God the companion. And in linking one's life with the experience and teaching of Jesus one discovers the "way" that traces one's thought of God from mystery to presence. Consequently, one is led to ask, "What was and is the truth about Jesus?" Sperry did not hide the premise of his inquiry: "If we could know the truth about him, we should know more of the truth about ourselves. We have not answered the problem of his person when we say he was a 'mere man'. For what we want to know above all else is what 'mere men' are and what the ultimate truth of them is."[7]

The Christological question for Sperry "seems to be in a state of arrest, and badly to need a non-apologetic reconsideration." He believed too much emphasis had been placed on the doctrine of the divinity of Christ which asserted itself with "pious indignation" whenever the custodians of its tradition were invited to explain what they mean.[8] He reserved his praise, however, for church fathers, such as Irenaeus and Athanasius who were "much bolder than the orthodoxy of our time; they did not hestitate to say that Christianity aims to make us divine in the same way and to the same degree that Jesus was divine." This is not entirely correct, for it is a generalization of a complex set of ideas, but has been expressed with a sense of selective usefulness in order to make a point. He appends the thought that "this was to their thinking the meaning and the intention of the Incarnation."[9]

Now Sperry confessed that he was not competent to propose a modern Christology "being neither a metaphysician nor the son of a metaphysician." He was prepared, however, to evaluate certain aspects of the situation which seems to be "furnishing the premises of our thinking" about Christology.[10] Sperry warned his dubious students at the Divinity School, "don't think because you find all ancient Christologies incredible or inadequate or perplexing, that there is no such problem and that it can be dismissed. In some sense Jesus remains a kind of test case for our humanity and its potential divinity... You have not solved the religious question by taking it off the person and shoulders of Jesus."[11]

On at least two counts Sperry examines the premises of Christology: the Christ of faith and the Jesus of history. First, Christ rather than Jesus is the figure who has moved Christians. In so far as the theological person Christ "was occasioned by and is to be identified with Jesus it has not been the historical man, but the cosmic figure who has influenced Christianity."[12] In his lecture notes Sperry explained to Divinity students his meaning that, "in general, the term Christ has become the personal name for all the idealism, devotion, aspiration of Christian character." The individual congnitive aspect of Christ, being highly subjective, yields a rich diversity of images. "My Christ and your Christ," he explains, "are different persons, that is because our natures and histories are different." In spite of the rival differences, "this one figure Christ comprehends them all. That is another way of saying that ultimately God comprehends them all, interprets them to each other and resolves their differences."

Secondly, Sperry in the face of growing opposition throughout his theological career maintained that "this Christ figure unless it is to become a Christian myth ought to be referred back constantly to its historical occasion, the Jesus of the first three Gospels." Here Sperry was also taking some exception to the Anglican incarnationalism that had carried over into William Temple's preference for the fourth Gospel, though the historical problems in it were also provocative. While Sperry knew well the futility of the search for the historical Jesus, he also conceded a pervading necessity that the quest not be abandoned. Sperry's line of thought in this regard jogs along smoothly, even in outline form: "No strict historical life of Jesus is possible. Not enough material to make this possible. We have to impute some theory to his life to make a consistent story. That he did die no doubt—but, what, what exactly did he hope to accomplish by it, how did he construe his own death." Sperry believed it was an important principle to recognize and accept that "every time we try to tell some truth about Jesus we inevitably tell a greater truth about ourselves." It is essential to a firsthand religious life that the interpretive skills not grow dull in examining the historical Jesus because "we are never wholly free of the necessity of trying to find out what he did and said. We shall go on with this, not merely out of historical curiosity but because the matter is more personal than that. It makes a difference what he thought and said."[13]

Sperry's dual concern for both the Jesus of history and the Christ of the creeds had grown a little out of fashion in many scholarly camps by the 1940s and has remained so for nearly forty years since. Only in the 1980s did his position show signs of being vindicated, but not before Sperry in his day paid the price of controversy and ridicule.[14] This last phase of his theological career is important not only because of what he said critically about neo-orthodoxy, but also for demonstrating the lasting impression Oxford had made on him so that the Continental challenge, no matter how persistent, could do little, if anything, to change his thinking. In 1949 Sperry lectured on Jesus at Northwestern University, the results of which were published that year as *Jesus Then and Now*. In the final sections Sperry noted a serious discrepancy between himself and the stylish neo-orthodoxy, occupying a different "mental world" than his.

Remembering his studies with Sanday and Streeter, Sperry said, "the premise of those proceedings was the assumption that if we could assure ourselves as to the *ipsissima verba* of Jesus of Nazareth we should have sufficient warrant at least for the beginnings of the Christian religion." Sperry hinted how in personal terms his belief had been helped by "those hours of patient inquiry, verse by verse, into the authenticity of the words of Jesus and the record of his life as found in the Synoptic Gospels." That experience, he said, "brought me nearer to what I believe to be the spirit of Jesus than most of the theological transactions in which I have been subsequently involved." In defense of the historical method, Sperry argued that no honest intellectual effort is ever wasted and to disparage that effort is to put Christianity "on precarious foundations."[15]

Meanwhile, having sampled Emil Brunner and W. A. Visser 't Hooft, Sperry entertained with "perplexity and honest concern the studied neglect of Jesus in the writings of the neo-orthodox theologians of our time." He did not question the piety of these theologians, but commented upon "the disproportion between space given to what Jesus himself is reported to have said and that given to what this encompassing cloud of [neo-or-thodox] witnesses have said." Sperry's indictment of neo-orthodoxy was derived from what he perceived as a lack of theological obligation to the ministry and sayings of Jesus, "that its cavalier neglect of the words and deeds of Jesus—apart from its emphasis upon his sacrificial death—is as partisan an account of Christianity as the critical and historical study of the gospels may have been at an earlier time."[16]

For these opinions, Sperry was so unexpectedly criticized by Amos N. Wilder, who was later Hollis Professor of Divinity at Harvard, in a review for *The Christian Century* that Sperry felt it to be unfairly severe. Wilder suggested that the Oxford school, given so much to the Synoptic problem, was passé and that Sperry's failure to mention Rudolf Bultmann's contribution to New Testament scholarship was negligent and perhaps belligerent or, by connotation an old man's crankiness, when there were obvious areas for fruitful conversation between the two rival interests. In subsequent issues of *The Christian Century* Wilder was subjected to counter-attack from Arthur Darby Nock, Sperry's closest friend and the one to whom the book in question was dedicated, and then from Edwin P. Booth of Boston University. Nock insisted in Sperry's defense that what one can find of use in Bultmann "is no more a product of neo-orthodoxy than it is of his political and economic convictions, whatever they be."[17]

Sperry received a kinder notice of *Jesus Then and Now* in *The Crozier Quarterly* from Harold R. Willoughby of The University of Chicago Divinity School, who also typified the older liberalism which hardly made him an impartial reviewer. Sperry wrote Willoughby a word of appreciation, but not without mention of Wilder's "very unfair review":

> I have never taken exception to anything which any reviewer has said about any of my books, but I broke the rule in the case of Amos. He says he did not mean it, but the general inference that one got from his review was that I was a rather old gentleman peddling out-of-date stock from shelves in the back shop. I told Amos that I thought that was hitting below the belt and had nothing to do with the relative merits of historical theology and dialectical theology.[18]

Because of his intellectual convictions about the continuing work to be done on Synoptic, Pauline and Johannine issues he was even disposed to consider in good humor the doctrine of immortality as the ultimate validation of pursuing the historical Jesus. In his Ingersoll Lecture in 1953 he said, "Whatever appeal the hope of immortality may have lies in the prospect that we may know more fully, love more truly and will more wisely. If there is a life after death, I personally hope that I may in some mysterious way know the man who wrote the Fourth Gospel and even ask him when and where he wrote it. I should like to have that baffling matter settled once for all."[19]

Sperry, in refusing to divorce the Word from the words, the Christ of faith from the Jesus of history, tried to overcome theologically the recurring difficulty of Christology. The entanglement is, as Sperry recounted, "that we may assume it to be a truth to be told only of Jesus and not pertinent for ourselves."

·❧·

Willard Sperry could not help feeling that he had been born too late, especially after his older liberalism, through his inconclusive airing of Christological and Synoptic problems, bumped up against neo-orthodoxy for the final time in the 1940s. This sense of being left behind was the general theme anticipated more than a decade earlier on the occasion of a Baccalaureate Sermon preached at Bryn Mawr on June 1, 1930. He found a companion mind in the writer of Ecclesiasticus (33:16, 17) who says that he had waked up in the world last of all, and that he was like one who must glean a field last of all after the great harvesters had passed. There were only a few odd straws left for him to pick up. This was one way Sperry came to perceive himself set in his times. The harvest was over and he was too late.

On second thought, however, he realized that selfish and cynical first thoughts would never be touched by what Wordsworth called "spots of time," the "local sympathy" of abstract ideas. Finally, the wise man of Israel imparted to Sperry, it seems in the most intimate terms, "his sober and steadying second thought"[20]—"I labour not for myself only, but for all them that seek learning."

As a case study of pre-1914 Anglo-American Protestant liberalism through the 1930s and beyond, Willard Sperry has much to teach the complex Protestant mind projecting itself toward the end of the modernist establishment's hegemony. He did his work during a formative period of the twentieth century in which he had gleaned the field from its beginning through its middle ground. Sperry anticipated the creeping pluralism which would catch up with the American mainline church by the 1980s. He recognized, on the one hand, that the future competition for liberal Protestantism would not come from other religious quarters necessarily, but from a secularism it had helped to develop through a pattern of cultural capitulation. While pointing to external threats, Sperry, on the other hand, predicted the spread of internal weaknesses along the lines which actually developed after the 1960s. As a generation in the last decade of the twentieth century is beginning to discover, the perils of weightless symbols and vacant language were ignored by the liberal Protestant church, in spite of warnings against bankrupt apologetics. Consequently, critics in the mid-1980s were saying that "liberal Protestantism faces its own crisis of identity and purpose from a position closer to the margin" largely because it failed in its custodial role in behalf of American culture.

Sperry was giving analysis and voice to an overlooked concern, that experimental trends such as neo-orthodoxy and humanism within liberal Protestant structures would eventually endanger the older, but modified conventional position which held the greatest prospect for longevity. The trouble was that the modifications, which Sperry represents, went unrecognized. The 1960s in American culture, of course, provided the force which enfeebled the mainline religious order. The result was, as Wade Roof and William McKinney argue and Sperry anticipated, a "vacuum in the culture created by the collapse of the middle."[21] That Sperry was a proponent of the middle ground which gave liberalism in religion its preponderant influence and security makes his awareness of the church's paradoxical fragility and durability seem prescient.

It is doubly ironic that neo-orthodoxy is with hindsight being interpreted, in part, as an alternate path to secularism. Similarly, it is curious that many, who embraced Reinhold Niebuhr for his political correctness, largely dismissed the theological foundations on which Niebuhr's position rested. One wonders if other theological expressions than neo-orthodoxy (an off-putting name) might have been able to hold a secular constituency drifting away from mainline religon. During the time of neo-orthodox reaction against the older, modified liberalism between 1930 and 1960, intellectual respectability for Protestant thought was an issue right at the place it might have had the best chance of gaining the broadest appeal—the middle ground. Instead, neo-orthodoxy not only drove supportive secularists away from its theological underpinnings, it contributed to the erosion of liberal religious thought which had been making self-corrections all along. Indeed, sin, irony and paradox were not the exclusive property of Niebuhrians.[22] Rather, the temporary alliance of neo-orthodoxy with the post-war liberal political and academic axis failed to carry with it the very terms which made Christian faith necessary: Jesus, worship and immortality, the themes of Sperry's later thought.

Willard Sperry died May 15, 1954, less than a year after his retirement from Harvard. At the end he was not embittered, but nevertheless felt cast aside and unwanted. An unfortunate published remark about being replaced by a more energetic young dean stung him at a moment of heightened personal sensitivity. He and Muriel sold their house on Francis Avenue near the Divinity School in favor of apartment living on Memorial Drive in Cambridge. He had made a number of false starts at an autobiography, all unsatisfactory attempts in the face of diminishing health. Pushing his limits, he collapsed with congestive heart failure not long after moving to new quarters. He did not die before being visited by his daughter, Henrietta, who made the urgent trip from England aboard the Queen Mary. Lady Wilson's memory of her father's last days are vividly evocative so that "in death that warm and kindly face was strangely stern: the Puritan strain revealed."

The funeral service was held in Memorial Church, which was full. Outside, the Yard was busy with students on a fine spring afternoon near the end of term. He was buried in Mount Auburn Cemetery where so many New England divines have been laid to rest and where he himself had taken so many burial services.

Sperry used to keep on his desk in Cambridge a brown notebook which served as an informal catalogue of his sermons, addresses, lectures and speeches. He readily confessed that the keeping of a casual record was necessary as a guard against "flagrant repetition" on his part, "at least within too short a time." The columns were labeled "What—Where—When." One day he scanned this book and discoverd that his wife had irreverently added a fourth heading to his titles, "Why?"—which he regarded as "a perfectly fair, but rather disconcerting query."[23]

As a person with a public life he sought an unsystematic, but methodical consistency in his private thoughts, laboring successfully to remain faithful to himself in purpose and expression. This kind of disciplined exercise, mindful of the abiding human question, "Why?" required not only lucidity but intimated courage to be a forthright self in the face of reality. Writing Henrietta on the occasion of her birthday he had once allowed that "to have lived at all—to have come to consciousness and self-consciousness is very much. Annihilation is as inconceivable as nothingness."[24]

Notes

Preface

1. WLS, *Signs of These Times* (Garden City, NY: Doubleday, Doran and Company, 1929), 6, 8.

2. Eugene Exman, *The House of Harper* (New York: Harper and Row, 1967).

3. Howard Mumford Jones to WLS, letter, January 15, 1953, Harvard University Archives, HUG 4808.

4. D. Elton Trueblood, *Essays in Gratitude* (Nashville, TN: Broadman Press, 1982), 113.

5. John Wesley Lord in "The Scribe," a student publication of the Harvard Divinity School, May 1953.

6. Bishop Tucker, *The American Oxonian*, XLI (April 1954), 125.

7. Alan Seaburg, "A Learned Ministry at Harvard: Willard Learoyd Sperry," *Harvard Theological Review*, vol. 80:2 (1987), 180.

8. Paul A. Carter, *Another Part of the Twenties*, New York: Columbia University Press, 1977), 41-61, 193.

9. Howard Mumford Jones.

10. WLS, *Signs of These Times*, vii.

11. WLS to Henrietta Wilson, letter, January 1940, in possession of author.

12. WLS to Henrietta Wilson, letter, February 1946, in possession of author.

13. James R. Moore, *The Post-Darwinian Controversies* (Cambridge: Cambridge University Press, 1979), 54.

14. WLS, *Signs of These Times*, 14-15.

15. WLS, *The Paradox of Religion* (London: Constable and Company, Ltd., 1927), x.

16. Robert Moats Miller, *Harry Emerson Fosdick: Preacher, Pastor, Prophet* (New York: Oxford University Press, 1985), 376.

17. WLS, *Signs of These Times*, 47-48.

18. H. Shelton Smith, "The Christocentric Liberals" (an introduction) in *American Christianity: An Historical Interpretation with Representative Docu-*

ments, vol.II, 1820-1960, H. Shelton Smith, Robert T. Handy and Lefferts A. Loetscher, eds. (New York: Charles Scribner's Sons, 1963), 255-65.

19. Jaroslav Pelikan in Kenneth Cauthen, *The Impact of American Religious Liberalism* (New York: Harper and Row, 1962), ix-x.

20. William R. Hutchison, *The Modernist Impulse in American Protestantism* (Cambridge: Harvard University Press, 1976), 8.

21. Claude Welch, *Protestant Thought in the Nineteenth Century*, vol. 2: 1870-1914, (New Haven: Yale University Press, 1985), 222.

22. Smith, Handy and Loetscher, 426ff.

Chapter 1

1. Willard L. Sperry in *Thirteen Americans: Their Spiritual Autobiographies*, ed. Louis Finkelstein, (New York: Harper and Brothers, 1953), 244.

2. WLS to George Miner Hall, letter, April 25, 1934, Harvard University Archives, HUG 4808.5. George Miner Hall wrote Sperry to ask if his father was the same man who was principal in Beverley during the 1870s. Hall had been a student there at the time and admired the senior Sperry.

3. *The Congregational Yearbook*, vol. 29, 1906, 38-39. In comparing the types of Congregationalism represented at Andover and Yale at the time Willard G. Sperry was a student, one finds a mix at both places of liberal and conservative forces, so that his theological training was not gained by the pairing of contrasts, but by adding complementary angles. Neither school was at its peak of institutional strength during those years. Andover had long been a bastion of conservative Calvinism, but had swung around to the liberal point of view. It was costly in the end with the heresy trial of Egbert C. Smyth (1886-92). Yale, perhaps, had a more congenial atmosphere than Andover and tolerated differences without resorting to theological litigation. cf. Daniel Day Williams, *The Andover Liberals: A Study in American Theology* (1941; reprint New York: Octagon Books, 1970) and Roland H. Bainton, *Yale and the Ministry* (New York: Harper and Brothers, 1957).

4. WLS, *Summer Yesterdays in Maine* (New York: Harper and Brothers, 1941), 8.

5. Ibid., 17.

6. Ibid.

7. Ibid., 18.

8. Ibid., 8.

9. A Sperry family geneaology summarized for me by Lady Henrietta Wilson, daughter of WLS. cf. Will of Richard Sperry, April 19, 1693 recorded in New Haven Probate Records, vol. 2, 230-31.

10. WLS to Pauline Sperry, letter, April 1911, Andover-Harvard Library, bMS 80/1:6.

11. Walt Whitman, "When Lilacs Last in the Dooryard Bloom'd," in John Frederick Nims, ed., *The Harper Anthology of Poetry* (New York: Harper and Row, 1981), 398.

12. WLS, *Summer Yesterdays in Maine*, 234.

13. Ibid., 9.

14. Ibid.

15. Ibid.

16. Ibid., 10.

17. Ibid.

18. WLS to Mrs. Edith H. MacFadden of New York City, letter, March 23, 1934, Harvard University Archives, HUG 4808.5.

19. WLS, *Summer Yesterdays in Maine*, 10.

20. WLS to W.H. Spence of Salem, Massachusetts, letter, January 4, 1926, Harvard University Archives, UAV 328.16.

21. WLS in Louis Finkelstein, ed. 232.

22. *Olivet, One Hundred Years, 1844-1944, A Commemorative History of College and Village* (Olivet, MI: Citizens of Olivet, 1944), 48.

23. *Charles G. Finney: An Autobiography*, (Old Tappan, NJ: Fleming H. Revell Co., 1876, 1908), 42.

24. WLS, *Religion in America* (New York: The Macmillan Company, 1946), 160.

25. WLS in Louis Finkelstein, 235.

26. WLS, *Religion in America*, 160.

27. Ibid., 161.

28. Jessie E. Sexton, "Congregationalism, Slavery and the Civil War" (pamphlet) Lansing, MI: Michigan Centennial Observance Commission, 1966, 9.

29. George A. Gordon, *My Education and Religion: An Autobiography* (Boston: Houghton Mifflin Company, 1925), 251.

30. Ibid., 252-53.

31. Richard Hofstadter, *The Age of Reform* (New York: Vintage Books, 1980), 150, 152; cf. William R. Hutchison, "Cultural Strain and Protestant Liberalism," *American Historical Review*, vol. 76, (April 1971): 386- 411.

32. Robert T. Handy, *A History of the Churches in the United States and Canada* (Oxford: Oxford University Press, 1976), 277-78.

33. Ibid., 279.

34. Sydney Ahlstrom, *A Religious History of the American People* (New Haven: Yale University Press, 1972), 867.

35. Willard G. Sperry, "The Vision of the Kingdom," Annual Sermon before the American Board of Commissioners for Foreign Missions, delivered at Manchester, NH, October 13, 1903, Boston: ABCFM, 1903, 3.

36. Ibid., 6.

37. Ibid., 7, 8.

38. Ibid., 10.

39. Ahlstrom, 866.

40. W. G. Sperry, 15.

41. Ibid., 12.

42. WLS, *Those of the Way* (New York: Harper and Brothers, 1945), 17-18.

43. WLS, *The Disciplines of Liberty* (New Haven: Yale University Press, 1921), 147.

44. WLS, "The Case for Foreign Missions," *Envelope Series* XVII: 3, ABCFM, October 14, 1914, 8, 17-18, 22.

45. William R. Hutchison, *Errand to the World: American Protestant Thought and Foreign Missions* (Chicago: University of Chicago Press, 1987), 158ff.

46. WLS to Pauline Sperry, letter, October 18, 1903, Andover-Harvard Library bMS 80/1.

47. Philip Greven, *The Protestant Temperament* (New York: Alfred A. Knopf, 1977), 16.

48. William R. Hutchison, "Cultural Strain and Protestant Liberalism," 406-11.

49. WLS in Louis Finkelstein, 231, 232, 233.

50. Henrietta Wilson to author, letter, May 22, 1986.

51. WLS in Louis Finkelstein, 234.

52. Lefferts A. Loetscher, *Facing the Enlightenment and Pietism: Archibald Alexander and the Founding of Princeton Theological Seminary* (Westport, CT: Greenwood Press, 1983), 172, 176, 68.

53. Ian Campbell, *Thomas Carlyle* (New York: Charles Scribner's Sons, 1974), 42-43, 175.

54. WLS to Agnes Thompson Starr, letter, December 31, 1952, Harvard University Archives, UAV 328.15.15, Box 7. See also WLS to Pauline Sperry, January 17, 1933, Andover-Harvard, bMS 80/2:11. The irony here is that as Sperry was nearing the end of his term as Dean at Harvard Divinity School, he was beset with the same kind of difficulty as his father in leading a school struggling for financial survival.

55. James L. Ash, Jr., *Protestantism and the American University: An Intellectual Biography of William Warren Sweet* (Dallas, TX: SMU Press, 1982), 16.

56. WLS to Pauline Sperry, letter, November 26, 1903, Andover-Harvard Library, bMS 80/1:1.

57. WLS to Pauline Sperry, letter, February 27, 1950, Andover-Harvard Library, bMS 80/3:11.

Chapter 2

1. Matthew Arnold, *St. Paul and Protestantism* (New York: The MacMillan Company, 1902), 70.

2. WLS, *Thirteen Americans: Their Spiritual Autobiographies*, Louis Finkelstein, ed. (New York: Harper and Brothers, 1953), 236.

3. WLS to Pauline Sperry, letter, undated, 1904, Andover- Harvard Library, bMS 80/1:2.

4. WLS to Pauline Sperry, letter, October 15, 1903, Andover-Harvard Library, bMS 80/1:1.

5. WLS to Pauline Sperry, letter, undated, 1903, Andover- Harvard Library bMS 80/1:1.

6. Ibid.

7. Thomas Hardy, *Jude the Obscure* (1895), chapter 4, part first.

8. WLS to Pauline Sperry, letter, undated, 1904, Andover- Harvard Library, bMS 80/1:2

9. Chairman Rhodes Scholarship Committee to WLS, letter, July 14, 1904, Harvard University Archives, HUG 4808.

10. WLS to Pauline Sperry, letter, undated, 1903, Andover-Harvard Library, bMS 80/1:1.

11. WLS, *Thirteen Americans*, 236.

12. Ibid., 236.

13. Walter Marshall Horton, *Contemporary English Theology* (New York: Harper and Brothers, 1936), 30.

14. B. H. Streeter, "The Historic Christ" in *Foundations*, B. H. Streeter, ed. (London: Macmillan Company, Ltd, 1913), 75-76, 127-38, 140.

15. Ibid., x.

16. Virginia Woolf as quoted in Thomas A. Langford, *In Search of Foundations: English Theology 1900-1910*, (Nashville, TN: Abingdon Press, 1969), 44.

17. Sperry apparently found the Modernist George Tyrrell generally more useful in Christology than Schweitzer. Tyrrell had tried to mediate the "strangeness" of Jesus out of the exclusive dehistorical approach of Weiss and Schweitzer because their method showed them "forced back very unwillingly in most cases, to eschatological and apocalyptic interpretations of the Gospel. Very unwilling, because it destroys the hope of smoothing away the friction between Christianity and the present age." Because Sperry was drawn first to Tyrrell's work, he was not going to find Schweitzer as compelling. This preference is not a repudiation of Schweitzer, but an adjustment of spirit. Tyrrell, however, harshly criticized the Jesus of liberal Protestantism, pointing out that "the Christ that Harnack sees, looking back through nineteen centuries of Catholic darkness, is only the reflection of a Liberal Protestant face, seen at the bottom of a deep well." This is essentially Schweitzer's message too. The emphases diverge. cf., George Tyrrell, *Christianity at the Cross-Roads* (London: Longmans, Green and Co., 1913) 43-44.

18. WLS, "The Choice of Course at Oxford," *The American Oxonian*, vol. III (January 1916), 16.

19. Jan Morris, *Oxford* (Oxford: Oxford University Press, 1978), 180.

20. Charles D. Cashdollar, *The Transformation of Theology, 1830-1890: Positivism and Protestant Thought in Britain and America* (Princeton, NJ: Princeton University Press), 115.

21. Walter M. Horton, 30.

22. WLS, *Thirteen Americans*, 236.

23. Lady Henrietta Wilson to author, letter, May 28, 1986.

24. L. W. Grensted, *Dictionary of National Biography* (1931-1940), 837.

25. L. E. Elliott-Binns, *English Thought 1860-1900: The Theological Aspect* (London: Longmans, Green and Company, 1956), 370.

26. Ibid., 371.

27. Thomas A. Langford, 263-64.

28. B. H. Streeter, *Foundations*, 5.

29. Thomas Carlyle, *Sartor Resartus*, Everyman's Edition (New York: Dutton, 1967), 125-26.

30. WLS to Pauline Sperry, letter, February 1, 1907, Andover-Harvard Library, bMS 80/1:5.

31. WLS to "Family," letter, December 29, 1906, Private Collection of Mrs. R. H. Milbraith of Guilford, Connecticut.

32. Ibid.

33. Henrietta Wilson confirms the place and time of her father's and mother's budding romance as Christmas vacation in Ireland, 1906: "It was there that he met my mother, striking and brilliant, one of the first women students at Trinity College Dublin. My grandfather [Bennett] ran an old-established auctioneering business, an occupation which was socially unacceptable to the land owning professional classes. My grandmother [Bennett] came of acceptable Hugenot stock, but after her marriage had to put up with occasional snubs from her snobbish relations. She married very young and had nine children, of whom my mother and Charles [Bennett, Sperry's roommate] were the youngest. . . When my father proposed to my mother he had to have an interview with my grandfather who, he said, asked him whether he would be able to keep my mother in the style to which she was accustomed. The style varied somewhat according to the state of my grandfather's business, but there were always maids. . ." Henrietta Wilson to author, letter, May 22, 1986.

34. WLS, *Thirteen Americans*, 237.

35. cf. Gabriel Daly, *Transcendence and Immanence: A Study in Catholic Modernism and Integralism*, (Oxford: Clarendon Press, 1980), 154-60.

36. WLS, "The Eschatology of the Synoptic Gospels: Its Fidelity to Religious Experience," *Harvard Theological Review*, 5:3 (1912), 386.

37. Ibid., 387.

38. Ibid., 388.

39. Ibid., 394-95.

40. Ibid., 388.

41. Ibid., 394.

42. B.H. Streeter, 7.

43. Ibid., 7.

44. Ibid., 514, 516.

45. Kenneth Cauthen, *The Impact of American Religious Liberals* (New York: Harper and Row, 1962).

46. Sydney Ahlstrom, "Continental Influence on American Christian Thought Since World War I," *Church History*, vol. 27 (September 1958), 269.

47. Charles S. Peirce, review of A. C. Fraser's edition of the *Works of Berkeley* in the *North American Review*, vol. 93 (October 1871), 449-72.

48. Louis White Beck, "German Philosophy," *The Encyclopedia of Philosophy* (New York: The Macmillan Company and the Free Press, volumes 3 & 4, 1972), 307. cf. WLS, *The Diciplines of Liberty* (New Haven: Yale University Press, 1921) 96.

49. Hans-Georg Gadamer, *Truth and Method* (New York: The Continuum Publishing Corporation, 1975), 26-30.

50. Sydney Ahlstrom, 256.

51. Ibid., 269.

52. Ibid., 268.

53. Walter M. Horton, 172.

54. William R. Hutchison, *The Modernist Impulse in American Protestantism* (Cambridge: Harvard University Press, 1976), 307-8.

55. cf. Walter M. Horton, 97.

56. cf. Nicholas Sagovsky, *Between Two Worlds: George Tyrrell's Relationship to the Thought of Matthew Arnold* (Cambridge: Cambridge University Press, 1983).

57. George Tyrrell, 5.

58. Ibid., 10.

59. Ibid., xx-xxi.

60. Ibid., xxi-xxii.

61. Ibid., 92 and John Ratte, *Three Modernists: Alfred Loisy, George Tyrrell and William Sullivan* (New York: Sheed and Ward, 1967), 218-19.

62. George Tyrrell as quoted by Lester R. Kurtz, *The Politics of Heresy: the Modernist Crisis in Roman Catholicism* (Berkeley: The University of California Press, 1986), 74.

63. George Tyrrell, 108.

64. George Tyrrell as quoted by Nicholas Sagovsky, 42.

65. WLS to Pauline Sperry, letter, February 1, 1907, Andover-Harvard Library, bMS 80/1:5.

66. George Tyrrell as quoted by WLS, *The Disciplines of Liberty*, 174- 75.

67. George Tyrrell as quoted by WLS, *Rebuilding Our World* (New York: Harper and Brothers, 1943), 91.

68. George Tyrrell, 107-8.

69. WLS, *Signs of the Times* (Garden City, NY: Doubleday, Doran and Company, 1929), 168.

70. George Tyrrell, *The Autobiography and Life of...*, ed., M. D. Petre, 2 vols. (London: 1912), vol. I, 153.

71. Henrietta Wilson to author, letter, May 22, 1986.

72. WLS, *Those of the Way* (New York: Harper and Brothers, 1945), 156n.

73. WLS to Pauline Sperry, letter, February 5, 1904, Andover-Harvard Library, bMS 80/1:2.

74. Henrietta Wilson to author, letter, April 21, 1986.

75. WLS to Pauline Sperry, letter, June 13, 1905, Andover-Harvard Library, bMS 80/1:3.

76. WLS to Henrietta Learoyd Sperry (Mother), letter, June 9, 1907, Andover-Harvard Library, bMS 80/1:5.

77. WLS to Henrietta and Pauline Sperry, letter, July 12, 1907, Andover-Harvard Library, bMS 80/4:3.

78. Henrietta Wilson to author, letter, April 21, 1986.

79. WLS to Pauline Sperry, letter, undated aboard RMS "Campania," 1905, Andover-Harvard Library, bMS 80/1:3.

80. WLS to Pauline Sperry, letter, November 23, 1906, Andover-Harvard Library, bMS 80/1:4.

81. WLS to Pauline Sperry, letter, April 28, 1907, Andover-Harvard Library, bMS 80/1:5.

82. WLS to Henrietta Learoyd Sperry, letter, June 9, 1907, Andover-Harvard Library, bMS 80/1:5.

Chapter 3

1. George Santayana, *Character and Opinion in the United States* (New York: George Braziller, 1955), 12-13.

2. WLS in *Thirteen Americans: Their Spiritual Autobiographies*, Louis Finkelstein, ed. (New York: Harper & Brothers, 1959), 239. For a review of Walker's career cf., Henry W. Borden, *Church History in the Age of Science: Historiographical Patterns in the United States, 1876-1918* (Chapel Hill: The University of North Carolina Press, 1971), 115-35.

3. Roland H. Bainton, *Yale and the Ministry* (New York: Harper & Brothers, 1957), 220.

4. Ibid., 220.

5. William Wordsworth, "Prefaces," *Wordsworth: Poetical Works*, Ernest de Selincourt, ed. (Oxford: Oxford University Press, 1978), 737.

6. Frank C. Porter, "The Place of the Sacred Book in the Christian Religion," in *Transactions of the Third International Congress for the History of Religions*, Oxford, 1908, II, 283-90; also same title in *Yale Divinity Quarterly*, V: 4, 266. cf., *Contemporary American Theology*, Vergilius Ferm, ed. (New York: Round Table Press, Inc., 1933), 197-242.

7. WLS, *Reality in Worship* (New York: The Macmillan Company, 1925), 207-208.

8. WLS in *Thirteen Americans*, 239.

9. Ibid., 240.

10. Peter Gordon Gowing, "Newman Smyth: New England Ecumenist," Th.D. dissertation, Boston University, 1960; William R. Hutchison, *The Modernist Impulse in American Protestantism* (Cambridge: Harvard University Press, 1976), 174-84.

11. WLS in *Thirteen Americans*, 241.

12. Martin Marty, *Modern American Religion: The Irony of It All* (volume I) (Chicago: The University of Chicago Press, 1986), 82-83.

13. WLS to John R. Mott, letter, February 25, 1938, Harvard University Archives, UAV 328.15.5.

14. For the most recent exposition on all this consult: Richard F. Gustafson, *Leo Tolstoy, Resident and Stranger: A Study in Fiction and Theology* (Princeton, NJ: Princeton University Press, 1986), 190, 264, 396-402. See also, *Lift Up Your Eyes: the Religious Writings of Leo Tolstoy* (New York: The Julian Press, 1960).

15. WLS to Henrietta Wilson, letter, dated only as 1938, in possession of author.

16. WLS to Henrietta Wilson, letter, probably late 1930s, in possession of author.

17. WLS in *Thirteen Americans*, 241; and WLS, "How My Mind Was Changed in This Decade," *The Christian Century*, vol. 56 (January 18, 1939), 83.

18. WLS in *Thirteen Americans*, 242.

19. WLS to Pauline Sperry, letter, April ?, 1911, Andover-Harvard Library, bMS 80/1:6.

20. WLS to Pauline Sperry, letter, undated 1911?, Andover-Harvard Library, bMS 80/1:6.

21. WLS to Pauline Sperry, letter, undated, 1911?, Andover-Harvard Library, bMS 80/1:6.

22. WLS to Pauline Sperry, letter, undated, 1911?, Andover-Harvard Library, bMS 80/1:6.

23. Ibid.

24. WLS in *Thirteen Americans*, 242.

25. WLS, "In Memoriam Rev. William Wisner Adams, D.D., 1831-1912," October 6, 1912, published sermon, 9-10.

26. Ibid., 11.

27. WLS to Pauline Sperry, letter, undated, 1911?, Andover-Harvard Library, bMS 80/1:6.

28. George Santayana, 32.

29. WLS to the Rev. William E. Gilroy, letter, July 10, 1923, Harvard University Archives, UAV 328.15, Box 1.

30. Granville Hicks, "The Parsons and the War," *American Mercury*, vol. X (February, 1927), 129.

31. Ray H. Abrams, *Preachers Present Arms* (New York: Round Table Press, 1933), 54.

32. S. Parkes Cadman and Henry Van Dyke as quoted in Granville Hicks, 133, 134.

33. Ibid., 133.

34. John E. Piper, Jr., *The American Churches in World War I* (Athens, Ohio: Ohio University Press, 1985), 12.

35. Edwin S. Gaustad, "The Pulpit and the Pews," in William R. Hutchison, ed., *Between the Times: The Travail of the Protestant Establishment in America, 1900-1960* (Cambridge: Cambridge University Press, 1989), 26-32.

36. Harry Emerson Fosdick, unpublished sermon, November 28, 1918, as quoted by Robert Moats Miller, *Harry Emerson Fosdick, Preacher, Pastor, Prophet* (New York: Oxford University Press, 1985), 78.

37. John E. Piper, Jr., 62-64.

38. Granville Hicks, 133.

39. John M. Mecklin, "The War and the Dilemma of the Christian Ethic," *American Journal of Theology*, vol. XXIII (January 1919), 33.

40. WLS, "Christ or Anti-Christ," published sermon, Thanksgiving 1914, Boston: The Pilgrim Press (pamphlet), 11, 20-21.

41. WLS, "Non-Resistance," published sermon, January 24, 1915, Boston: The Pilgrim Press (pamphlet), 8-10.

42. Ibid., 12.

43. Ibid., 16-17.

44. WLS, "Christ Our Peace," published sermon, Janurary 31, 1915, Boston: The Pilgrim Press (pamphlet), 7.

45. Ibid., 11.

46. Ibid., 16.

47. Ibid., 19.

48. Ibid., 20-21.

49. WLS to mother, letter, May 5, 1915, private source shared with author by Mr. R. H. Milbraith.

50. John Haynes Holmes, *I Speak for Myself*, (New York: Harper & Brothers, 1959), 181-86; also Ray H. Abrams, 199.

51. Margaret Hope Bacon, *Let This Life Speak, the Legacy of Henry Joel Cadbury* (Philadelphia: University of Pennsylvania Press, 1987), 32-49.

52. WLS to mother, letter, April 16, 1916, private source (Mrs. R. H. Milbraith).

53. WLS in *Thirteen Americans*, 244.

54. WLS to Pauline Sperry, letter, July 21, 1917, Andover-Harvard Library, bMS 80/1:7.

55. WLS to Pauline Sperry, letter, December 19, 1917, Andover-Harvard Library, bMS 80/1:7.

56. WLS in *Thirteen Americans*, 244.

57. Richard Hofstadter, *The Age of Reform* (pb) (New York: Vintage Press, 1980), 272.

58. Reinhold Niebuhr, *Leaves from the Notebook of a Tamed Cynic* (Chicago: Willet, 1929), 47.

59. Richard Wightman Fox, *Reinhold Niebuhr* (New York: Pantheon Books, 1985), 35, 43.

60. Ibid., 36.

61. Harry Emerson Fosdick, as quoted by Robert Moats Miller, 88.

62. Harry Emerson Fosdick, "What the War Did to My Mind," *The Christian Century*, vol. XLV (January 5, 1928), 11.

63. Robert Moats Miller, 497.

64. WLS to Harry Emerson Fosdick, letter, December 31, 1924, Harvard University Archives, UAV 328.15.5, Box 3.

65. WLS to Harry Emerson Fosdick, letter, May 12, 1939, Harvard University Archives, UAV 328.15.5, Box 3.

66. WLS to Pauline Sperry, letter, October 14, 1935, Andover-Harvard Library, bMS 80/2:13; WLS to Pauline Sperry, letter, December 18, 1937, Andover-Harvard Library bMS 80/2:15; WLS to Pauline Sperry, letter, February 28, 1939, Andover-Harvard Library, bMS 80/2:17.

67. WLS, "The Feel of This War," *Christendom: An Ecumenical Review*, vol. VIII (Autumn 1943), 476, 483.

68. WLS, *Wordsworth's Anti-Climax* (Cambridge: Harvard University Press, 1935), 12.

69. Ibid., 161; cf. WLS, "The Casting Out of Prussianism," privately published sermon, April 14, 1918, 9.

70. Leslie Stephen, as quoted in WLS, *Wordsworth's Anti-Climax*, 203.

71. Randolph Bourne, *War and the Intellectuals* (New York: Harper, 1964), 6.

72. Benjamin Jowett as quoted in Charles D. Cashdollar, *The Transformation of Theology, 1830-1890: Positivism and Protestant Thought in Britain and America* (Princeton, NJ: Princeton University Press 1989), 376.

73. WLS, "Bridging the Gulf," *The Atlantic Monthly*, vol. 123 (March 1919), 314.

74. Ibid., 315-16.

75. William R. Hutchison, *The Modernist Impulse*, 308- 309.

76. WLS, *The Disciplines of Liberty* (New Haven: Yale University Press, 1921), 59-80.

77. WLS, "The Meaning of God in the Life of Lincoln," published sermon, Boston: Central Church, February 12, 1922.

78. Lewis F. Stearns, *Present Day Theology* (London: James Nisbet and Company, 1893), 593.

79. Ibid., 534.

80. Ibid., 541.

81. William R. Hutchison, *The Modernist Impulse*, 304.

82. WLS, "The Paradox of Religion," *The Hibbert Lectures* (London: Constable and Company Ltd, 1927), 14-15, 17.

83. Ibid., 23-24.

84. Ibid., 28.

85. WLS, "How My Mind Was Changed in This Decade," *The Christian Century* vol. 56 (January 18, 1939), 84.

86. cf., Horton Davies, *Worship and Theology in England*, vol. V (Princeton, NJ: Princeton University Press, 1965), 150, 155, 158.

87. WLS, "Three Hundred Years—And After," (Convocation Address), *Harvard Divinity School Bulletin*, vol. XXXIV (April 24, 1937), 55.

88. WLS, "The Divine Reticence," The Essex Hall Lecture, 1927 (London: The Lindsey Press, 1927), 9, 13.

89. Ibid., 45.

90. WLS, "Three Hundred Years— And After,", 55-56

91. Horton Davies, 159.

92. WLS, "The Paradox of Religion," 58.

93. WLS, "The Divine Reticence," 25-27, 50.

94. WLS, *The Disciplines of Liberty*, 5-6.

95. Ibid., 61.

96. Ibid., 59-62.

97. Ibid., 65.

98. Ibid., 66.

99. Ibid., 67.

100. WLS, *Strangers and Pilgrims* (Boston: Little Brown and Company, 1939), 9.

101. Ibid., 10, 12.

102. WLS, "A Credible Doctrine of Man," in *The Nature of Man*, Simon Doniger, ed. (New York: Harper & Brothers, 1962), 87.

103. Ibid., 87.

104. WLS, "How My Mind Was Changed in This Decade," 82.

105. Ibid., 84.

106. WLS to Pauline Sperry, letter, November 26, 1939, Andover-Harvard Library, bMS 80/2:17.

107. WLS, "How My Mind Was Changed in This Decade," 84.

Chapter 4

1. WLS, "My Reasons," *Central Church Bulletin*, vol. VIII (June 1922).

2. Ibid.

3. WLS, *Thirteen Americans: Their Spiritual Autobiographies*, Louis Finkelstein, ed. (New York: Harper and Brothers, 1953), 245.

4. Levering J. Reynolds, "The Later Years," in *The Harvard Divinity School: Its Place in Harvard University and in American Culture*, George H. Williams, ed. (Boston: The Beacon Press, 1954), 210ff.

5. Henry J. Cadbury, George H. Williams and Arthur Darby Nock, Harvard University Memorial Minute from the Records of the Faculty of Arts and Sciences, October 19, 1954.

6. WLS, "My Reasons," 1922.

7. Ibid.

8. Mason Hammond, interview with author, July 10, 1986, Harvard University, Widener Study H.

9. Charles Forman, interview with author, July 29, 1986, Plymouth, Massachusetts.

10. WLS, *Thirteen Americans. . .*, 246.

11. Ibid., 246.

12. WLS, "How My Mind Has Changed in This Decade," *The Christian Century* vol. 56 (January 18, 1939): 84.

13. Theodore H. White, "Harvard Lies At the End of the Subway," in *The Harvard Book*, William Bentinck-Smith, ed., (Cambridge: Harvard University Press, 1982), 84.

14. Henrietta Wilson to author, private letter, March 16, 1986.

15. Mason Hammond, interview with author, July 10, 1986.

16. Paul G. Kuntz, "Willard L. Sperry: A Life of Natural Piety," unpublished manuscript, 1982. Kuntz was interviewed by the author on the telephone and corresponded with him, July 21, 1982. His 17 page essay cited above contains the insight, "Sperry was hurt by the shift from Lowell to Conant. He [Sperry] pointed out that there was a President's Pew in Memorial Church, just in front of the eagle lectern. The squire in an English country church had the privilege of reading the epistle lesson. Lowell used to do that. Why was Conant so conspicuously absent? 'Conant,' he tried to explain to us, 'had been brought up a Swedenborgian and had had so much religion forced upon him that he rebelled. It was entirely understandable,'

said the Dean. 'I myself had set out to be a biologist and many are the wrongs of the dogmatic theologian blind to new truth that seemed to threaten old orthodoxy.' Sperry must have told Conant that scientific truth had a claim in its own right."

Kuntz also points out that the Conants enjoyed hearing Reinhold Niebuhr preach at Harvard because they respected him intellectually. This is corroborated in Richard Wightman Fox, *Reinhold Niebuhr: A Biography* (New York: Pantheon Books, 1985), 211.

17. James B. Conant, "Baccalaureate Address to Harvard University Class of 1950," Harvard University Archives, 1950.

18. Howard Mumford Jones to WLS, letter, June 1, 1944, Harvard University Archives, UAV 328.15, Box 8.

19 WLS to Pauline Sperry, letter, January 8, 1929, Andover-Harvard Library, bMS 80/2:7.

20. WLS to Pauline Sperry, letter, September 1, 1929, Andover-Harvard Library, bMS 80/2:9.

21. WLS to Pauline Sperry, letter, March 2, 1943, Andover-Harvard Library, bMS 80/3:4.

22. WLS, "The Alumnus: Indubitably American, there is nothing like him in any other land," *Harvard Alumni Bulletin*, vol. 49 (1947): 589.

23. WLS to Pauline Sperry, letter, October 9, 1926, Andover-Harvard Library, bMS 80/2:4.

24. WLS to Pauline Sperry, letter, August 5, 1928, Andover-Harvard Library, bMS 80/2:6. The British Unitarian, L. P. Jacks (1860-1955) became one of Sperry's most important contacts with the academic and theological scene abroad. Jacks stood in the line of tradition that ran back through Stopford Brooke and James Martineau. In fact, Jacks married Brooke's fourth daughter, Olive Cecilia. He moved in literary circles as well, knowing Oscar Wilde and George Bernard Shaw. It has been said by Lance A. Garrard who prepared the article on Jacks for the *Dictionary of National Biography (1951-1960)* that "he is best thought of as the last of the Victorian prophets in the line of Thomas Carlyle whom he greatly venerated. (539) This single description goes far to explain the reason why Jacks was a significant figure in Sperry's orbit.

Jacks became Principal of Manchester College in 1915 and edited the influential Hibbert Journal "brilliantly" until 1947, sixteen years after retiring from his small Nonconformist Oxford college. Among Jack's several honors he had conferred upon him the D.D. degree by Harvard which Sperry surely had helped to effect.

Jacks had built a house outside the city of Oxford called "Great Stones, Headington," which Sperry and his wife happily rented for many summers. Muriel Sperry had dubbed Jacks "the sage of Shotover" and "the man of property," but her irreverence did not stop there. Because "Great Stones" incorporated and was extended from an old brick kiln, on heavy clay soil, Muriel came up with another name for it: "Big Bricks." Muriel also made it known, at least to Charles Forman (interview with author, July 29, 1986) that "the biggest thing about Jacks was his ego."

Jacks and Sperry had a serious falling out during the early forties over the conditions of tenancy at Great Stones. Sperry had sublet the property, presumably with permission from Jacks, but the arrangement somehow ran afoul to the annoyance of Sperry who had received notice from Jacks that the contents of the house had to be removed at once. This while Sperry was at Harvard!

Sperry wrote his sister in the spring of 1943, "Jacks is proceeding against me via his lawyer, to collect some unpaid rent, due from a defaulting sub-tenant, as well as two hundred and fifty pounds for dilapidation to the property, and his legal cost included. The whole proposed bill is $2,500. I am probably liable for something, in view of all the facts... He has turned mean and nasty on me... Behind it all, on the part of the tenant in default and Jacks there is the old delusion about the 'rich American'."[letter to Pauline Sperry, April 7, 1943, Andover-Harvard Library, bMS 80/3:4]

Given that Sperry had dedicated his work, *Yes, But* (1931) to Jacks and that Jacks had dedicated his book, *My American Friends* (1933) to Sperry, the riff between such close friends seems not only unfortunate, but unnecessary. Even with Sperry's "pro-British ardor cooled off at the moment," his feelings ran deep: "it is the end of any friendship with Jacks or any slightest desire ever to see that part of Oxford again." Sperry's daughter cannot recall whether Jacks and her father ever patched up the breach.[Henrietta Wilson to author, private letter, May 22, 1986]. There is, however, more than a trace of reconciliation before the two men died. Jacks sent Sperry a copy of his final book, *Near the Brink: Observations of a Nonagenerian*, inscribed, "to Willard L. Sperry with every good wish, Christmas 1953" (copy in Andover-Harvard Library).

25. Charles Forman, interview with author, July 29, 1986.

26. Paul G. Kuntz remembers "He did not look kindly on my reading of Kant's *Critique of Pure Reason*. He responded, 'I guess I'm still an Hegelian. Do read Collingwood's *Speculum Mentis*.' I wish I had pressed him on why he had preferred the idealism of the Nineteenth Century tradition, particularly of Britain and America. But then I knew what he felt: the idealists found God in the community. This was, and this may have been, Sperry's favorite quotation from Josiah Royce, 'the beloved community of memory and hope'."

27. WLS, "Preparation for the Ministry in a Nondenominational School," in George H. Williams, ed., *The Harvard Divinity School*, 276.

28. WLS, *The Disciplines of Liberty* (New Haven: Yale University Press, 1921), 164.

29. Ibid., 136.

30. WLS, "Preparation for the Ministry in a Nondenominational School," 292.

31. WLS, "The Double Loyalty of the Christian Ministry," *Harvard Theological Review* vol. XIII (April 1920): 102.

32. Ibid., 103, 105, 108, 112, 113-14.

33. Nietzsche as quoted in W. H. Auden and Louis Kronenberg, eds., *The Viking Book of Aphorisms* (New York: Penguin Books, pb), 323.

34. WLS, "The Mental Habits of the Minister," *Rochester Theological Seminary Bulletin* (June 1928): 6.

35. WLS, "The Double Loyalty of the Christian Ministry," 115.

36. WLS, "The Call to the Ministry," *Harvard Theological Review*, vol. XV (July 1922): 5, 7-9, 13, 15- 16.

37. WLS, "The Call of the Modern Ministry," *The Congregationalist and Advance*, vol. 105, March 4, 1920 295.

38. Herbert W. Schneider, *Religion in Twentieth Century America* (Cambridge: Harvard University Press, 1967), 145.

39. Bernard E. Meland, *Modern Man's Worship* (New York: Harper and Brothers, 1934), 20; Albert W. Palmer, *The Art of Conducting Public Worship* (New York: The Macmillan Co., 1957), 204; Andrew W. Blackwood, *The Fine Art of Public Worship* (Nashville: Abingdon- Cokesbury Press, 1939), 239; George Hedley, *Christian Worship: Some Meanings and Means* (New York: The Macmillan Co., 1953), 249; and Luther D. Reed, *Worship: A Study of Corporate Devotion* (Philadelphia: Muhlenberg Press, 1959), 386.

40. WLS to Edward Caldwell Moore, letter, March 16, 1927, Andover-Harvard Library, bMS 95/17:52.

41. Horton Davies, *Worship and Theology in England*, vol. V (Princeton: Princeton University Press, 1965),125f.

42. Ibid., 133.

43. WLS, "The Ethical and the Aesthetic in Religion," *Christendom*, vol. I (1935), 156.

44. T. J. Jackson Lears, *No Place of Grace* (New York: Pantheon Books, 1981), 185.

45. Ibid., 194-95.

46. WLS, *Reality in Worship: A Study of Public Worship and Private Religion* (New York: The Macmillan Company, 1925), 9.

47. Ibid., 23, 28-29, 30, 43, 57.

48. Ibid., 68. On the need for "objectivity" in worship see also: WLS, "Liberalism In Contemporary Religion," *Jewish Institute of Religion Bulletin*, vol. 3 (November 1924), 7.

49. Ibid., 70, 72-73, 74, 76.

50. Sperry, as a representative of the Congregational and Christian Churches, attended the World Conference on Faith and Order in Oxford, 1935 and Edinburgh, 1937 and was Chairman of the Commission dealing with "The Church's Unity in Life and Worship." Through this work he met a number of internationally known people, "reviving an old friendship with William Temple who was a don at Queens and is now Archbishop of York," later Archbishop of Canterbury. [WLS to Pauline Sperry, letter, August 20, 1935, Andover-Harvard Library bMS 80/2:13].

It is with notable irony that when Temple came to visit Harvard and the diocese of Boston he stayed with his low church friend, Sperry. Sperry remarks to his sister: "The Archbishop of York and wife are staying with us nearly a week... Put up a prayer for us! Muriel will love it [she being Anglican], and I like him, as he was 'Billy Temple' of Queens days. Still a very decent sort. But all the local Episcopalians are curled crooked with perplexity and jealousy as to why a super-Episcopalian has elected to lodge with a mere Congregationalist. 'Friend go up higher.' Or as Mother used to say, 'seest thou a man diligent in his business, he shall entertain archbishops'." [WLS to Pauline Sperry, letter, December 6, 1935, Andover-Harvard Library, bMS 80/2:13]. Clearly the Temple-Sperry friendship was based more on common ground theologically than the critical terms of Emerson's dictum on friendship being a kind of beautiful enmity.

Sperry eulogized the Archbishop during the Sunday morning service in Memorial Church for October 29, 1944, shortly after Temple's death. At that occasion he said that "his native humanity and his capacity for friendship were to the last unimpaired by the high office he held." cf., WLS, "A Tribute to the Late Archbishop of Canterbury," *Federal Council Bulletin* (December 1944).

51. WLS, *Reality in Worship*, 76-77, 10, 93, 94f, 90- 91, 151, 149.

52. Ibid., 152-58.

53. Ibid., 254f, 271, 260.

54. T. J. Jackson Lears, 174-75.

55. Ibid., 195.

56. Ibid., 196. Evidence of Sperry's interest in returning to a medieval paradigm is found in his article, "Relgion In Contemporary America," *The Yale Review* (October 1926): 22-23.

57. WLS to Edward Caldwell Moore, letter, March 16, 1927, Andover-Harvard Library, bMS 95/17:52.

58. WLS, "The Ethical and the Aesthetic in Religion," 152.

59. WLS to Edward Caldwell Moore, letter, undated, perhaps 1930, Andover-Harvard Library, bMS 95/17:52.

60. James Luther Adams, "Taking Time Seriously," (from *The Christian Century*, September 6, 1939) in *The Prophethood of All Believers*, George K. Beach, ed. (Boston: The Beacon Press, 1986), 38.

61. WLS, *The Paradox of Religion* (London: Constable and Co.,Ltd., 1927), 46; and WLS, *Reality in Worship*, 118-19. The image is originally from *Theologica Germanica*.

62. Horton Davies, 135.

63. WLS, *The Paradox of Religion*, 53-54.

64. Ibid., 56.

65. William James, *The Principles of Psychology*, vol. 2 (New York: Dover Press, 1950), 297-98. cf., WLS, "The Importance of William James," *The Journal of Pastoral Care*, vol. VII (Fall 1953): 148-52.

66. Josiah Royce, *The Problem of Christianity* (Chicago: The University of Chicago Press, 1968) 216-17. cf., also Bruce Kuklick, *The Rise of American Philosophers: Cambridge, Massachusetts, 1860-1930* (New Haven: Yale University Press, 1977), 351-69.

67. WLS to William Ernest Hocking, letter, October 30, 1941, Harvard University Archives, UAV 328.15.5, Box 1.

68. Sperry papers, Harvard University Archives, UAV 328.15, Box 2.

69. William Ernest Hocking, *The Meaning of God in Human Experience* (New Haven: Yale University Press, 1912), 411, 414-15, 416, 419-20,424-25; cf., also WLS, "William Ernest Hocking," *Advance*, 136 (February 1944): 6-7; Bruce Kuklick, *The Rise of American Philosophers*, 481- 95.

70. William Ernest Hocking in Charles A. Bennett, *The Dilemma of Religious Knowledge* (New Haven: Yale University Press, 1931), ix.

71. Ibid., x, 16-17.

72. WLS, *Reality in Worship*, 206-7.

73. Ibid., 253.

74. WLS to The Reverend Murray Shipley Howland, letter, January 7, 1926, Harvard University Archives, UAV 328.16.

75. WLS, *Reality in Worship*, 263.

76. W. Norman Pittenger to WLS, letter, October 10, 1929, Harvard University Archives, UAV 328.16.

77. William A. Clebsch, *American Religious Thought: A History*, (Chicago: University of Chicago Press, 1973), 50, 55.

78. WLS, *Reality in Worship*, 283f.

79. Ibid., 323.

80. WLS, *Prayers for Private Devotion in War-Time* (New York: Harper and Brothers, 1943), 52.

81. WLS, "The Whole Act of Man," unpublished lecture MS, 1936?, Harvard University Archives HUG 4808.

82. WLS, "Christian Prayer," umnpublished lecture MS, 1936?, Harvard University Archives HUG 4808.

83. WLS, *Reality in Worship*, 322-23.

84. WLS to Elmore M. McKee, letter, November 24, 1928, Harvard University Archives, UAV 328.15, Box 11.

85. WLS, *We Prophesy in Part* (New York: Harper and Brothers, 1938), 102.

86. Ibid., 104, 112, 133, 125.

87. Williams, Bixler and Nock.

88. WLS, *We Prophesy in Part*, 104, 175, 162.

89. Joseph Fort Newton, ed., *If I Had Only One Sermon to Prepare* (New York: Harper Brothers, 1932), 161-68.

90. Ibid.

91. WLS to Pauline Sperry, letter, January 3, 1939, Andover-Harvard Library, bMS 80/2:17.

92. Henrietta Wilson, a commentary on a student paper written at Harvard by Richard Tafel, April 1987. Lady Wilson shared her remarks with the author, most of which took Tafel to task for various "ill considered" and false assumptions about the Sperry marriage, their friendship with Arthur Darby Nock and Muriel's complex personality. In an April 21, 1986 communication to the author, Lady Wilson responded to a questionnaire, saying of her mother: "Looking back at her now, in my old age, I feel that she was a somewhat frustrated woman with an insufficient outlet for an active mind.... Nowadays she could have combined an academic post with marriage and been fulfilled. Perhaps as a result of this frustration, she was of uncertain temper, her tongue was sharp and at times indiscreet."

Howard Mumford Jones, according to Charles Forman (interview by the author, July 29, 1986), once told one of Sperry's students (probably the Unitarian minister, Alan Deale) that in all of Cambridge Muriel Sperry had the greatest grasp of the Irish Renaissance poets of the 1920s. Jones writes in his autobiography (Madison: WI The University of Wisconsin Press, 1979, 192), "Mrs. Sperry... had Strong Views on almost everything. She was a gifted writer too, but she never finished the book she had begun, to be entitled Dear Dead Women [the phrase coming from Browning's "A Toccata of Galuppi's": "Dear dead women...what's become of all the gold / Used to hang and brush their bosoms? I feel chilly and grown old."] I read the two or three sketches she had accumulated towards the proposed volume and found them moving and accurate."

Lady Wilson concludes, "So she was not an easy wife, and my father's uncompromising attitude to divorce may have stemmed not only from his Puritan background but also from the tensions in his own marriage. He remarked to me that it would be very dull to know everything about one's wife, and that he had no use for the kind of woman who says: 'my husband thinks and I think too.' He certainly never suffered from that."

93. Henrietta Wilson, to author, letter, April 21, 1986.

94. Paul G. Kuntz.

95. WLS to W. Norman Pittenger, letter, October 8, 1929, Harvard University Archives, UAV 328.16. Sperry wrote: "No man with as strong a feeling as Mr. Lippmann has for outer reality, or with as much concern as

he discloses for disinterested correspondence with a reality-not-ourselves, can be called a humanist in the stricter sense of that word... meanwhile his [Lippmann's] profound conception of life as correspondence with reality is the substance of a religion at once older and newer than of most contemporary humanism." WLS, "From Pure Science to High Religion," *The Yale Review*, vol. XIX (1929): 161-63.

96. Paul G. Kuntz.

97. Josiah Royce, *Basic Writings*, vol. 2 (Chicago: The University of Chicago Press, 1968), 966.

98. WLS to Pauline Sperry, letter, February 2, 1930, Andover-Harvard Library bMS 80/2:8.

Chapter 5

1. William Wordsworth, "Preface to the Lyrical Ballads," *Poetical Works*, Ernest de Selincourt, ed. (Oxford: Oxford University Press, 1978), 738.

2. James Luther Adams, "Fishing With Nets," an ordination sermon, *The Prophethood of All Believers*, George K. Beach, ed. (Boston: Beacon Press, 1986), 252.

3. WLS, "Modern Religion and American Citizenship," *The Yale Review*, vol. XVII (April 1928): 422.

4. Ibid., 422-23.

5. Ibid., 429-30.

6. WLS, *The Disciplines of Liberty*(New Haven: Yale University Press, 1921), 3-6.

7. Ibid., 3.

8. Ibid., 4.

9. Ibid., 66-67.

10. Ibid., 3, 73.

11. Ibid., 75.

12. Ibid., 75.

13. James R. Moore, *The Post-Darwinian Controversies* (Cambridge: Cambridge University Press, 1979), 68, 81.

14. WLS, *The Disciplines of Liberty*, 68.

15. Vilhelm Gronbech, as quoted in James R. Moore, 68.

16. James R. Moore, 76, 111. By the turn of the century, Huxley himself was surprised that any other battle lines could possibly be drawn between science and the church. He writes in response to a faint challenge made

from a few Anglican clergy pronouncing scriptural inerrancy, "Within the pale of the Anglican establishment, I venture to doubt, whether, at this moment, there are as many thorough-going defenders of 'plenary inspiration' as there were timid questioners of that doctrine, half a century ago." Thomas Henry Huxley in *Science and Christian Tradition* (New York: D. Appleton and Company, 1898), 24.

17. James R. Moore, 81.

18. T. H. Huxley, as quoted, Ibid., 349 and in WLS, *The Disciplines of Liberty*, 68.

19. James R. Moore, 349.

20. Daniel Day Williams, *The Andover Liberals: A Study in American Theology*, (New York: King's Crown Press, 1941), 74.

21. Ibid., 74, 158.

22. James R. Moore, 350.

23. Ibid., 350.

24. WLS, *The Disciplines of Liberty*, 124.

25. WLS, "Religion in An Age of Science," *The Journal of Religion*, vol. XV (July 1935): 264.

26. T. H. Huxley, as quoted in WLS, *The Disciplines of Liberty*, 125-26.

27. WLS, "On the Side Lines," *The Atlantic Monthly*, vol. 133 (1924): 767.

28. Frank M. Turner, *The Greek Heritage in Victorian Britain* (New Haven: Yale University Press, 1981), 414, 383.

29. WLS, "Religion in An Age of Science," 267.

30. Bruce Kuklick, *Churchmen and Philosophers* (New Haven: Yale University Press, 1985), 192.

31. Ibid., 196n.

32. Ibid., 257.

33. Ralph Barton Perry, *Present Conflict of Ideals*, as quoted by WLS in *The Disciplines of Liberty*, 127.

34. James Ward Smith, "Religion and Science in American Philosophy," in *The Shaping of American Religion*, James Ward Smith and Leland Jamison, eds. (Princeton, NJ: Princeton University Press, 1961), 430.

35. Bruce Kuklick, 250, 256.

36. WLS, "Religion in An Age of Science," 254.

37. WLS, *The Disciplines of Liberty*, 66.

38. Bruce Kuklick, 261.

39. WLS, untitled sermon on I Corinthians 1:14,16, unpublished MS, February 15, 1930, Andover-Harvard Library, bMS 80/5:13.

40. Ibid.

41. WLS, *Religion in America* (New York: The Macmillan Company, 1946), 254.

42. WLS, *The Disciplines of Liberty*, 126-27.

43. Ibid., 79-80.

44. WLS, *We Prophesy in Part*, (New York: Harper and Brothers Publishers, 1938), 142.

45. WLS, "On the Side Lines," 769-70, 771.

46. WLS, *Yes, But: The Bankruptcy of Apologetics* (New York: Harper and Brothers, 1931), 2.

47. Ibid., 2-3.

48. William R. Hutchison, *The Modernist Impulse in American Protestantism* (Cambridge: Harvard University Press, 1976), 2.

49. Ibid., 311.

50. Ibid., 251-253.

51. WLS, *Yes, But*, 6-7.

52. L. P. Jacks as quoted in Ibid., 14.

53. Ibid., 15-18, 21.

54. Ibid., 23-27.

55. Ibid., 30-32.

56. William R. Hutchison, 256.

57. Ibid., 311.

58. WLS, *Yes, But*, 39.

59. Ibid., 83.

60. Ibid., 73-74.

61. Ibid., 40, 42.

62. Ibid., 119, 122; N.B. Sperry's point on Darwin's artistic "illiteracy" is given exposition in WLS, "Art, Science and the Good Life," *The Yale Review*, vol. XVIII (December 1928): 215-16.

63. WLS, *Yes, But*, 120-21.

64. Ibid., 129-32.

65. Ibid., 136.

66. Ibid., 145.

67. Ibid., 147-48.

68. Henry Nelson Wieman to WLS, letter, April 10, 1935, Harvard University Archives, HUG 4808.4.

69. WLS, "Religion in an Age of Science," 255.

70. Ibid., 259.

71. Ibid., 260; cf., WLS, "Our Moral Chaos: Can Science and Religion Together Establish New Moral Universals," *Fortune*, vol. 25 (May 1942): 102ff.

72. Ibid., 262, 263-64.

73. WLS, *Yes, But*, 249.

74. Walter Lippmann, *A Preface to Morals* (New York: The Macmillan Company, 1929): 9, 6, 7.

75. Ronald Steel, *Walter Lippmann and the American Century* (Boston: Little, Brown and Company, 1980), 262.

76. Walter Lippmann, 77, 324, 327-28.

77. Ronald Steel, 264.

78. WLS, "From Pure Science to High Religion," *The Yale Review* vol. XIX (1930): 163.

79. Ibid., 161-63.

80. WLS, "Religion in an Age of Science," 265.

81. WLS, "From Pure Science to High Religion," 163.

82. WLS, "The New Asceticism," *The Atlantic Monthly*, vol. 151 (1933): 30.

83. Ibid., 33.

84. Ibid., 34, 35.

85. WLS to C. Leslie Glenn, letter, April 14, 1933, Harvard University Archives, UAV 328.15.5, Box 4.

86. WLS, "Humanism Against Romanticism," *The Yale Review*, vol. XIX (1930): 825.

87. WLS to L. L. Rice, letter, January 13, 1933, Harvard University Archives, UAV 328.16.

88. WLS, "Francis Thompson," unpublished lecture, December 2, 1935, Andover-Harvard Library, bMS 80/5:42; WLS, *Wordsworth's Anti-Climax* (Cambridge: Harvard University Press, 1935), 191.

89. WLS to Pauline Sperry, letter, February 11, 1923, Andover-Harvard Library, bMS 80/2:2.

90. John Stuart Mill, *Autobiography*, Harvard Classics Edition, vol. 25, (New York: P.F. Collier and Son, 1909), 96-97.

91. WLS, "Humanism Against Romanticism," 824.

92. Ibid., 825.

93. Ibid., 826.

94. WLS, *Wordsworth's Anti-Climax* (Cambridge: Harvard University Press, 1935), 227.

95. WLS, *Yes, But*, 146.

96. Ibid., 154-55.

97. WLS, *Wordsworth's Anti-Climax*, 187, 189f, 191.

98. Ibid., 197.

99. William Wordsworth, "The Prefaces," 737, 738.

100. WLS, *Wordsworth's Anti-Climax*, 199-202. cf., WLS, "Wordsworth's Religion" in *Wordsworth: Centenary Studies*, Gilbert T. Dunklin, ed. (Princeton, NJ.: Princeton University Press, 1951), 153-163.

101. WLS, "The Mind of Christ and the Tempers of Science," *Commencement Bulletin of the Newton Theological Institution*, vol. 14 (June 1922).

102. WLS, *Yes, But*, 180.

103. WLS to Henrietta Wilson, private letter, ? 1938, in possession of author.

104. WLS, untitled sermon on Job 14:14, unpublished MS preached at Princeton University, April 14, 1935, Andover-Harvard Library bMS 80/5:39.

105. WLS, "Immortality," unedited, unpublished lecture notes, Harvard University Archives, HUG 4808.

106. WLS, "Man's Destiny In Eternity," in *Man's Destiny in Eternity* (Boston: Beacon Press, 1951), 213-14.

107. Ibid., 212.

108. John Hick, *Death and Eternal Life* (San Francisco: Harper and Row, 1976), 215-16.

109. George Matheson as quoted by WLS, *The Disciplines of Liberty*, 19; "Man's Destiny In Eternity," 217.

Epilogue

1. WLS to Henrietta Wilson, letter, April 2, 1945, in possession of the author.

2. WLS to Henrietta Wilson, letter, July 1942, in possession of the author.

3. George Santayana, *The Last Puritan* (New York: Charles Scribner's Sons, 1936), 512-13.

4. Ibid., 422, 424.

5. WLS, "The Mind of Christ and the Tempers of Science," *Commencement Bulletin of the Newton Theological Institution*, vol. 14 (June 1922): 28.

6. WLS, *The Disciplines of Liberty* (New Haven: Yale University Press, 1921), 33, 40-41.

7. WLS, "Jesus," unedited, unpublished lecture notes, Harvard University Archives, HUG 4808.

8. WLS, *Yes, But* (New York: Harper, 1931), 157-58.

9. Ibid., 159.

10. Ibid., 162.

11. WLS, "Jesus," unpublished lecture notes.

12. WLS, *Yes, But*, 165.

13. WLS, "Jesus," unpublished lecture notes.

14. As indicative of a new "quest" cf., Leander E. Keck, *A Future for the Historical Jesus* (Philadelphia: Fortress Press: 1980); and James M. Robinson, *A New Quest of the Historical Jesus* (Philadelphia: Fortress Press, 1983).

15. WLS, *Jesus Then and Now* (New York: Harper and Brothers: 1949), 192, 194.

16. Ibid., 195, 199, 204-5.

17. Amos N. Wilder, Arthur Darby Nock and Edwin P. Booth in *The Christian Century*, September 7, 1949, October 12, 1949 and November 9, 1949 respectively.

18. WLS to Harold R. Willoughby, letter, January 18, 1950, Harvard University Archives, UAV 328.15.5 Box 7.

19. WLS, "Approaches to the Idea of Immortality," The Ingersoll Lecture on the Immortality of Man for 1952- 1953, April 14, 1953, *The Harvard Divinity School Bulletin* (1953-1954), 21.

20. WLS, unpublished sermon MS on Ecclesiasticus 33:16, 17, Andover-Harvard Library, bMS 80/4:25.

21. Wade Clark Roof and William Mckinney, *American Mainline Religion* (New Brunswick, NJ: Rutgers University Press, 1987), 240, 9.

22. R. Laurence Moore in William R. Hutchison, ed., *Between the Times: the Travail of the Protestant Establishment in America, 1900-1960* (Cambridge: Cambridge University Press, 1989), 245-48.

23. WLS, *Summer Yesterdays in Maine* (New York: Harper and Brothers, 1941), 1.

24. Henrietta Wilson to the author, letter, April 21, 1986.

INDEX

Abbot Academy, 3
Abrams, Ray N., 80, 87, 213, 214
Adams, Henry, 28, 134
Adams, James Luther, 56, 137, 151, 222, 225
Adams, William Wisner, 71, 75-78, 100, 213
Addams, Jane, 72
aesthetics, 2
Ahlstrom, Sydney, 19, 21, 53-55, 206, 210
American Board of Commissioners for Foreign Missions (ABCFM), 15, 16-18, 19, 23, 24, 206
Andover-Newton Theological Seminary, 110
Andover Theological Seminary, 3, 16, 109
apologetics, xx, 26, 95, 145, 162-164, 166-167, 168, 171, 199, 227
Arnold, Matthew, 27, 52, 58, 60, 93, 181, 207, 210
art, 44, 130, 131, 135-136, 145, 166, 168, 171, 178, 193, 227
asceticism, 177-181, 228
Athanasian Creed, See under THEOLOGY
Atlantic Monthly, 95, 164, 178, 215, 226, 228

Bainton, Roland, 204, 212
Barth, Karl, 97, 99, 100, 101, 106, 157
Beck, Lewis White, 54, 210
Bellamy, Joseph, 143
Bennett, Charles A., 46-47, 139-141, 209, 223
Bennett, John C., 167
Booth, Edwin P., 197
Boston, xi, xii, 4, 7, 8, 11, 13, 15, 23, 76, 78, 79, 119, 139, 162, 179, 180, 197, 221
Bourne, Randolph, 94, 215
Brooke, Stopford, 218
Brooks, Phillips, 144
Brown, William Adams, 53
Browning, Robert, 27, 28, 46, 93, 181, 224
Brunner, Emil, 196
Buchman, Frank N. D., 42, 57
Buchmanism, 13-14
Bushnell, Horace, 11, 16, 21, 69

Cadbury, Henry J., 86, 214, 217
Cadman, S. Parkes, 80, 213
Caird, Edward, 159
Calvin, John, 77, 100, 102, 124

Calvinism, 1, 2, 9, 20, 67, 97, 102, 124, 151, 153, 155-157, 160-162, 204
Campbell, R. J., 37, 41, 128, 207
Carlyle, Thomas, xv, 27-28, 45-47, 49, 61, 69, 167, 181, 207, 209, 218
Carter, Paul A., xiii, xiv
Cashdollar, Charles D., 41, 208, 215
Cauthen, Kenneth, xiv, xviii, 53, 210
Central Congregational Church, 78, 110
Christian Century, 90, 100, 106, 107, 197, 212, 215, 222
Christian Socialism, 22
Christology, See under THEOLOGY
Civil War, See under WAR
Clarke, Samuel, 26
Clarke, William Newton, 16, 112
Clebsch, William A., 143, 223
Colgate, 112
Collins, Anthony, 26
Common Sense, 12, 26, 54-55, 148
Conant, James B., xiii, 115-118, 217, 218
Congregationalism, 9, 15, 16, 57, 69 Congregationalists, 18, 142
Cushman, Arthur, 16

Darwinism, 156-157
Davies, Horton, 101, 128-129, 216, 221, 222
Dewey, John, 160-162
Drummond, William, H. 98

ecclesiasticism, 153
ecclesiology, See under THEOLOGY
ecumenism, xii, xix, 71
Edwards, Jonathan, 26, 107, 142-143, 155, 160, 161
Edwards, Jonathan, Jr., 143
Einstein, Albert, 174, 175, 184
Eliot, Charles W., 115, 117
Eliot, T. S., 179, 180
Elliott-Binns, L. E., 43, 208
Emerson, Ralph Waldo, xiv, xvii-xix, 78, 113, 188, 222
Episcopalians, 41, 67, 70, 221
eschatology, See under THEOLOGY
ethics, xii, xx, 2, 72, 73, 95, 104, 121, 129, 141, 154, 177

evangelicalism, 57
Exman, Eugene, xii

Fall River, 47, 71, 76-78, 100
Fausset, Hugh, 183
Finkelstein, Louis, 204, 205, 206, 207, 211, 217
Finney, Charles Grandison, 10-14, 26, 31, 205
First World War, *See under WAR*
Forman, Charles, 113, 119, 217, 219, 224
Forsyth, P. T., 41, 100
Fosdick, Harry Emerson, xii, xiv, xvii, xviii, xix, 53, 55, 74, 80, 81, 85, 89, 90, 91, 145, 147, 149, 167, 213, 214, 215
Foundations, 37, 38, 42, 44, 45, 47, 48, 51, 52, 53, 57, 196, 199, 208, 209
Fox, Richard Wightman, 214, 218
French Revolution, 93
fundamentalism, 90
future probation, 16

Gadamer, Hans-Georg, 54, 210
Garrard, Lance A., 218
Garrison, William Lloyd, 83
Garrod, H. W., 74
Gaustad, Edwin S., 213
Gilroy, William E., 213
Gladden, Washington, 16
Glenn, C. Leslie, 228
Goffe, William, 6
Gordon, George A., 15-20, 85, 205, 212
Gore, Charles, 132
Greven, Philip, 24, 206

Hammond, Mason, 113, 115, 217
Hardy, Thomas, 33, 34, 63, 207
Harnack, Adolph, xvi, 131, 174, 208
Harvard Divinity School, xi, 2, 109-110, 111, 114, 137, 151, 207, 216, 217, 220
Harvard University, 109, 112, 217
Hick, John, 189, 229
Hicks, Granville, 80, 213
Higher Criticism, 76
Hocking, William Ernest, 24, 139-141, 152, 223
Hofstadter, Richard, 18, 89, 206, 214
Holmes, Oliver Wendell, 180
Hopkins, Samuel, 143 Horton, Walter Marshall, 55, 56, 106, 167, 208, 210
humanism, xiv, xvi, 141, 148, 172-174, 176, 177, 179, 180, 183, 184, 199, 225, 228, 229

human nature, *See under THEOLOGY*
Hutchison, William R., xiii, xiv, xviii, xix, 25, 42, 50, 51, 56, 96, 97, 100, 165, 166, 169, 171, 206, 210, 212, 213, 215, 227
Huxley, T. H., 104, 153, 154-159, 170, 172, 225, 226

idealism, xviii, 51, 52, 57, 72, 73, 82, 87, 89, 93, 132, 152, 195, 220
immanentism, xix, 41, 42, 50, 100, 128, 137, 171
immortality, *See under THEOLOGY*
Inge, William Ralph, 137
irony, xx, 88, 90, 101, 102, 113, 143, 191, 199, 207, 212

Jacks, L. P., 56, 57, 98, 119, 166, 172, 174, 177, 218-219, 227
James, William, 31, 49, 51, 89, 107, 135, 138, 139, 222
Jesus, *See under THEOLOGY*
Jones, Howard Mumford, xii, xiii, 113, 116, 218, 224
Jowett, Benjamin, 39, 40, 94, 159, 215
just war, *See under WAR*

Kant, Immanuel, 220
Keats, John, 180, 181
Kingdom of God, *See under THEOLOGY, eschatology*
King's Chapel, 162
Krutch, Joseph Wood, 142
Kuklick, Bruce, 160-162, 222, 223, 226
Kuntz, Paul G., 115, 120, 148, 149, 217, 218, 220, 224, 225

Lake, Kirsopp, 189
Langford, Thomas A., 44, 208, 209
Learoyd, John, 3
Learoyd, Sarah S. 3
Lears, T. J. Jackson, 129, 130, 135, 221, 222
liberalism, *See under THEOLOGY*
Lincoln, Abraham, 97, 98, 99, 215
Lincoln College, 52
Lippmann, Walter, xiv, 97, 136, 142, 148, 149, 175-178, 224, 225, 228
Logos, *See under THEOLOGY*
Loisy, Alfred, 210
Longfellow, Henry Wordsworth, 180

Lowell, A. Lawrence, 109-111, 114, 115, 119, 180, 217
Luccock, Halford E., 89, 106

Macintosh, Douglas Clyde, 89
Manchester, New Hampshire, 3-5, 15, 153, 206
Manchester College (Oxford), 42, 119, 127, 218
Martineau, James, 218
Marty, Martin, 212
Matheson, George, 189, 229
Matthews, Shailer, 53, 80, 85
McAfee, Joseph E., 21, 22
McGiffert, Arthur Cushman, 16
McKee, Elmore M., 145, 223
McKinney, William, 199
Mecklin, John M., 81, 214
Memorial Church, xi, 111, 113, 115, 116, 119, 136, 139, 145, 200, 217, 222
Mill, John Stuart, 45, 182, 228
Miller, Robert Moats, 213, 214, 215
ministry, xi, xx, 3, 8, 9, 15, 22, 24, 31, 35, 65, 67, 68, 69-72, 74, 76-78, 81, 110-114, 120-126, 145, 163, 181, 196, 204, 212, 220modernism, xv, xviii, xix, 15, 38, 41, 50, 51, 57, 58, 71, 162, 165, 166, 167, 169, 174, 209
Moody, Dwight L., 12, 13, 31
Moore, Edward Caldwell, 111, 127, 221, 222
Moore, James R., 154, 155, 156, 170, 225, 226
morality, 154, 183
Morrison, Charles Clayton, 106
Mott, John R., 72, 212
mysticism, xvi, 35, 58, 61, 62, 63, 102, 133, 134, 135, 137-140, 142, 160, 170, 177

neo-orthodoxy, See under THEOLOGY
New Haven, 6, 69, 70, 76
New Theology, xix, 10, 16
Newton, Joseph Fort, 146, 223
Newton Theological Institution, 110, 193
Niebuhr, Reinhold, 53, 55, 56, 74, 89, 106, 145, 161, 162, 214, 218
Niebuhr, H. Richard, 75
Nietzsche, Friedrich Wilhelm, 27, 73, 74, 123, 220
Nock, Arthur Darby, 112, 115, 197, 217, 223, 224

"objective reality", 160
Olivet College, 5, 7, 10-12, 14, 15, 18, 26, 28, 29, 31, 34, 45, 205
Oman, John, 41
original sin, See under THEOLOGY
Oxford, xv, xvi, xx, 14, 18, 26, 29, 31, 33-43, 45, 46, 47, 52, 56, 57, 61, 63-69, 76, 79, 92, 94, 100, 107, 110, 119, 121, 127, 154, 159, 166, 191, 192, 196, 197, 208, 218, 219, 221
Oxford Group, 13, 42, 57

pacifism, See under WAR
Paley, William, 26
paradox, xvii, xviii, 38, 59, 96, 97, 98, 99, 101, 102, 106, 122, 123, 124, 133, 134, 138, 140, 146, 149, 157, 185, 189, 191, 199, 216, 222
Park, Edwards A., 16, 70
Pascal, Blaise, 106, 173, 174, 184
Peabody, Francis Greenwood, 85, 112
Peirce, Charles S., 54, 210
Perry, Ralph Barton, 161, 226
Phillips Academy, 3
Piper, John E. J., 80, 213
Pittenger, W. Norman, 142, 223, 224
poetry, 1, 69, 151, 157, 164, 171, 178, 180, 185, 186, 205
Porter, Frank C., 68, 69, 212
positivism, 61, 208, 215
post-war, See under WAR
pragmatism, 134, 138
prayer, xx, 62, 120, 121, 126, 127, 143-145, 221, 223
preaching, xi, xx, 7, 35, 71, 78, 80, 83, 97, 111, 113, 120, 121, 125, 126, 129, 142, 143-147, 162, 186
Princeton Theological Seminary, xv, 12, 127, 206
Princeton University, xi, 112, 186, 229
prophesy, 26, 82, 143, 156, 170, 223, 227
Puritanism, 183

Queens College, 35, 36, 140

Rauschenbusch, Walter, xviii
Religion in America, 205, 227
revivalism, 13, 14
Rhodes Scholars, 33
Rice, L. L., 228
Ritschl, Albrecht, 94

Ritschlians, 48
Romanticism, 102, 152, 163, 173, 182-185, 228, 229
Roof, Wade Clark, 199
Royce, Josiah, 122, 133, 138, 139, 140, 149, 220, 222, 225

Sanday, William, 37, 40, 43, 44, 51, 76, 196
Santayana, George, 78, 191, 192, 211, 213
Sartor Resartus, 27, 45-47, 209
Schneider, Herbert W., 126, 220
Schweitzer, Albert, xviii, 37, 39, 49, 77, 164, 208
science, xii, xx, 28, 34, 35, 44, 48-51, 58, 59, 61, 104, 116, 117, 126, 130, 131, 145, 151, 152, 154, 155, 156, 158, 159, 160, 161, 163, 164, 166-171, 174-179, 181, 182, 185, 186, 192, 193, 211, 225, 226, 227, 228, 229
Seaburg, Alan, xii
Second Thought, xvii, xix, 28, 67, 88, 94, 105, 138, 198
Second World War, See under WAR
Secular models, 157
Sedgwick, Ellery, 95, 164
sentimentalism, 181, 184, 185
Shakespeare, William, 93
Shaw, George Bernard, 46, 61, 104, 153, 154, 218
Shelley, John, 181
sin, See under THEOLOGY
Smith College, 5, 46
Smith, James Ward, 161, 226
Smyth, Newman, 16, 70, 71, 204, 212
Social Gospel, xviii, 9, 15, 19, 73, 78, 80, 123
Sockman, Ralph W., 89
Sperry, Henrietta Learoyd (mother of WLS), 3, 5, 10, 25, 211
Sperry, Henry, 3
Sperry, Mehitable, 3
Sperry, Pauline, 4, 205, 206, 207, 209, 210, 211, 213, 214, 215, 216, 218, 219, 221, 225, 228
Sperry, Richard, 6, 205
Sperry, Willard Gardner, 2-5, 8, 9, 11, 12, 15, 17-24, 25, 29, 31, 204, 206
Sperry, Willard Learoyd,
    Adams, William Wisner as mentor of, 71, 75-76
    birth of, 2
    death of, 200
    death of father, 46
    evangelical influences, 12-14
    foreign missions, 22-24
    funeral of, 200
    genealogy of, 6
    at Harvard, 109-120
    marriage to Muriel Bennett, 69, 224
    as minister, 47, 70, 71, 78
    as witness to modernist controversy, 36-39
    New England roots of, 7-9
    at Oxford, 63-66
    religious training at home, 10
    as Rhodes Scholar, 33-35
    theology as method, 94-95
    thoughts on
        Barth, Karl, 99-100
        biblical scholarship, 39-40
        Calvinism, 41, 100-104, 124, 151-157, 162
        Carlyle, Thomas, 27, 45, 47
        Eliot, T. S., 179-180
        eschatology, 48-49
        immortality, 185-109
        Jacks, L. P., 172, 218-219
        Jesus, 194-197
        Lincoln, Abraham, 98-99
        ministry, 120-126
        Niehbur, Reinhold, 161-162
        Nietzsche, 74
        Olivet College, 28-29
        pacifism, 79-88, 90-91
        preaching, 143-149, 163-164
        Tolstoi, 72-73
        Tyrrell, George, 75-63, 106, 121, 122
        Wordsworth, William, 181-185
        worship, 126-142
    at Yale, 67-69
    as YMCA secretary, 31-33
Starr, Agnes Thompson, 207
Stearns, Lewis French, 97, 215
Steel, Ronald, 228
Streeter, B. H., 35-38, 40, 42-47, 48, 57, 64, 70, 76, 121, 166, 167, 196, 208, 209
Sullivan, William, 210
Sunday, Billy, 13
Sweet, William Warren, 29, 207
Synoptic Problem, 36-39, 43, 48, 197
Systematic Theology, See under THEOLOGY

Temple, William, 40, 46, 56, 100, 133, 159, 221, 222
Tennyson, Alfred Lord, 27, 28, 180
THEOLOGY
  Athanasian Creed, 172
  Christology, xi, xviii, 39, 95, 194, 195, 198, 208
  ecclesiology, xvi
  eschatology, 48-52, 60, 209
    Kingdom of God, xviii, 42, 51, 129, 145
  human nature, 53, 88, 96, 102, 104, 105, 106, 152, 163, 170
  immortality, xx, 164, 184-189, 197, 200, 229
  Jesus, xx, 12, 24, 37-39, 48, 49, 50, 70, 73, 74, 75, 77, 82, 85, 91, 153, 166, 186, 188, 192, 194-198, 200, 208
  liberalism, xiv, xv, xvii-xx, 11, 14, 21, 25, 29, 52, 57, 68, 74, 92, 94, 96, 97, 101, 105, 106, 112, 124, 133, 142, 143, 156-159, 164, 165, 168, 172-175, 181, 182, 184-185, 192, 197, 198, 199, 206, 221
  Logos, 193
  neo-orthodoxy, xiv, xv, xvi, xix, 53, 96, 101, 106, 123, 157, 162, 165, 169, 184, 196-199
  original sin, 96, 102-104, 156
  sin, 11, 25, 56, 81, 95, 96, 103, 106, 128, 157, 159, 199
  Systematic Theology, 10, 79, 95, 189

Thompson, Francis, 180, 228
Tillich, Paul, 161, 189
Tittle, Ernest F., 89
Tolstoi, Leo, 72, 73, 77, 82, 83
Trueblood, D. Elton, xii
Turner, Frank M., 159, 226
Tyrrell, George, 37, 38, 41, 43, 47, 48, 57-63, 71, 106, 107, 121, 122, 128, 208, 210, 211

Underhill, Evelyn, 127, 137, 138
Unitarians, 110, 142

Van Dyke, Henry, 80, 112, 213
Visser't Hooft, W. A., 196
von Hügel, Friedrich, 41, 137, 138, 142

Walker, Williston, 68, 76, 211
WAR
  Civil War, 11, 30, 64, 97, 99, 205
  First World War, 23, 30, 38, 39, 41, 51, 52, 55, 56, 57, 72, 74, 77, 79-83, 85, 87-94, 105, 114, 127-129, 133, 152, 183, 210, 213, 214, 215
  general, xiv, 52, 57, 80-87, 89-95, 99, 102, 127, 152, 155, 169, 180, 215, 223
  just war, 81, 89
  pacifism, xii, 73, 79, 80, 81, 82, 85, 87, 88, 89, 91, 92, 94
  post-war, 90, 199
  Second World War, 92, 105, 157

Weigle, Luther A., 158
Weiss, Johannes, 48
Welch, Claude, xix
Wells, H. G., 83, 104, 107, 153
Westcott, B. F., 132, 133
Whalley, Edward, 6
Whitehead, Alfred North, 28, 105, 146, 194
Whitman, Walt, 7, 205
Whittier, John Greenleaf, 180
Wieman, Henry Nelson, 53, 174, 228
Wilde, Oscar, 152, 218
Wilder, Amos N., 197
Williams, Daniel Day, 157, 204, 226
Williams College, 136
Willoughby, Harold R., 197
Wilson, Henrietta Sperry, 63, 115, 148, 200, 205, 206, 208, 209, 211, 212, 217, 219, 224, 229
Woolf, Virginia, 38, 208
Wordsworth, William, 1, 69, 93, 94, 151, 152, 157, 174, 178, 180, 181, 182, 184, 185, 189, 212, 215, 225, 228, 229
Worship, xi, xx, 14, 78, 114, 120, 121, 126-146, 149, 172, 200, 212, 216, 220, 221, 222, 223

Yale, xi, xv, 3, 35, 46, 65, 67-70, 85, 109, 110, 140, 145, 151, 158, 164, 204, 212
Yale Review, 148, 152, 177, 225, 227
Y.M.C.A, 13, 15, 24, 29, 31, 32-34, 88

DATE DUE

HIGHSMITH 45-220